# Bruschetta with Basil

*Perfect for those who can't eat dairy, this appetizer will also have cheese lovers reaching for seconds of this tofu-topped bread. If you can't find a ciabatta loaf, try a baguette, or even a focaccia.*

| | | |
|---|---|---|
| Ciabatta bread loaf, cut into 1/2 inch (12 mm) slices | 1 | 1 |
| Olive oil | 1/4 cup | 60 mL |
| Garlic clove, halved | 1 | 1 |
| Medium Roma (plum) tomatoes, seeds removed and chopped | 6 | 6 |
| Finely chopped firm tofu | 2/3 cup | 150 mL |
| Finely chopped fresh basil | 1/4 cup | 60 mL |
| Olive oil | 3 tbsp. | 50 mL |
| Balsamic vinegar | 1 tbsp. | 15 mL |
| Garlic clove, minced | 1 | 1 |
| Salt1/4 tsp. | 1 mL | |
| Pepper | 1/2 tsp. | 2 mL |

Lightly brush both sides of bread slices with first amount of olive oil. Place on baking sheet. Broil on top rack in oven for 2 to 3 minutes, turning once, until lightly browned. Rub both sides of bread slices with garlic.

Combine remaining 8 ingredients in medium bowl. Just before serving, spoon tomato mixture onto bread slices. Serves 6.

*1 serving:* 349 Calories; 20.1 g Total Fat (12.6 g Mono, 3.5 g Poly, 3.0 g Sat); 0 mg Cholesterol; 34 g Carbohydrate; 3 g Fibre; 10 g Protein; 446 mg Sodium

Most Loved

Most Loved Appetizers

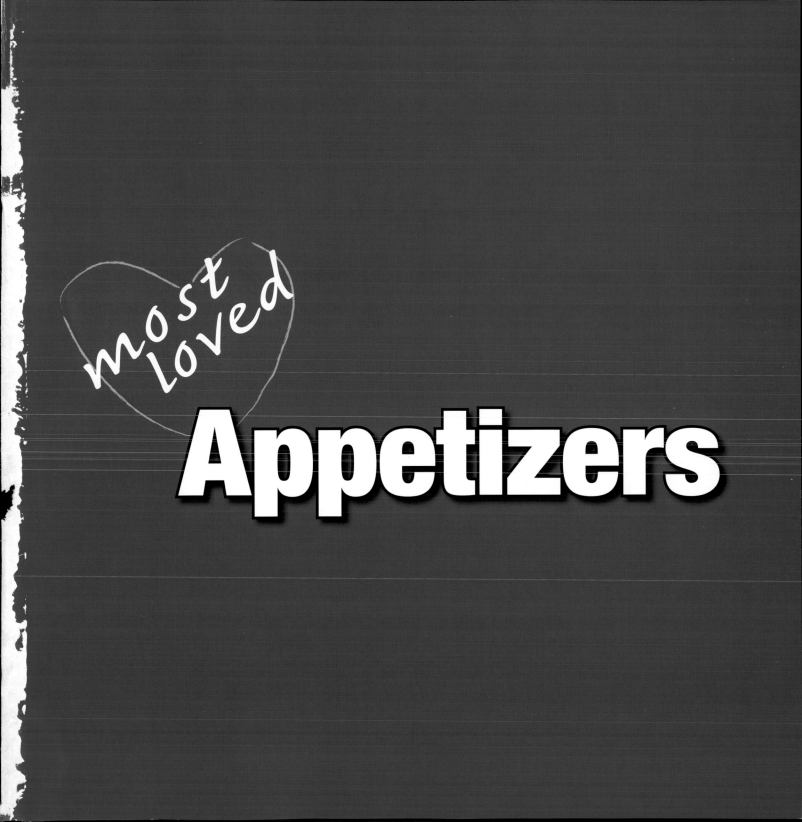

**Divider Photo:**
Chili Lemon Shrimp, page 64

*We gratefully acknowledge the following suppliers for their generous support of our Test and Photography Kitchens:*

*Corelle®*
*Lagostina®*
*Tupperware®*

*Our special thanks to the following businesses for providing props for photography:*

*Anchor Hocking Canada*
*Browne & Co. Ltd.*
*Canhome Global*
*Cherison Enterprises Inc.*
*Chintz & Company*
*Danesco Inc.*
*Exquisite Sewing Centre*
*Island Pottery Inc.*
*La Cache*
*Le Gnome*
*Mikasa Home Store*
*Pfaltzgraff Canada*
*Scona Clayworks*
*Stokes*
*The Bay*

**Pictured from left:** Sesame Sticks, page 11; Bruschetta, page 90; Shrimp Salad Wraps, page 82; Jalapeño Cheese, page 24

# table of contents

# the Company's Coming story

*"never share a recipe you wouldn't use yourself"*

Jean Paré (pronounced "jeen PAIR-ee") grew up understanding that the combination of family, friends and home cooking is the best recipe for a good life. From her mother, she learned to appreciate good cooking, while her father praised even her earliest attempts in the kitchen. When Jean left home, she took with her a love of cooking, many family recipes and an intriguing desire to read cookbooks as if they were novels!

In 1963, when her four children had all reached school age, Jean volunteered to cater the 50th Anniversary of the Vermilion School of Agriculture, now Lakeland College, in Alberta, Canada. Working out of her home, Jean prepared a dinner for more than 1,000 people, which launched a flourishing catering operation that continued for over 18 years. During that time, she had countless opportunities to test new ideas with immediate feedback—resulting in empty plates and contented customers! Whether preparing cocktail sandwiches for a house party or serving a hot meal for 1,500 people, Jean Paré earned a reputation for good food, courteous service and reasonable prices.

As requests for her recipes mounted, Jean was often asked the question, "Why don't you write a cookbook?" Jean responded by teaming up with her son, Grant Lovig, in the fall of 1980 to form Company's Coming Publishing Limited. The publication of *150 Delicious Squares* on April 14, 1981 marked the debut of what would soon become one of the world's most popular cookbook series.

The company has grown since those early days when Jean worked from a spare bedroom in her home. Today, she continues to write recipes while working closely with the staff of the Recipe Factory, as the Company's Coming test kitchen is affectionately known. There she fills the role of mentor, assisting with the development of recipes people most want to use for everyday cooking and easy entertaining. Every Company's Coming recipe is *kitchen-tested* before it's approved for publication.

Jean's daughter, Gail Lovig, is responsible for marketing and distribution, leading a team that includes sales personnel located in major cities across Canada. In addition, Company's Coming cookbooks are published and distributed under licence in the United States, Australia and other world markets. Bestsellers many times over in English, Company's Coming cookbooks have also been published in French and Spanish.

Familiar and trusted in home kitchens around the world, Company's Coming cookbooks are offered in a variety of formats. Highly regarded as kitchen workbooks, the softcover Original Series, with its lay-flat plastic comb binding, is still a favourite among readers.

Jean Paré's approach to cooking has always called for *quick and easy recipes* using *everyday ingredients.* That view has served her well. The recipient of many awards, including the Queen Elizabeth Golden Jubilee medal, Jean was appointed a Member of the Order of Canada, her country's highest lifetime achievement honour.

Jean continues to gain new supporters by adhering to what she calls The Golden Rule of Cooking: *"Never share a recipe you wouldn't use yourself."* It's an approach that works—*millions of times over!*

# foreword

*Most Loved Appetizers* brings together more than two decades of our very best appetizer recipes. With this handy book on your shelf, you'll never be caught without something to make for your guests.

Serving appetizers is an easy way to get a party started and to get the conversation flowing. Tasty morsels can whet the appetite for the meal to follow or simply satisfy the munchies over cocktails. In *Most Loved Appetizers*, we've included everything from our old favourites, such as Surprise Spread, page 6, to some of our more recent hits.

Contrary to popular belief, appetizers don't have to be fussy to make. Many delicious starters can be created with a minimum amount of ingredients and time. We've also suggested some additional time savers and make ahead tips.

One of the best things about appetizers is that they offer new and experienced cooks the opportunity to be adventuresome. Let your imagination run wild and have fun experimenting with different shapes, sizes and, above all, flavours. These savoury snacks can be as much fun to make as they are to eat!

When preparing appetizers, remember that visual appeal is a must—they should be small and inviting. Experiment with a variety of textures, colours and tastes; serve them hot or cold, simple or elegant. If you are throwing a large party, you might want to invest in some decorative cocktail picks and platters. The preparation can be time-consuming but worth the effort!

Turn the great results that you will achieve with *Most Loved Appetizers* into a great beginning for your next cocktail party, baby shower, office gathering or community event. With this collection of treasured treats, you can kick off any gathering with style—and you'll always be ready when company's coming!

*Jean Paré*

## nutrition information

Each recipe has been analyzed using the most up-to-date version of the Canadian Nutrient File from Health Canada, which is based on the United States Department of Agriculture (USDA) Nutrient Data Base. If more than one ingredient is listed (such as "hard margarine or butter"), then the first ingredient is used in the analysis. Where an ingredient reads "sprinkle," "optional," or "for garnish," it is not included as part of the nutrition information.

Margaret Ng, B.Sc. (Hon.), M.A.
Registered Dietitian

*You'll be tempted to eat this very popular spread by the spoonful. Everybody loves this one! It shows up at party, after party, after party....*

### note

An economical substitution for 3 cans of small shrimp is 2 1/4 cups (550 mL) frozen small shrimp, thawed.

### dippers

Assorted tortilla chips, Toast Points, page 31

# Surprise Spread

| | | |
|---|---|---|
| Block of cream cheese, softened | 8 oz. | 250 g |
| Sour cream | 1/2 cup | 125 mL |
| Salad dressing (or mayonnaise) | 1/4 cup | 60 mL |
| Cans of small shrimp (4 oz., 113 g, each), rinsed and drained (see Note, this page) | 3 | 3 |
| Seafood cocktail sauce | 1 cup | 250 mL |
| Grated mozzarella cheese | 2 cups | 500 mL |
| Medium green pepper, chopped | 1 | 1 |
| Green onions, chopped | 3 | 3 |
| Medium tomato, diced | 1 | 1 |

Combine cream cheese, sour cream and salad dressing in small bowl. Spread in ungreased 12 inch (30 cm) pizza pan or on serving platter.

Scatter shrimp over cream cheese mixture.

Layer remaining 5 ingredients, in order given, over shrimp. Cover. Chill until ready to serve. Serves 10 to 12.

*1 serving:* 286 Calories; 21.4 g Total Fat (7.3 g Mono, 2.4 g Poly, 10.4 g Sat); 107 mg Cholesterol; 9 g Carbohydrate; 1 g Fibre; 14 g Protein; 572 mg Sodium

Pictured on page 7.

*If you like things hot, add more cayenne pepper to this dip. It has a pleasant flavour and an attractive browned top.*

### dippers

Tortilla Chips, page 10, Tortilla Crisps, page 10

### black bean dip

Substitute 2 cans of black beans (19 oz., 540 mL, each), rinsed and drained, for the kidney beans.

# Kidney Bean Dip

**BOTTOM LAYER**

| | | |
|---|---|---|
| Cans of kidney beans (14 oz., 398 mL, each), drained | 2 | 2 |
| Sliced green onion | 1/2 cup | 125 mL |
| Salsa | 6 tbsp. | 100 mL |
| Parsley flakes | 2 tsp. | 10 mL |
| White vinegar | 1 tsp. | 5 mL |
| Chili powder | 1 tsp. | 5 mL |
| Onion powder | 1/2 tsp. | 2 mL |
| Salt | 1/2 tsp. | 2 mL |
| Cayenne pepper | 1/4 tsp. | 1 mL |
| Garlic powder | 1/4 tsp. | 1 mL |

**TOP LAYER**

| | | |
|---|---|---|
| Grated medium Cheddar cheese | 1 cup | 250 mL |
| Grated Monterey Jack cheese | 1 cup | 250 mL |
| Chili powder | 1 tsp. | 5 mL |

**Bottom Layer:** Mash kidney beans with fork in medium bowl.

Add next 9 ingredients. Mix well. Spread in ungreased 9 inch (22 cm) pie plate or shallow casserole.

**Top Layer:** Layer all 3 ingredients, in order given, over salsa mixture. Bake, uncovered, in 350°F (175°C) oven for 30 minutes. Makes about 4 cups (1 L).

*2 tbsp. (30 mL): 48 Calories; 2.4 g Total Fat (0.7 g Mono, 0.1 g Poly, 1.5 g Sat); 7 mg Cholesterol; 4 g Carbohydrate; 1 g Fibre; 3 g Protein; 158 mg Sodium*

Pictured on page 9.

Top Centre: Tortilla Crisps, page 10
Top Right: Tortilla Chips, page 10
Bottom: Kidney Bean Dip, above

*These are so easy to make and the result is very tasty.*

### serving suggestion

Serve as a dipper for Mexican-type dips, such as Kidney Bean Dip, page 8, and Refried Bean Dip, page 52.

# Tortilla Crisps

| | | |
|---|---|---|
| Hard margarine (or butter), softened | 3/4 cup | 175 mL |
| Grated Parmesan cheese | 1/2 cup | 125 mL |
| Sesame seeds | 1/4 cup | 60 mL |
| Parsley flakes | 2 tsp. | 10 mL |
| Dried whole oregano | 1/2 tsp. | 2 mL |
| Onion powder | 1/4 tsp. | 1 mL |
| Garlic powder | 1/4 tsp. | 1 mL |
| Flour tortillas (6 inch, 15 cm, diameter) | 12 | 12 |

Combine first 7 ingredients in small bowl.

Divide and spread thick layer of Parmesan cheese mixture on each tortilla. It will seem like too much but once cooked they will be just right. Cut each tortilla into 8 wedges. Arrange in single layer on ungreased baking sheets. Bake in 350°F (175°C) oven for 12 to 15 minutes until crisp and golden. Makes 96 crisps.

*4 crisps: 129 Calories; 7.8 g Total Fat (4.5 g Mono, 1.1 g Poly, 1.8 g Sat); 2 mg Cholesterol; 12 g Carbohydrate; trace Fibre; 3 g Protein; 182 mg Sodium*

Pictured on page 9.

*The wonderful thing about these appetizers is that you can deep-fry or bake them—either way they're delicious!*

### oven tortilla chips

Arrange tortilla wedges in single layer on ungreased baking sheets. Brush lightly with water. Sprinkle with salt. Bake in 400°F (205°C) oven for 8 minutes. Turn wedges over. Bake for about 3 minutes until crisp and golden.

# Tortilla Chips

| | | |
|---|---|---|
| Corn tortillas (6 inch, 15 cm, diameter) | 12 | 12 |
| Cooking oil, for deep-frying | | |
| Salt (or seasoned salt), sprinkle | | |

Cut each tortilla into 8 wedges. Deep-fry, several at a time, in hot (375°F, 190°C) cooking oil, turning occasionally, until crisp. Remove to paper towels to drain.

Sprinkle with salt. Makes 96 chips.

*4 chips: 72 Calories; 3.8 g Total Fat (1.8 g Mono, 0.9 g Poly, 0.2 g Sat); 0 mg Cholesterol; 9 g Carbohydrate; 1 g Fibre; 1 g Protein; 35 mg Sodium*

Pictured on page 9.

# Sesame Sticks

| | | |
|---|---|---|
| Mashed potatoes | 1 cup | 250 mL |
| Hard margarine (or butter), softened | 1/2 cup | 125 mL |
| Seasoned salt | 1/4 tsp. | 1 mL |
| All-purpose flour | 1 cup | 250 mL |
| Large egg, fork-beaten | 1 | 1 |
| Water | 1 tbsp. | 15 mL |
| Salt | 1/2 tsp. | 2 mL |
| Sesame seeds | 4 tsp. | 20 mL |

Combine potatoes, margarine and seasoned salt in medium bowl.

Add flour. Mix well. Chill for several hours or overnight for ease of handling. Roll out on lightly floured surface to 1/4 inch (6 mm) thickness.

Mix egg and water in cup. Brush over top.

Sprinkle with salt and sesame seeds. Cut into 4 inch (10 cm) strips, about 1⁄2 inch (12 mm) wide. Transfer carefully with lifter to greased baking sheet. Bake in 400°F (205°C) oven for about 20 minutes until crisp and golden. Makes 34 bread sticks.

*2 bread sticks: 100 Calories; 6.5 g Total Fat (4 g Mono, 0.8 g Poly, 1.3 g Sat); 13 mg Cholesterol; 9 g Carbohydrate; 1 g Fibre; 2 g Protein; 173 mg Sodium*

Pictured on this page.

*The crispy exterior has a delicious buttery, nutty flavour.*

## serving suggestion

Serve as a dipper for your favourite sauce or as an accompaniment to soup.

*Serve this special dip hot from the oven and watch it disappear. It will become a regular at all your gatherings.*

### dippers

Assorted crackers, assorted tortilla chips

### double devil's dip

Add 2 tbsp. (30 mL) chili powder to the first 6 ingredients. Mix well.

# Devil's Dip

| | | |
|---|---|---|
| Block of cream cheese, softened | 8 oz. | 250 g |
| Sour cream | 1 cup | 250 mL |
| Can of jalapeño bean dip | 10 1/2 oz. | 298 g |
| Drops of hot pepper sauce | 10 | 10 |
| Dried chives | 3 tbsp. | 50 mL |
| Parsley flakes | 2 tsp. | 10 mL |
| Chili powder | 1 tsp. | 5 mL |
| Grated Monterey Jack cheese | 1 1/2 cups | 375 mL |
| Grated medium Cheddar cheese | 1 1/2 cups | 375 mL |
| Chili powder, sprinkle | | |
| Pickled jalapeño pepper slices, for garnish | | |

Put first 6 ingredients into medium bowl. Mix well. Spread in ungreased 9 x 13 inch (22 x 33 cm) pan.

Layer next 4 ingredients, in order given, over bean dip mixture. Bake in 350°F (175°C) oven for 20 to 40 minutes until crispy.

Garnish with jalapeño pepper slices. Makes 4 cups (1 L).

*2 tbsp. (30 mL): 92 Calories; 7.2 g Total Fat (2.1 g Mono, 0.3 g Poly, 4.5 g Sat); 22 mg Cholesterol; 3 g Carbohydrate; trace Fibre; 4 g Protein; 118 mg Sodium*

Pictured on page 13.

*This classic appetizer is a true favourite.*

### make ahead

Make several days ahead. Double to make 1 larger ball or to make 2—1 for the freezer and 1 to chill for tomorrow's party.

# Sauced Crab Ball

| | | |
|---|---|---|
| Block of cream cheese, softened | 4 oz. | 125 g |
| Can of crabmeat, drained and cartilage removed, flaked | 4 oz. | 113 g |
| Lemon juice | 1 tsp. | 5 mL |
| Onion powder | 1/4 tsp. | 1 mL |
| Hot pepper sauce, dash | | |
| Seafood cocktail sauce | 1/3 cup | 75 mL |
| Chopped fresh chives, for garnish | | |

(continued on next page)

Put first 5 ingredients into small bowl. Beat until well combined. Shape into ball. Cover. Chill. Makes about 1 cup (250 mL).

Just before serving, place on serving plate. Pour cocktail sauce over crab ball. Garnish with chives. Add more cocktail sauce as needed. Serves 8.

*1 serving: 71 Calories; 5.4 g Total Fat (1.5 g Mono, 0.2 g Poly, 3.3 g Sat); 16 mg Cholesterol; 3 g Carbohydrate; trace Fibre; 3 g Protein; 256 mg Sodium*

Pictured below.

Top: Devil's Dip, page 12
Bottom Right: Sauced Crab Ball, page 12

### dippers

Assorted crackers

### homemade cocktail sauce

Combine 1/4 cup (60 mL) ketchup, 1 – 2 tsp. (5 – 10 mL) prepared horseradish and 1 tsp. (5 mL) lemon juice in small bowl. Chill for 1 hour. Makes 1/4 cup (60 mL) sauce. Easily doubled or tripled.

*A sweet vegetable dip. Use half and freeze half of this large recipe so that it's ready at a moment's notice.*

## note

Dark corn syrup adds a bit more colour than light corn syrup but either can be used.

## make ahead

Freeze for up to 6 months.

## presentation idea

Cut carrots and cucumbers with a crinkle cutter to make ruffled edges. Use a citrus stripper to create "stripes" on radishes, mushrooms, cucumbers, oranges and lemons.

# Best Vegetable Dip

| | | |
|---|---|---|
| Block of cream cheese, softened | 8 oz. | 250 g |
| Dark corn syrup (see Note, this page) | 1/2 cup | 125 mL |
| Granulated sugar | 1/2 cup | 125 mL |
| Cooking oil | 1 cup | 250 mL |
| White vinegar | 1/4 cup | 60 mL |
| Minced onion flakes | 1/4 cup | 60 mL |
| Lemon juice | 1 tbsp. | 15 mL |
| Dry mustard | 1 tsp. | 5 mL |
| Celery seed | 1 tsp. | 5 mL |
| Salt | 1/2 tsp. | 2 mL |
| Paprika | 1/4 tsp. | 1 mL |

Put cream cheese, corn syrup and sugar into medium bowl. Beat until well combined.

Add cooking oil. Mix.

Add remaining 7 ingredients. Beat until combined. Chill until ready to serve. Makes 3 cups (750 mL).

*2 tbsp. (30 mL):* 156 Calories; 12.8 g Total Fat (6.5 g Mono, 2.9 g Poly, 2.9 g Sat); 11 mg Cholesterol; 11 g Carbohydrate; trace Fibre; 1 g Protein; 86 mg Sodium

Pictured on page 15.

*This wonderful sauce has a bite that lingers!*

**dippers**

Spring Rolls, page 88, Green Onion Cakes, page 116, Pot Stickers, page 118

# Spicy Dipping Sauce

| | | |
|---|---|---|
| Apple juice | 1/2 cup | 125 mL |
| Soy sauce | 2 tbsp. | 30 mL |
| Red wine vinegar | 2 tbsp. | 30 mL |
| Chili sauce | 1 tbsp. | 15 mL |
| Garlic cloves, minced (or 1/2 tsp., 2 mL, powder) | 2 | 2 |
| Dried crushed chilies, finely crushed | 1 tsp. | 5 mL |
| Granulated sugar | 1/4 tsp. | 1 mL |
| Pepper | 1/16 tsp. | 0.5 mL |

Combine all 8 ingredients in small saucepan. Bring to a simmer on medium-low. Cover. Simmer for 10 minutes. Serve at room temperature. Makes 1/3 cup (75 mL).

*1 tbsp. (15 mL): 23 Calories; 0.1 g Total Fat (0 g Mono, trace Poly, trace Sat); 0 mg Cholesterol; 5 g Carbohydrate; trace Fibre; 1 g Protein; 425 mg Sodium*

Pictured on page 17.

*Very quick to make. It will be gone before it cools!*

**dippers**

Assorted crackers, potato chips, Toast Triangles, page 31

**serving suggestion**

Transfer hot dip from pie plate to chafing dish to keep warm, or assemble in an attractive shallow stoneware dish and serve straight from oven. Be sure to set it on a trivet!

# Hot Crab Dip

| | | |
|---|---|---|
| Block of cream cheese, softened | 8 oz. | 250 g |
| Cans of crabmeat (4 oz., 113 g, each), drained and cartilage removed, flaked | 2 | 2 |
| Finely chopped onion | 2 tbsp. | 30 mL |
| Milk | 2 tbsp. | 30 mL |
| Creamed horseradish | 1/2 tsp. | 2 mL |
| Salt | 1/4 tsp. | 1 mL |
| Pepper | 1/16 tsp. | 0.5 mL |
| Sliced almonds | 1/3 cup | 75 mL |

Put cream cheese and crab into medium bowl. Mash well.

Add next 5 ingredients. Mix well. Spread in ungreased 9 inch (22 cm) pie plate.

Sprinkle with almonds. Bake in 375°F (190°C) oven for about 15 minutes until heated through. Makes 2 cups (500 mL).

*2 tbsp. (30 mL): 76 Calories; 6.5 g Total Fat (2.2 g Mono, 0.4 g Poly, 3.4 g Sat); 17 mg Cholesterol; 1 g Carbohydrate; trace Fibre; 4 g Protein; 170 mg Sodium*

Pictured on page 17.

# Dilly Dip

| | | |
|---|---|---|
| Salad dressing (or mayonnaise) | 1 cup | 250 mL |
| Sour cream | 1 cup | 250 mL |
| Onion flakes | 2 tsp. | 10 mL |
| Parsley flakes | 2 tsp. | 10 mL |
| Dill weed | 2 tsp. | 10 mL |
| Seasoned salt | 1 tsp. | 5 mL |

**Chopped fresh dill, for garnish**

Mix first 6 ingredients in small bowl. Chill until ready to serve.

Just before serving, transfer to serving bowl. Sprinkle with dill. Makes 2 cups (500 mL).

*2 tbsp. (30 mL): 125 Calories; 13.3 g Total Fat (6.8 g Mono, 3.8 g Poly, 2.3 g Sat); 14 mg Cholesterol; 1 g Carbohydrate; trace Fibre; 1 g Protein; 150 mg Sodium*

Pictured below.

*A classic recipe for one of the best all around dips you will find! A good spur-of-the-moment choice.*

## dippers

Bread sticks, fresh vegetables (such as baby carrots, broccoli florets, cauliflower florets, celery sticks, cherry or grape tomatoes, radishes, whole mushrooms), potato chips

Top Left: Dilly Dip, this page
Top Right: Hot Crab Dip, page 16
Bottom: Spicy Dipping Sauce, page 16

*A block of cream cheese is marinated in soy sauce, ginger and green onion. Very yummy!*

### note

To toast sesame seeds, spread evenly in ungreased shallow pan. Bake in 350°F (175°C) oven for 5 to 10 minutes, stirring or shaking often, until desired doneness.

### time saver

Cut block of cream cheese in half horizontally. Marinate both halves in refrigerator for only 12 hours (or up to 24 hours).

# Oriental Cheese Spread

| | | |
|---|---|---|
| Soy sauce | 1/2 cup | 125 mL |
| Icing (confectioner's) sugar | 1/4 cup | 60 mL |
| Finely chopped green onion | 3 tbsp. | 50 mL |
| Minced crystallized ginger | 1 1/2 tbsp. | 25 mL |
| Dried crushed chilies | 1 tsp. | 5 mL |
| Garlic clove, minced (or 1/4 tsp., 1 mL, powder) | 1 | 1 |
| Block of cream cheese | 8 oz. | 250 g |
| Sesame seeds, toasted (see Note, this page) | 3 tbsp. | 50 mL |

Put first 6 ingredients into small bowl. Stir until icing sugar is dissolved. Pour into resealable freezer bag. Makes 3/4 cup (175 mL) marinade.

Add cream cheese block. Seal bag. Turn until coated. Marinate in refrigerator for 3 days, turning occasionally.

Drain and discard marinade. Spread sesame seeds on waxed paper or large plate. Press cream cheese block into sesame seeds until completely coated. Place on serving plate. Sprinkle any remaining sesame seeds over top. Serves 8 to 10.

*1 serving: 138 Calories; 12.6 g Total Fat (3.7 g Mono, 1.1 g Poly, 7.1 g Sat); 34 mg Cholesterol; 3 g Carbohydrate; 1 g Fibre; 3 g Protein; 367 mg Sodium*

Pictured below.

# Caramel Fruit Dip

| | | |
|---|---|---|
| Sour cream | 1 cup | 250 mL |
| Brown sugar, packed | 1 tbsp. | 15 mL |
| Coffee-flavoured liqueur (such as Kahlúa) | 1 tbsp. | 15 mL |

**Caramel sauce, for garnish**

Combine first 3 ingredients in small bowl.

Drizzle with caramel sauce. Makes 1 cup (250 mL).

*2 tbsp. (30 mL): 57 Calories; 4.1 g Total Fat (1.2 g Mono, 0.2 g Poly, 2.5 g Sat); 11 mg Cholesterol; 4 g Carbohydrate; 0 g Fibre; 1 g Protein; 13 mg Sodium*

Pictured on page 20.

# Easy Fruit Dip

| | | |
|---|---|---|
| Plain yogurt | 1 cup | 250 mL |
| Icing (confectioner's) sugar | 3 tbsp. | 50 mL |
| Finely grated lemon zest | 1/2 tsp. | 2 mL |

Combine all 3 ingredients in small bowl. Makes 1 cup (250 mL).

*2 tbsp. (30 mL): 30 Calories; 0.5 g Total Fat (0.1 g Mono, trace Poly, 0.3 g Sat); 2 mg Cholesterol; 5 g Carbohydrate; trace Fibre; 2 g Protein; 22 mg Sodium*

Pictured on page 21.

# Peanut Butter Dip

| | | |
|---|---|---|
| Smooth peanut butter | 1 cup | 250 mL |
| Vanilla ice cream, softened | 2 cups | 500 mL |

**Chopped peanuts, for garnish**

Measure peanut butter and ice cream into medium bowl. Mix until ice cream is melted and well blended.

Sprinkle with peanuts. Serve immediately. Makes 2 1/2 cups (625 mL).

*2 tbsp. (30 mL): 105 Calories; 8.2 g Total Fat (3.6 g Mono, 1.9 g Poly, 2.3 g Sat); 6 mg Cholesterol; 6 g Carbohydrate; 1 g Fibre; 4 g Protein; 72 mg Sodium*

Pictured on page 20/21.

*These fruit dips will make an excellent trio on your table. Surround them with a gigantic platter of fruit and let your guests enjoy the varied flavours. These dips are so easy to make and can easily be doubled.*

## dippers

Fresh fruit (such as apple wedges tossed in lemon juice, banana chunks tossed in lemon juice, cantaloupe pieces, Cape gooseberries, fresh pineapple pieces, grapes, honeydew pieces, kiwifruit pieces, orange segments, watermelon chunks, whole strawberries)

## variations

Omit the liqueur in the Caramel Fruit Dip if you prefer and double the amount of brown sugar.

For less tang in the Easy Fruit Dip, use only 1/4 tsp. (1 mL) grated lemon zest.

Provide cocktail picks and a shallow dish with 1 cup (250 mL) crushed peanuts along with the Peanut Butter Dip for those who would like to dip and roll!

*Relish is a tasty addition to a cheese ball. The two flavours complement each other nicely—like a cheese sandwich and a dill pickle!*

### make ahead

Make 1 or 2 days ahead to allow flavours to blend, or make 2 smaller balls and freeze 1 for later use.

### dippers

Assorted crackers

*Try this versatile spread or dip the next time you entertain.*

### serving suggestion

This recipe is thick enough to serve as a spread with dark cocktail-size bread slices or as a dip with a selection of fresh vegetables.

# Relish Cheese Ball

| | | |
|---|---|---|
| Blocks of light cream cheese (8 oz., 250 g, each), softened | 2 | 2 |
| Grated medium Cheddar cheese | 2 cups | 500 mL |
| Sweet pickle relish, drained | 1/2 cup | 125 mL |
| Onion powder | 1/8 tsp. | 0.5 mL |
| Finely chopped pecans (or walnuts) | 1 cup | 250 mL |

Put first 4 ingredients into medium bowl. Beat on low until well mixed. Shape into ball. If too soft to shape into ball, chill for at least 1 hour.

Roll ball in pecans until coated. Chill for at least 1 hour. Makes 1 cheese ball, 3 1/2 cups (875 mL).

*2 tbsp. (30 mL): 100 Calories; 8.5 g Total Fat (3.5 g Mono, 0.9 g Poly, 3.6 g Sat); 17 mg Cholesterol; 2 g Carbohydrate; trace Fibre; 4 g Protein; 232 mg Sodium*

Pictured on page 23.

# Cuke Spread 'R Dip

| | | |
|---|---|---|
| Block of light cream cheese, softened | 8 oz. | 250 g |
| Peeled, seeded and finely chopped cucumber | 2 cups | 500 mL |
| Seasoned salt | 1 tsp. | 5 mL |
| Cayenne pepper | 1/16 tsp. | 0.5 mL |

Mash cream cheese with fork in medium bowl.

Add cucumber, seasoned salt and cayenne pepper. Mix well. Chill for at least 2 hours to blend flavours. Makes 3 cups (750 mL).

*2 tbsp. (30 mL): 22 Calories; 1.7 g Total Fat (0.5 g Mono, 0.1 g Poly, 0.9 g Sat); 5 mg Cholesterol; 1 g Carbohydrate; trace Fibre; 1 g Protein; 150 mg Sodium*

Pictured on page 23.

**Pictured on Previous Page:**
Top Left: Caramel Fruit Dip, page 19
Top Right: Easy Fruit Dip, page 19
Centre: Peanut Butter Dip, page 19

Top Left: Relish Cheese Ball, above
Centre Right: Cuke Spread 'R Dip, above

*Hah-lah-PEH-nyoh jelly is a unique, tasty spread. Its clear, shimmery look is like a jewel on the table.*

## jalapeño cheese

Place block of cream cheese, or turn out a tub of spreadable cream cheese, onto shallow plate. Cover with Jalapeño Jelly, this page. Serve with a variety of crackers and provide a cocktail spreader.

Pictured on this page.

# Jalapeño Jelly

| | | |
|---|---|---|
| Chopped pickled jalapeño pepper | 1/4 cup | 60 mL |
| Chopped red pepper | 3/4 cup | 175 mL |
| White vinegar | 1 cup | 250 mL |
| Lemon juice | 3 tbsp. | 50 mL |
| Granulated sugar | 5 cups | 1.25 L |
| Pouch of liquid pectin | 3 oz. | 85 mL |

Put jalapeño and red pepper into blender. Add 1/2 of vinegar. Process until smooth. Pour into large saucepan.

Add remaining vinegar, lemon juice and sugar. Bring to a rolling boil on medium-high, stirring often. Boil, uncovered, for 3 minutes.

Add pectin. Stir. Bring to a rolling boil. Boil, uncovered, for 1 minute. Remove from heat. Skim off foam. Pour into sterilized half-pint (250 mL) jars to within 1/4 inch (6 mm) of top. Place sterilized metal lids on jars and screw metal bands on securely. For added assurance against spoilage, process in boiling water bath for 15 minutes. Makes 4 half-pint (250 mL) jars.

*2 tbsp. (30 mL): 130 Calories; trace Total Fat (0 g Mono, 0 g Poly, 0 g Sat); 0 mg Cholesterol; 34 g Carbohydrate; trace Fibre; trace Protein; 16 mg Sodium*

Pictured below.

# Mint Papaya Salsa

| | | |
|---|---|---|
| Medium papayas, peeled, seeded and diced | 2 | 2 |
| Finely diced red onion | 1/2 cup | 125 mL |
| Chopped fresh mint leaves | 1/4 cup | 60 mL |
| Lime juice | 2 tsp. | 10 mL |
| Salt | 1/4 tsp. | 1 mL |
| Pepper, sprinkle | | |

Combine all 6 ingredients in medium bowl. Cover. Chill for at least 2 hours to blend flavours. Makes 3 cups (750 mL).

*2 tbsp. (30 mL): 11 Calories; trace Total Fat (trace Mono, trace Poly, trace Sat); 0 mg Cholesterol; 3 g Carbohydrate; trace Fibre; trace Protein; 28 mg Sodium*

Pictured below.

*An excellent make-ahead salsa for your next barbecue bash.*

## make ahead

Keep a supply in refrigerator for up to 5 days.

*Both of these very popular dips can be served at room temperature in a small bowl or heated in the Bread Bowl, described below.*

## bread bowl

Cut top from round or oblong bread loaf. Remove bread from inside, leaving about 1 inch (2.5 cm) thick shell. Reserve removed bread for dipping. Fill hollowed loaf with your choice of either Spinach Dip. Replace top. (You may need to double the recipe if loaf is large.) Wrap filled loaf in foil. Bake in 300°F (150°C) oven for 2 hours. Remove from oven and turn foil back. Remove top.

## dippers

Fresh vegetables, reserved bread chunks

## variation

To reduce fat, use lower-fat versions of the dairy products.

# Spinach Dip #1

| | | |
|---|---|---|
| Salad dressing (or mayonnaise) | 1/2 cup | 125 mL |
| Blocks of cream cheese (8 oz., 250 g, each), softened | 2 | 2 |
| Grated medium Cheddar cheese | 1 cup | 250 mL |
| Box of frozen chopped spinach, thawed, drained and squeezed dry | 10 oz. | 300 g |
| Bacon slices, cooked crisp and crumbled | 6 | 6 |
| Finely chopped onion | 1/4 cup | 60 mL |
| Dill weed | 2 tsp. | 10 mL |
| Garlic powder | 1/4 tsp. | 1 mL |

Grated medium Cheddar cheese, for garnish
Chopped cooked bacon, for garnish

Beat salad dressing and cream cheese in medium bowl until smooth.

Add next 6 ingredients. Mix well.

Garnish with Cheddar cheese and bacon. Makes 3 cups (750 mL).

*2 tbsp. (30 mL): 126 Calories; 11.8 g Total Fat (4.1 g Mono, 1.2 g Poly, 5.9 g Sat); 30 mg Cholesterol; 2 g Carbohydrate; trace Fibre; 4 g Protein; 152 mg Sodium*

Pictured on page 27.

# Spinach Dip #2

| | | |
|---|---|---|
| Box of frozen chopped spinach, thawed, drained and squeezed dry | 10 oz. | 300 g |
| Sour cream | 1 cup | 250 mL |
| Salad dressing (or mayonnaise) | 1 cup | 250 mL |
| Chopped green onion | 1/2 cup | 125 mL |
| Parsley flakes | 1 tsp. | 5 mL |
| Lemon juice | 1 tsp. | 5 mL |
| Seasoned salt | 1/2 tsp. | 2 mL |

Green onion slices, for garnish
Paprika, sprinkle

*(continued on next page)*

Put spinach, sour cream and salad dressing into medium bowl. Stir.

Add next 4 ingredients. Mix well. Chill until ready to serve.

Garnish with green onion slices. Sprinkle with paprika. Serve warm or at room temperature. Makes about 3 cups (750 mL).

*2 tbsp. (30 mL): 86 Calories; 8.9 g Total Fat (4.5 g Mono, 2.6 g Poly, 1.6 g Sat); 9 mg Cholesterol; 1 g Carbohydrate; trace Fibre; 1 g Protein; 84 mg Sodium*

Pictured below.

Top Right: Spinach Dip # 2, page 26
Bottom Left: Spinach Dip #1, page 26

*It only takes 30 minutes to assemble and bake this exceptionally good dip. Everybody loves this one!*

### note

To toast almonds, spread evenly in ungreased shallow pan. Bake in 350°F (175°C) oven for 5 to 10 minutes, stirring or shaking often, until desired doneness.

### dippers

Baguette slices, French bread chunks, pita wedges, potato chips

*The spicy soy flavour that dominates this hot dip goes well with Spring Rolls, page 88, Green Onion Cakes, page 116, and Pot Stickers, page 118.*

### note

To toast sesame seeds, spread evenly in ungreased shallow pan. Bake in 350°F (175°C) oven for 5 to 10 minutes, stirring or shaking often, until desired doneness.

# Artichoke Dip

| Ingredient | | |
|---|---|---|
| Can of artichoke hearts, drained and finely chopped | 14 oz. | 398 mL |
| Salad dressing (or mayonnaise) | 3/4 cup | 175 mL |
| Sour cream | 1/4 cup | 60 mL |
| Grated Parmesan cheese | 1/2 cup | 125 mL |
| Onion salt | 1/16 tsp. | 0.5 mL |
| Garlic powder | 1/16 tsp. | 0.5 mL |
| Hot pepper sauce | 1/16 tsp. | 0.5 mL |
| Sliced almonds, toasted (see Note, this page) | 1/2 cup | 125 mL |
| Paprika | 1/2 tsp. | 2 mL |

Mix first 7 ingredients well in medium bowl. Turn into ungreased 9 inch (22 cm) pie plate. Bake, uncovered, in 350°F (175°C) oven for 15 to 20 minutes until hot.

Sprinkle with almonds and paprika. Makes 2 cups (500 mL).

*2 tbsp. (30 mL):* 96 Calories; 8.1 g Total Fat (4.3 g Mono, 2.1 g Poly, 1.4 g Sat); 7 mg Cholesterol; 4 g Carbohydrate; 1 g Fibre; 2 g Protein; 173 mg Sodium

Pictured on page 29.

# Soy Fire Dip

| Ingredient | | |
|---|---|---|
| Soy sauce | 1/4 cup | 60 mL |
| Apple cider vinegar | 2 tbsp. | 30 mL |
| Ketchup | 2 tsp. | 10 mL |
| Garlic clove (or 1/4 tsp., 1 mL, powder) | 1 | 1 |
| Dried crushed chilies | 1 tsp. | 5 mL |
| Sesame seeds, toasted (see Note, this page), for garnish | | |

Process first 5 ingredients in blender until smooth. Transfer to serving bowl. Let stand at room temperature for about 1 hour to blend flavours.

Garnish with sesame seeds. Makes 1/2 cup (125 mL).

*2 tbsp. (30 mL):* 19 Calories; 0.1 g Total Fat (0 g Mono, 0 g Poly, 0 g Sat); 0 mg Cholesterol; 3 g Carbohydrate; trace Fibre; 2 g Protein; 1091 mg Sodium

Pictured on page 29.

Top: Artichoke Dip, above
Bottom: Soy Fire Dip, above

*An easy-to-make spread that will become a winter favourite. One of those deceptively delicious recipes that you can't judge by reading the recipe—you must try it.*

**note**

If you are unable to find the 6 1/2 oz. (184 g) can of corned beef, this size is equivalent to 3/4 cup (175 mL) flaked corned beef.

**serving suggestion**

Serve with assorted crackers, Toast Cups, page 31, or Toast Points, page 31.

# Corned Beef Mousse

| | | |
|---|---|---|
| Envelope of unflavoured gelatin (equivalent to 1 tbsp., 15 mL) | 1 | 1 |
| Cold water | 1/4 cup | 60 mL |
| Can of condensed cream of mushroom soup | 10 oz. | 284 mL |
| Block of cream cheese, softened | 8 oz. | 250 g |
| Curry powder | 1/4 tsp. | 1 mL |
| Salad dressing (or mayonnaise) | 1 cup | 250 mL |
| Finely chopped onion | 1/2 cup | 125 mL |
| Finely chopped celery | 1/2 cup | 125 mL |
| Can of corned beef (see Note, this page), mashed | 6 1/2 oz. | 184 g |

Sprinkle gelatin over cold water in large saucepan. Let stand for 1 minute.

Add mushroom soup, cream cheese and curry powder. Heat and stir on medium until smooth. Chill until slightly thickened.

Add salad dressing, onion and celery. Fold in corned beef. Pour into 6 cup (1.5 L) mold. Chill for at least 1 hour to set. Just before serving, unmold onto serving plate. Makes about 5 cups (1.25 L).

*2 tbsp. (30 mL): 82 Calories; 7.8 g Total Fat (3.5 g Mono, 1.9 g Poly, 2.2 g Sat); 14 mg Cholesterol; 1 g Carbohydrate; trace Fibre; 2 g Protein; 151 mg Sodium*

Pictured on page 33.

---

*Expect rave reviews when you serve this savoury spread.*

**note**

An economical substitution for 2 cans of small shrimp is 1 1/2 cups (375 mL) frozen small shrimp, thawed.

# Shrimp Spread

| | | |
|---|---|---|
| Salad dressing (or mayonnaise) | 1/2 cup | 125 mL |
| Butter (not margarine), softened | 1/2 cup | 125 mL |
| Cans of small shrimp (4 oz.,113 g, each), drained (see Note, this page) | 2 | 2 |
| Minced onion flakes | 1 tbsp. | 15 mL |
| Garlic powder | 1/8 tsp. | 0.5 mL |
| Lemon juice | 1 tbsp. | 15 mL |

*(continued on next page)*

Cream salad dressing and butter in medium bowl.

Add shrimp, onion flakes, garlic powder and lemon juice. Mix. Spread in small serving dish. Makes about 2 cups (500 mL).

*2 tbsp. (30 mL): 118 Calories; 11.7 g Total Fat (4.8 g Mono, 2.2 g Poly, 4.2 g Sat); 41 mg Cholesterol; trace Carbohydrate; trace Fibre; 3 g Protein; 116 mg Sodium*

Pictured on page 33.

# Toast Cups

**White (or whole wheat) sandwich bread**     9                9
   **slices, crusts removed**

Cut each bread slice into 4 squares or 2 1/2 inch (6.4 cm) circles. Press into ungreased muffin cups. Bake on bottom rack in 350°F (175°C) oven for about 15 minutes until browned. Cool. Makes 36 toast cups.

**1 toast cup:** 15 Calories; 0.2 g Total Fat (0.1 g Mono, trace Poly, 0.1 g Sat); trace Cholesterol; 3 g Carbohydrate; trace Fibre; trace Protein; 30 mg Sodium

Pictured on page 33 and on back cover.

### TOAST POINTS

Arrange uncut bread slices on ungreased baking sheet. Broil, 1 side only, until lightly toasted. (Diagram #1) Cut each slice down the centre to make 2 rectangles. Cut each rectangle diagonally to make 4 elongated triangles.

Diagram 1

### TOAST SQUARES

Arrange uncut bread slices on ungreased baking sheet. Broil, 1 side only, until lightly toasted. (Diagram #2) Cut each slice into 4 squares.

Diagram 2

### TOAST TRIANGLES

Arrange uncut bread slices on ungreased baking sheet. Broil, 1 side only, until lightly toasted. (Diagram #3) Cut each slice diagonally from corner to corner into 4 even triangles.

Diagram 3

---

## shrimp ball

Mix all 6 ingredients well. Shape into ball. Roll in 1/4 cup (60 mL) chopped fresh parsley and 2 tbsp. (30 mL) paprika.

*Quick and easy "containers" for a dip, mousse or spread.*

## make ahead

Cool completely. Put into plastic bag or other airtight container. Do not freeze if buttered.

## serving suggestion

Serve Toast Cups (or any of the variations) with Surprise Spread, page 6, Hot Crab Dip, page 16, Corned Beef Mousse, page 30, Shrimp Spread, page 30, Crab Mousse, page 32, Ham And Cheese Ball, page 34, or Antipasto, page 46.

*Looks so fancy when shaped in a mold. Lightly spray mold with non-stick cooking spray to make it easier to remove mousse.*

## serving suggestion

Surround with assorted crackers and Toast Cups, page 31. Provide a cocktail spreader or small spoon.

## presentation idea

To add great colour, lightly blanch fresh asparagus spears. Cut red and yellow peppers into slivers. Arrange asparagus and peppers, standing up, in a small cup and set in centre of unmolded mousse.

# Crab Mousse

| | | |
|---|---|---|
| Envelope of unflavoured gelatin (equivalent to 1 tbsp., 15 mL) | 1 | 1 |
| Cold water | 1/4 cup | 60 mL |
| Can of condensed cream of mushroom soup | 10 oz. | 284 mL |
| Block of cream cheese, softened | 8 oz. | 250 g |
| Salad dressing (or mayonnaise) | 2/3 cup | 150 mL |
| Finely chopped celery | 3/4 cup | 175 mL |
| Can of crabmeat, drained and cartilage removed, flaked | 4 oz. | 113 g |
| Worcestershire sauce | 1 1/2 tsp. | 7 mL |
| Onion flakes | 1 tsp. | 5 mL |

Sprinkle gelatin over cold water in large saucepan. Let stand for 1 minute.

Add mushroom soup, cream cheese and salad dressing. Heat and stir on medium until smooth. Remove from heat. Chill until slightly thickened.

Add remaining 4 ingredients. Stir well. Pour into lightly greased 4 cup (1 L) ring mold or fish mold. Chill for at least 1 hour to set. Just before serving, unmold onto serving plate. Makes about 3 1/2 cups (875 mL).

*2 tbsp. (30 mL): 84 Calories; 8.1 g Total Fat (3.4 g Mono, 1.9 g Poly, 2.5 g Sat); 13 mg Cholesterol; 1 g Carbohydrate; trace Fibre; 2 g Protein; 170 mg Sodium*

Pictured on page 33.

Top Left: Corned Beef Mousse, page 30
Top Right: Shrimp Spread, page 30
Bottom Left: Toast Cups, page 31
Bottom Right: Crab Mousse, above

*You probably have all of the ingredients on hand for this delicious spread.*

## ham roll canapés

Shape into log (rather than ball), slightly smaller in diameter than your favourite round cracker. Chill for 2 hours. Just before serving, cut into 1/4 inch (6 mm) slices and place on crackers.

Pictured on this page.

## ham and cheese spread

Use only 1 can of flaked ham, making it creamier and just right for spreading. Serve in a bowl.

Left: Ham And Cheese Ball, this page
Right: Ham Roll Canapés, above

# Ham And Cheese Ball

| | | |
|---|---|---|
| Block of cream cheese, softened | 8 oz. | 250 g |
| Cans of flaked ham (6 1/2 oz., 184 g, each) | 2 | 2 |
| Dried chives | 2 tsp. | 10 mL |
| Lemon juice | 2 tsp. | 10 mL |
| Worcestershire sauce | 1/2 tsp. | 2 mL |
| Chopped fresh parsley | 1 cup | 250 mL |

Put cream cheese and ham into small bowl. Beat or mash until well mixed.

Add chives, lemon juice and Worcestershire sauce. Shape into ball. If too soft to shape into ball, chill for at least 1 hour.

Roll ball in parsley until coated. Chill for at least 1 hour. Makes 1 ball, 2 1/2 cups (625 mL).

*2 tbsp. (30 mL):* 66 Calories; 5.5 g Total Fat (1.8 g Mono, 0.3 g Poly, 3.1 g Sat); 21 mg Cholesterol; 1 g Carbohydrate; trace Fibre; 4 g Protein; 223 mg Sodium

Pictured below.

# Brie In Pastry

| Frozen puff pastry patty shells (from 10 1/2 oz., 300 g, package of 6), thawed (see Note, this page) | 2 | 2 |
|---|---|---|
| Small Brie cheese round (with rind) | 4 oz. | 125 g |
| Large egg, fork-beaten | 1 | 1 |
| Medium red apples, cut into thin wedges | 2 | 2 |

Roll 1 pastry shell out on lightly floured surface to 5 1/2 to 6 inch (14 to 15 cm) circle.

Place cheese round in middle of pastry. Bring up sides, pleating dough around edge. Roll out second pastry shell. Cut circle to fit top, using Brie tin. Crimp and seal edges. Make decorative shapes from scraps of pastry. Place on top.

Brush pastry with egg. Place on greased baking sheet. Bake in 450°F (230°C) oven for 15 minutes. Reduce heat to 350°F (175°C). Bake for about 5 minutes until golden brown. Transfer to serving plate.

Place apple wedges around pastry. Serves 6.

*1 serving:* 200 Calories; 13.1 g Total Fat (3.4 g Mono, 4 g Poly, 4.8 g Sat); 57 mg Cholesterol; 15 g Carbohydrate; 1 g Fibre; 7 g Protein; 183 mg Sodium

Pictured below.

*Fruit and hot cheese make a great appetizer.*

## note

All 6 shells may be used to make 3 Brie pastries for a larger party. Simply triple the recipe.

## make ahead

Assemble but don't brush with egg. Wrap and freeze. Thaw and bake as directed just before serving.

*What an impressive appetizer—summer or winter!*

## notes

Use gloves when chopping hot peppers, as the caustic, oily compound called capsaicin (kap-SAY-ih-sihn) permeates the skin and causes an intense burning sensation.

If cilantro is not your favourite herb, double the amount of chopped parsley and omit the cilantro.

## serving suggestion

Use Fruity Salsa as an accompaniment for chicken, fish or pork as well.

## variation

If you don't have an electric grill or gas barbecue, toast baguette slices on both sides under broiler. Heat Brie cheese rounds in 325°F (160°C) oven for 5 to 10 minutes until softened.

# Grilled Brie And Fruit Crostini

## FRUITY SALSA

| | | |
|---|---|---|
| Diced mango | 1/2 cup | 125 mL |
| Diced red apple (with peel) | 1/2 cup | 125 mL |
| Canned white kidney beans, drained, rinsed and coarsely chopped | 1/2 cup | 125 mL |
| Finely chopped red onion | 2 tbsp. | 30 mL |
| Small hot pepper (your choice), seeded and finely diced (see Note, this page), optional | 1 | 1 |
| Balsamic vinegar | 2 tbsp. | 30 mL |
| Granulated sugar | 1 tsp. | 5 mL |
| Chopped fresh parsley | 1 tbsp. | 15 mL |
| Chopped fresh cilantro (see Note, this page) | 1 tbsp. | 15 mL |
| Baguette bread slices, cut 1/2 inch (12 mm) thick | 24 | 24 |
| Small Brie cheese rounds (with rind), 4 oz. (125 g) each | 2 | 2 |
| Olive (or cooking) oil | 1/4 cup | 60 mL |

**Fruity Salsa:** Combine first 9 ingredients in small bowl. Cover. Let stand at room temperature for 1 hour, stirring several times, to blend flavours. Makes 2 cups (500 mL) salsa.

Preheat lightly greased electric grill to medium. Lightly brush baguette slices and cheese rounds with olive oil on both sides. Place baguette slices on grill. Cook for about 1 minute, turning to toast both sides. Increase heat to medium-high. Place cheese rounds on grill. Cook for 4 to 5 minutes on each side, turning carefully, until soft to touch. Arrange on serving platter with Fruity Salsa and baguette slices. Makes 24 servings.

*1 serving: 92 Calories; 5.6 g Total Fat (2.7 g Mono, 0.4 g Poly, 2.2 g Sat); 10 mg Cholesterol; 7 g Carbohydrate; 1 g Fibre; 3 g Protein; 133 mg Sodium*

Pictured on page 37.

*An easy, one-step recipe using ingredients that you will probably have on hand. Serve warm.*

### dippers

Blisters, this page, Cheese Thins, page 39, corn chips

### variation

Substitute a few finely chopped slices of jalapeño pepper for the hot pepper sauce. Then you really will have fire!

*The best kind of blisters to have! People are intrigued by the name.*

### make ahead

Bake up to 3 days ahead. Cool completely. Store in airtight container or freeze for up to 6 months.

### serving suggestion

Serve with Spreading Forest Fire, this page.

# Spreading Forest Fire

| | | |
|---|---|---|
| Can of baked beans in tomato sauce, drained and mashed | 14 oz. | 398 mL |
| Grated sharp Cheddar cheese | 1 cup | 250 mL |
| Hard margarine (or butter) | 1/2 cup | 125 mL |
| Very finely chopped onion | 1/2 cup | 125 mL |
| Hot pepper sauce | 1/2 tsp. | 2 mL |
| Garlic powder | 1/4 tsp. | 1 mL |
| Salt | 1/4 tsp. | 1 mL |
| Pepper | 1/8 tsp. | 0.5 mL |

Finely diced peppers (your choice), for garnish

Put first 8 ingredients into medium saucepan. Heat and stir until cheese and margarine are melted.

Transfer to serving bowl. Garnish with diced peppers. Makes 3 cups (750 mL).

*2 tbsp. (30 mL): 71 Calories; 5.5 g Total Fat (3 g Mono, 0.5 g Poly, 1.8 g Sat); 5 mg Cholesterol; 4 g Carbohydrate; 1 g Fibre; 2 g Protein; 167 mg Sodium*

Pictured on page 39.

# Blisters

| | | |
|---|---|---|
| All-purpose flour | 1 1/4 cups | 300 mL |
| Salt | 1/4 tsp. | 1 mL |
| Hard margarine (or butter) | 6 tbsp. | 100 mL |
| Grated Havarti cheese | 1 cup | 250 mL |
| Cold water | 1/3 cup | 75 mL |
| Worcestershire sauce | 1 tsp. | 5 mL |

Combine flour and salt in medium bowl. Cut in margarine until crumbly. Add cheese. Stir.

Combine cold water and Worcestershire sauce in small cup. Add to flour mixture. Stir until dough forms a ball. Divide dough into 8 portions. Roll each portion into paper-thin circle on lightly floured surface, turning over a few times to prevent sticking. Cut each circle into 8 wedges. Arrange in single layer on ungreased baking sheet. Bake on rack in top third of 350°F (175°C) oven for about 10 minutes until browned. Makes 64 wedges.

*1 wedge: 25 Calories; 1.6 g Total Fat (0.8 g Mono, 0.1 g Poly, 0.5 g Sat); 2 mg Cholesterol; 2 g Carbohydrate; trace Fibre; 1 g Protein; 37 mg Sodium*

Pictured on page 39.

# Cheese Thins

| | | |
|---|---|---|
| All-purpose flour | 2 cups | 500 mL |
| Grated sharp Cheddar cheese | 1 cup | 250 mL |
| Granulated sugar | 1 tbsp. | 15 mL |
| Baking soda | 1/2 tsp. | 2 mL |
| Salt | 1/2 tsp. | 2 mL |
| Onion powder | 1/4 tsp. | 1 mL |
| Cayenne pepper | 1/16 tsp. | 0.5 mL |
| Water | 1/2 cup | 125 mL |
| Cooking oil | 1/4 cup | 60 mL |

Put first 7 ingredients into medium bowl. Stir well.

Add water and cooking oil. Mix until dough forms a ball. Cover. Let stand for 20 minutes. Divide dough into 8 portions. Roll each portion into paper-thin circle on lightly floured surface. Cut each circle into 8 wedges. Arrange in single layer on ungreased baking sheet. Bake in 375°F (190°C) oven for about 10 minutes until crisp and browned. Makes 64 wedges.

*1 wedge: 31 Calories; 1.6 g Total Fat (0.7 g Mono, 0.3 g Poly, 0.5 g Sat); 2 mg Cholesterol; 3 g Carbohydrate; trace Fibre; 1 g Protein; 40 mg Sodium*

Pictured below.

*These large, thin wafers are nice and crisp. Make a showy basketful.*

## serving suggestion

Serve with Dilly Dip, page 17, or Spreading Forest Fire, page 38.

Left: Cheese Thins, this page
Centre: Blisters, page 38
Right: Spreading Forest Fire, page 38

*A hot and spicy dip with a definite mushroom and onion presence. This will be a huge hit at any gathering!*

## make ahead

Assemble but don't bake. Cover and chill for up to 2 days.

## dippers

Assorted crackers, bread sticks, fresh vegetables (such as broccoli florets, carrot sticks, cherry or grape tomatoes, olives, pickled peppers, zucchini slices), pita wedges

## variation

Serve cold if a thicker dip is desired.

# Hot Mushroom Dip

| | | |
|---|---|---|
| Hard margarine (or butter) | 2 tbsp. | 30 mL |
| Finely chopped onion | 1 cup | 250 mL |
| Garlic clove, minced (or 1/4 tsp., 1 mL, powder), optional | 1 | 1 |
| Chopped fresh white mushrooms | 3 cups | 750 mL |
| Block of cream cheese, softened and cut into 8 pieces | 8 oz. | 250 g |
| Seasoned salt | 1/2 tsp. | 2 mL |
| Dill weed | 1/2 tsp. | 2 mL |
| Pepper, heavy sprinkle | | |
| Grated Monterey Jack With Jalapeño cheese | 1 1/2 cups | 375 mL |
| Mayonnaise (not salad dressing) | 1/2 cup | 125 mL |
| Sliced fresh mushrooms, for garnish | | |

**Chopped chives, for garnish**

Melt margarine in large frying pan on medium. Add onion, garlic and chopped mushrooms. Cook for about 10 minutes until liquid is evaporated and mushrooms are golden. Remove from heat.

Add next 4 ingredients. Stir until cream cheese is melted.

Add Monterey Jack cheese and mayonnaise. Mix well. Spread in ungreased 9 inch (22 cm) pie plate or shallow casserole. Sprinkle with sliced mushrooms. Bake in 350°F (175°C) oven for about 30 minutes until heated through.

Sprinkle with chives. Makes 2 1/2 cups (625 mL).

*2 tbsp. (30 mL): 131 Calories; 12.5 g Total Fat (5.2 g Mono, 1.9 g Poly, 4.9 g Sat); 24 mg Cholesterol; 2 g Carbohydrate; trace Fibre; 3 g Protein; 153 mg Sodium*

Pictured on page 41.

*Pronounced kon-KAY-soh. No need to go south of the border to enjoy this Mexican favourite.*

**dippers**

Fresh vegetables, tortilla chips

# Chili Con Queso

| | | |
|---|---|---|
| Can of stewed tomatoes (with juice), broken up | 14 oz. | 398 mL |
| Chopped onion | 1 cup | 250 mL |
| Garlic powder | 1/4 tsp. | 1 mL |
| Can of diced green chilies (with liquid) | 4 oz. | 113 g |
| Pasteurized cheese loaf (such as Velveeta), cut up | 17 1/2 oz. | 500 g |

Put first 4 ingredients into medium saucepan. Stir. Cook, uncovered, on medium until liquid is evaporated.

Add cheese. Heat and stir on low until melted. Makes 4 cups (1 L).

*2 tbsp. (30 mL):* 51 Calories; 3.4 g Total Fat (1 g Mono, 0.1 g Poly, 2.1 g Sat); 9 mg Cholesterol; 2 g Carbohydrate; trace Fibre; 3 g Protein; 273 mg Sodium

Pictured above.

# Chili Cheese Log

| Ingredient | Imperial | Metric |
|---|---|---|
| Grated medium Cheddar cheese | 3 cups | 750 mL |
| Block of cream cheese, softened | 4 oz. | 125 g |
| Worcestershire sauce | 3/4 tsp. | 4 mL |
| Garlic salt | 1/2 tsp. | 2 mL |
| Pepper | 1/4 tsp. | 1 mL |
| Chili powder | 1/4 cup | 60 mL |

Put first 5 ingredients into medium bowl. Beat until smooth. Roll into 2 logs. Make diameter slightly smaller than your favourite cracker so slices will fit on top.

Spread chili powder on waxed paper or plate. Roll each log in chili powder until coated. Wrap in waxed paper or plastic wrap. Chill for 3 or 4 days to blend flavours. Cuts into 48 to 60 slices.

*1 slice:* 41 Calories; 3.5 g Total Fat (1 g Mono, 0.1 g Poly, 2.2 g Sat); 11 mg Cholesterol; 1 g Carbohydrate; trace Fibre; 2 g Protein; 74 mg Sodium

Pictured below.

*An unusual, but delicious, appetizer that is easy to make and fun to serve.*

## make ahead

Prepare 3 or 4 days ahead to give flavours time to blend, or wrap tightly and freeze for up to 6 months.

## serving suggestion

Place pre-cut slices on crackers or serve log with cheese knife and assorted crackers and let your guests help themselves.

*Garnish with sour cream.*

**make ahead**

Prepare day before. Store in refrigerator until ready to serve.

**serving suggestion**

Serve with assorted breads and crackers, or serve in wedges as a first course for a sit-down dinner.

# Blue Cheesecake

| | | |
|---|---|---|
| Fine dry bread crumbs | 2 tbsp. | 30 mL |
| Grated Parmesan cheese | 1 tbsp. | 15 mL |
| Bacon slices, diced | 8 | 8 |
| Finely chopped onion | 1 cup | 250 mL |
| Blocks of cream cheese (8 oz., 250 g, each), softened | 3 | 3 |
| Blue cheese, crumbled | 4 oz. | 113 g |
| Large eggs | 4 | 4 |
| Sour cream | 1/2 cup | 125 mL |
| Hot pepper sauce | 1/4 tsp. | 1 mL |

Combine bread crumbs and Parmesan cheese in small bowl. Grease bottom and side of 9 inch (22 cm) springform pan. Coat with crumb mixture, shaking off excess.

Cook bacon in frying pan on medium for 3 minutes. Add onion. Cook and stir until onion is soft and bacon is crisp. Drain.

Beat cream cheese, blue cheese and 1 egg in medium bowl until smooth. Little bits of blue cheese will remain. Add remaining eggs, 1 at a time, beating only until blended.

Add sour cream. Beat until well mixed. Add hot pepper sauce and bacon mixture. Stir. Pour into prepared pan. Bake in 325°F (160°C) oven for 1 to 1 1/2 hours until centre jiggles slightly when shaken. Immediately run sharp knife around top edge to allow cheesecake to settle evenly. Cool. Cover. Chill for 4 hours or overnight. Cuts into 20 thin wedges.

*1 wedge:* 197 Calories; 17.9 g Total Fat (5.4 g Mono, 0.9 g Poly, 10.6 g Sat); 93 mg Cholesterol; 3 g Carbohydrate; trace Fibre; 7 g Protein; 255 mg Sodium

Pictured on page 45.

*Use some, freeze some—you'll always be prepared for unexpected entertaining. Make this traditional recipe with a friend. Share one batch or double the recipe and divide it.*

### note

Jar sizes of the sweet mixed pickles may vary. Buy whatever is closest to 12 oz. (341 mL).

### serving suggestion

Serve with assorted crackers and Toast Cups, page 31, or spoon about 1 tsp. (5 mL) into croustades.

### presentation idea

Antipasto makes the perfect gift for a dinner host, for new parents (for all those relatives and friends who drop by to take a peek at the new baby) or for a friend who did you a favour. Put a fancy lid on the jar, make a fabric topper, or simply tie a pretty ribbon around the lid. Attach a label that says "Can be stored in refrigerator for up to 1 week after thawing or opening."

# Antipasto

| | | |
|---|---|---|
| Finely chopped cauliflower | 1 cup | 250 mL |
| Finely chopped pitted ripe olives | 1/2 cup | 125 mL |
| Chopped pickled onion | 1/2 cup | 125 mL |
| Finely chopped pimiento-stuffed olives | 1/4 cup | 60 mL |
| Cooking oil | 1/4 cup | 60 mL |
| Can of mushroom stems and pieces, drained and chopped | 10 oz. | 284 mL |
| Small green pepper, finely chopped | 1 | 1 |
| Ketchup | 2 1/4 cups | 550 mL |
| Jar of sweet mixed pickles, juice reserved, finely chopped (see Note, this page) | 12 oz. | 341 mL |
| Finely chopped red pepper (optional) | 1/4 cup | 60 mL |
| Reserved sweet pickle juice | 3 tbsp. | 50 mL |
| Can of flaked tuna, drained | 6 1/2 oz. | 184 g |
| Can of small shrimp, drained | 4 oz. | 113 g |

Put first 5 ingredients into large saucepan. Cook, uncovered, on medium for 10 minutes, stirring occasionally.

Add next 6 ingredients. Bring to a boil. Reduce heat to medium-low. Simmer, uncovered, for 10 minutes, stirring often.

Add tuna and shrimp. Stir. Chill. Makes 6 cups (1.5 L).

*2 tbsp. (30 mL): 39 Calories; 1.6 g Total Fat (0.9 g Mono, 0.4 g Poly, 0.2 g Sat); 5 mg Cholesterol; 5 g Carbohydrate; trace Fibre; 2 g Protein; 242 mg Sodium*

Pictured on page 47 and on back cover.

*Your guests will be impressed with this homemade, colourful salsa.*

# Quick Salsa

| | | |
|---|---|---|
| Small garlic clove | 1 | 1 |
| Jalapeño pepper, halved and seeded (see Note, this page) | 1 | 1 |
| Medium green or yellow pepper, cut into chunks | 1/2 | 1/2 |
| Medium red onion, cut into chunks | 1/2 | 1/2 |
| Medium roma (plum) tomatoes, quartered | 6 | 6 |
| Fresh cilantro, to taste (optional) | | |
| Salt | 1/2 tsp. | 2 mL |
| Ground cumin | 1/8 tsp. | 0.5 mL |
| Pepper, sprinkle | | |
| Can of diced green chilies, drained | 4 oz. | 113 g |
| Lime juice | 2 tsp. | 10 mL |

Secure knife blade in food processor bowl. With motor running, drop garlic clove and jalapeño pepper through feed chute. Turn off.

Remove lid. Add green pepper and red onion to processor bowl. Secure lid. Pulse with on/off motion 8 to 10 times until coarsely diced. Scrape down processor bowl with spatula.

Add tomato, cilantro, salt, cumin and pepper. Secure lid. Pulse several times. Scrape sides down. Pulse several times until salsa is desired texture. Transfer to medium bowl.

Stir in green chilies and lime juice. Cover. Let stand at room temperature for 1 hour to blend flavours. Makes 3 1/2 cups (875 mL).

*2 tbsp. (30 mL): 5 Calories; 0.1 g Total Fat (trace Mono, trace Poly, trace Sat); 0 mg Cholesterol; 1 g Carbohydrate; trace Fibre; trace Protein; 71 mg Sodium*

Pictured on page 49.

*Your guests will appreciate these colourful little alternatives to baguette slices or crackers.*

### serving suggestion

Accompany these with a soft cheese, such as Brie or Camembert, for easy spreading. Especially good with Layered Camembert, this page.

# Welsh Cakes

| | | |
|---|---|---|
| All-purpose flour | 2 cups | 500 mL |
| Granulated sugar | 1/2 cup | 125 mL |
| Baking powder | 2 tsp. | 10 mL |
| Salt | 1/2 tsp. | 2 mL |
| Ground nutmeg | 1/4 tsp. | 1 mL |
| Ground cinnamon | 1/4 tsp. | 1 mL |
| Hard margarine (or butter) | 1/2 cup | 125 mL |
| Currants | 1/2 cup | 125 mL |
| Cut mixed peel, finely chopped | 1/4 cup | 60 mL |
| Large egg, fork-beaten | 1 | 1 |
| Milk | 1/3 cup | 75 mL |

Combine first 6 ingredients in large bowl. Cut in margarine until crumbly.

Stir in currants and peel.

Add egg and milk. Stir until dough forms a ball. Roll on lightly floured surface to 1/4 inch (6 mm) thickness. Cut into 2 or 3 inch (5 or 7.5 cm) rounds. Heat frying pan on medium-low. Cook cakes, in batches, until both sides are browned. Pan should be lower temperature than for cooking pancakes. Serve cold. Makes 24 to 36 small cakes.

*1 cake: 113 Calories; 4.4 g Total Fat (2.7 g Mono, 0.5 g Poly, 0.9 g Sat); 9 mg Cholesterol; 17 g Carbohydrate; 1 g Fibre; 2 g Protein; 132 mg Sodium*

Pictured on page 51.

*An excellent way to dress up this soft cheese. Very pretty for a wedding or baby shower.*

### serving suggestion

Serve with crackers or Welsh Cakes, this page. Provide a cocktail spreader.

# Layered Camembert

| | | |
|---|---|---|
| Small Camembert cheese round | 4 oz. | 125 g |
| Block of cream cheese, softened | 4 oz. | 125 g |
| Orange juice | 1 tbsp. | 15 mL |
| Sliced almonds | 2 tbsp. | 30 mL |
| Seedless red grapes, sliced | 2 tbsp. | 30 mL |

*(continued on next page)*

Cut cheese round in half horizontally.

Mash cream cheese in small bowl. Stir in orange juice.

Add almonds and grapes. Mix well. Spread all but 1 tbsp. (15 mL) cream cheese mixture over bottom layer of cheese round. Place top layer of cheese round over top. Spread remaining cream cheese mixture over top. Serves 8 to 10.

*1 serving: 160 Calories; 13.9 g Total Fat (4.3 g Mono, 0.6 g Poly, 8.3 g Sat); 40 mg Cholesterol; 1 g Carbohydrate; trace Fibre; 8 g Protein; 309 mg Sodium*

Pictured below.

## presentation idea

Place in centre of serving plate. Arrange Welsh Cakes, page 50, on either side. Add clusters of seedless grapes for colour.

Left: Welsh Cakes, page 50
Right: Layered Camembert, page 50

*This is so quick and so easy to make. Enjoy!*

## dippers

Assorted colours of tortilla chips, Tortilla Chips, page 10, Tortilla Crisps, page 10

# Refried Bean Dip

| Can of refried beans | 14 oz. | 398 mL |
| Salsa | 2 tsp. | 10 mL |
| Lean ground beef | 1 lb. | 454 g |
| Salsa | 1/2 cup | 125 mL |
| Salt, sprinkle | | |
| Grated medium Cheddar cheese | 1 cup | 250 mL |
| Salsa | 1/2 cup | 125 mL |
| Non-fat sour cream | 1 cup | 250 mL |
| Finely chopped green onion | 2 tbsp. | 30 mL |
| Shredded iceberg lettuce | 1 cup | 250 mL |
| Medium tomato, seeded and chopped | 1 | 1 |

Combine beans and first amount of salsa in small bowl. Spread evenly in ungreased 10 inch (25 cm) pie plate.

Scramble-fry ground beef in non-stick frying pan until no longer pink. Drain off fat.

Add second amount of salsa and salt to beef. Cook on medium for 5 minutes. Spread beef mixture evenly over bean mixture.

Sprinkle with cheese. Bake in 350°F (175°C) oven for about 15 minutes until cheese is melted and beans are hot. Cool for 10 minutes.

Spread with third amount of salsa.

Combine sour cream and green onion in separate small bowl. Spread over salsa.

Sprinkle with lettuce and tomato. Makes 4 cups (1 L).

*2 tbsp. (30 mL): 56 Calories; 2.6 g Total Fat (0.9 g Mono, 0.1 g Poly, 1.3 g Sat); 11 mg Cholesterol; 4 g Carbohydrate; trace Fibre; 5 g Protein; 96 mg Sodium*

Pictured on page 53.

Top Left: Refried Bean Dip, above
Bottom Right: Mexican Snackies, page 54

*A colourful appetizer with an easy biscuit crust. Watch out for the nip in the taste!*

## make ahead

Prepare and bake biscuit crust ahead of time. Place in resealable freezer bag or wrap in plastic wrap. Chill for up to 24 hours or freeze for up to 2 months.

# Mexican Snackies

| | | |
|---|---|---|
| Biscuit mix | 2 cups | 500 mL |
| Chopped fresh cilantro (or fresh parsley) | 1/4 cup | 60 mL |
| Water | 1/2 cup | 125 mL |
| Lean ground beef | 1/2 lb. | 225 g |
| Can of refried beans with green chilies | 14 oz. | 398 mL |
| Non-fat sour cream | 1 cup | 250 mL |
| Envelope of taco seasoning mix | 1 1/4 oz. | 35 g |
| Grated medium Cheddar cheese | 1 1/2 cups | 375 mL |
| Medium tomato, seeded and finely diced | 1 | 1 |
| Finely chopped green onion | 1/2 cup | 125 mL |
| Finely chopped green pepper | 1/4 cup | 60 mL |
| Finely chopped red pepper | 1/4 cup | 60 mL |
| Finely chopped pitted ripe whole olives | 1/4 cup | 60 mL |

Combine biscuit mix and cilantro in medium bowl. Add water. Stir until soft dough forms. Turn out onto surface coated lightly with biscuit mix. Knead 10 times. Press in ungreased 10 x 15 inch (25 x 38 cm) jelly roll pan. Dough will be very thin. Bake in 400°F (205°C) oven for about 10 minutes until golden and firm. Cool.

Scramble-fry ground beef in non-stick frying pan until no longer pink. Drain.

Add refried beans. Mix. Cool slightly. Spread on crust.

Combine sour cream and seasoning mix in small bowl. Spread on beef mixture. Sprinkle with cheese.

Combine remaining 5 ingredients in separate medium bowl. Sprinkle over cheese. Pack down lightly. Chill for 1 hour. Cut into 1 1/2 x 2 inch (3.8 x 5 cm) pieces. Makes 40 appetizers.

*1 appetizer: 79 Calories; 3.3 g Total Fat (1.2 g Mono, 0.4 g Poly, 1.4 g Sat); 8 mg Cholesterol; 9 g Carbohydrate; trace Fibre; 4 g Protein; 264 mg Sodium*

Pictured on page 53.

# Cheese Cubes

| | | |
|---|---|---|
| White sandwich bread loaf (unsliced) | 1 | 1 |
| Grated sharp Cheddar cheese | 1 cup | 250 mL |
| Hard margarine (or butter) | 1/2 cup | 125 mL |
| Block of cream cheese | 4 oz. | 125 g |
| Egg whites (large), room temperature | 2 | 2 |

Cut crusts from bread loaf. Cut bread into 1 inch (2.5 cm) cubes. Put into resealable freezer bag. Put into freezer until ready to dip.

Put Cheddar cheese, margarine and cream cheese into top of double boiler. Heat over boiling water, stirring often, until melted. Remove from heat.

Beat egg whites in small bowl until stiff peaks form. Fold into cheese mixture. Dip bread cubes into cheese mixture with fork until all sides are coated. Use knife to help spread if needed. Arrange in single layer on ungreased baking sheet. Chill overnight. Just before serving, bake in 400°F (205°C) oven for about 10 minutes until golden brown. Makes about 60 cheese cubes.

*1 cheese cube: 50 Calories; 3.3 g Total Fat (1.6 g Mono, 0.3 g Poly, 1.3 g Sat); 4 mg Cholesterol; 4 g Carbohydrate; trace Fibre; 1 g Protein; 80 mg Sodium*

Pictured below.

*You'll love these when they're hot and enjoy the leftovers cold—if there are any!*

## make ahead

Freeze, unbaked, on baking sheet until firm. Transfer frozen cubes to resealable freezer bag. Freeze for up to 2 months. Just before serving, thaw and bake as directed.

## variation

Use Swiss cheese instead of Cheddar cheese for a lighter colour and a milder flavour.

*These are a winner every time.*

**make ahead**

Freeze baked tarts (in foil cups) in airtight container for up to 3 months. Just before serving, reheat thawed tarts in 325°F (160°C) oven for 15 to 20 minutes (or 30 to 40 minutes if still frozen) until heated through. Remove from foil cups.

# Cheese Tarts

| | | |
|---|---|---|
| Milk | 1/2 cup | 125 mL |
| Large egg | 1 | 1 |
| Grated medium Cheddar cheese | 1/2 cup | 125 mL |
| Grated Havarti (or other white) cheese | 1/2 cup | 125 mL |
| Chopped onion | 1 tbsp. | 15 mL |
| Salt | 1/4 tsp. | 1 mL |
| Pepper, just a pinch | | |
| Dry mustard, just a pinch | | |
| Frozen mini-tart shells, thawed | 24 | 24 |

Process first 8 ingredients in blender until smooth.

Place tart shells on ungreased baking sheet. Divide cheese mixture among tart shells. Bake in 350°F (175°C) oven for 20 to 25 minutes until set. Remove tarts from foil cups. Makes 24 tarts.

*1 tart: 59 Calories; 4.1 g Total Fat (1.7 g Mono, 0.6 g Poly, 1.6 g Sat); 14 mg Cholesterol; 3 g Carbohydrate; trace Fibre; 2 g Protein; 111 mg Sodium*

Pictured on page 57.

*This combination of salmon and ham creates a tasty topping.*

**note**

Red salmon is best for colour. If using red salmon, omit the paprika.

**make ahead**

Prepare and chill spread up to 2 days ahead or freeze for up to 3 months.

# Salmon Canapés

| | | |
|---|---|---|
| Cans of salmon (7 1/2 oz., 213 g, each), drained and round bones removed, flaked (see Note, this page) | 2 | 2 |
| Block of cream cheese, softened | 8 oz. | 250 g |
| Can of flaked ham | 6 1/2 oz. | 184 g |
| Lemon juice | 2 tsp. | 10 mL |
| Prepared horseradish | 1 tsp. | 5 mL |
| Liquid smoke | 1 tsp. | 5 mL |
| Onion powder | 1/4 tsp. | 1 mL |
| Paprika (use with pink, not red, salmon) | 2 tsp. | 10 mL |
| Crackers (or small cocktail-size bread slices) | 60 | 60 |
| Chopped fresh parsley, for garnish | | |

*(continued on next page)*

Put first 8 ingredients into medium bowl. Mix well. Makes 3 cups (750 mL) spread.

Spread about 2 tsp. (10 mL) salmon mixture on each cracker.

Sprinkle with parsley. Makes 60 canapés.

*1 canapé: 43 Calories; 2.8 g Total Fat (1 g Mono, 0.4 g Poly, 1.2 g Sat); 9 mg Cholesterol; 2 g Carbohydrate; trace Fibre; 2 g Protein; 103 mg Sodium*

Pictured below.

### serving suggestion

As an alternative, serve salmon mixture in a bowl and crackers à la carte. Let everyone make their own canapés.

Left: Cheese Tarts, page 56
Centre Left: Salmon Canapés, page 56
Centre Right: Zippy Canapés, page 58
Right: Cheesy Meat Canapés, page 58

*Visually impressive with red, green and white on dark bread.*

### make ahead

Freeze spread for up to 3 months.

### presentation idea

To garnish, cut red and orange peppers into thin slices. Cut each slice on the diagonal to make small diamond shapes.

*Keep these ingredients on hand for a quick and delicious last-minute appetizer.*

### make ahead

Prepare spread in morning and chill. Just before serving, assemble and bake as directed. Spread can also be frozen for up to 6 months if beef and sausage were not previously frozen.

# Zippy Canapés

| | | |
|---|---|---|
| Block of light cream cheese, softened | 8 oz. | 250 g |
| Dried chives | 2 tbsp. | 30 mL |
| Seasoned salt | 1/2 tsp. | 2 mL |
| Finely chopped pimiento | 1 tbsp. | 15 mL |
| Small cocktail-size bread slices (such as pumpernickel) | 48 | 48 |

Put cream cheese, chives and seasoned salt into small bowl. Mix well. Add pimiento. Stir. Makes 1 cup (250 mL) spread.

Spread or pipe about 1 tsp. (5 mL) cream cheese mixture on each bread slice. Makes 48 canapés.

*1 canapé: 28 Calories; 1 g Total Fat (0.3 g Mono, 0.1 g Poly, 0.5 g Sat); 3 mg Cholesterol; 4 g Carbohydrate; trace Fibre; 1 g Protein; 104 mg Sodium*

Pictured on page 57 and on back cover.

# Cheesy Meat Canapés

| | | |
|---|---|---|
| Lean ground beef | 1 lb. | 454 g |
| Sausage meat | 1 lb. | 454 g |
| Pasteurized cheese loaf, cut up | 17 1/2 oz. | 500 g |
| Small cocktail-size bread slices (such as pumpernickel) | 64 | 64 |

Scramble-fry ground beef and sausage meat in frying pan until no longer pink. Drain well.

Add cheese. Stir until melted. Makes 4 cups (1 L) spread.

Spread about 1 tbsp. (15 mL) meat mixture on each bread slice. Place on ungreased baking sheets. Bake in 350°F (175°C) oven for about 15 minutes until hot. Makes 64 canapés.

*1 canapé: 71 Calories; 4.3 g Total Fat (1.5 g Mono, 0.3 g Poly, 2.1 g Sat); 13 mg Cholesterol; 4 g Carbohydrate; trace Fibre; 4 g Protein; 185 mg Sodium*

Pictured on page 57.

# Devilled Eggs

| | | |
|---|---|---|
| Large hard-boiled eggs (see Notes, this page) | 6 | 6 |
| Salad dressing (or mayonnaise) | 2 tbsp. | 30 mL |
| Sweet pickle relish | 2 tbsp. | 30 mL |
| Onion powder | 1/4 – 1/2 tsp. | 1 – 2 mL |

**Paprika, sprinkle**

Cut eggs in half lengthwise. Remove yolks to small bowl. Place egg white halves on large plate.

Add salad dressing, relish and onion powder to egg yolks. Mash well with fork. Spoon or pipe into egg white halves.

Sprinkle with paprika. Makes 12 devilled eggs.

*1 devilled egg: 54 Calories; 3.9 g Total Fat (1.7 g Mono, 0.8 g Poly, 0.9 g Sat); 108 mg Cholesterol; 2 g Carbohydrate; 0 g Fibre; 3 g Protein; 67 mg Sodium*

Pictured below.

*These are an all-season favourite.*

## notes

To make perfect hard-boiled eggs, poke wider end of each egg with an egg piercer. Put eggs into cold water in saucepan large enough to hold in single layer. Bring water to a boil on medium-high. Reduce heat to medium. Boil for exactly 10 minutes. Cool eggs under cold, running water until no heat can be felt when egg is held for 10 seconds. Refrigerate immediately (with or without shells).

When slicing hard-boiled eggs, wet knife first to keep yolk from crumbling, or purchase an egg slicer that has thin wire cutters.

*This won't last long! Be prepared to refill the bowl several times. Also good for bag lunches and birthday parties.*

### make ahead

Cool completely. Freeze in airtight container for up to 6 months.

### variation

Add 2 cups (500 mL) peanuts to popped corn before adding syrup mixture.

### special caramel corn

Add 2 cups (500 mL) peanuts to the popped corn but make 1 1/2 times the syrup. Makes about 26 1/2 cups (6.6 L).

Pictured on this page.

# Caramel Popcorn

| | | |
|---|---|---|
| Popped corn (about 1 cup, 250 mL, unpopped) | 24 – 28 cups | 6 – 7 L |
| Hard margarine (or butter) | 1 cup | 250 mL |
| Brown sugar, packed | 2 cups | 500 mL |
| Corn syrup | 1/2 cup | 125 mL |
| Salt | 1 tsp. | 5 mL |
| Vanilla | 1 tsp. | 5 mL |
| Baking soda | 1/2 tsp. | 2 mL |

Put popped corn into extra-large bowl.

Combine margarine, brown sugar, corn syrup and salt in large heavy saucepan. Heat and stir on medium until boiling. Boil, without stirring, for 5 minutes.

Add vanilla and baking soda. Stir. Mixture will bubble and foam. Pour over popped corn. Toss until all pieces are coated. Spread on 2 large ungreased baking sheets. Bake in 250°F (120°C) oven for 1 hour, stirring every 15 minutes. Cool completely. Break apart. Store in resealable freezer bags. Makes about 24 cups (6 L).

*1 cup (250 mL): 199 Calories; 8.4 g Total Fat (5.3 g Mono, 1 g Poly, 1.7 g Sat); 0 mg Cholesterol; 31 g Carbohydrate; 0 g Fibre; 1 g Protein; 237 mg Sodium*

Pictured below.

Top Left: Caramel Popcorn, this page
Bottom Right: Special Caramel Corn, above

# Snackin' Potato Skins

| | | |
|---|---|---|
| Medium baking potatoes, baked and cooled | 5 | 5 |
| Hard margarine (or butter), melted | 1/4 cup | 60 mL |
| Seasoned salt, sprinkle | | |

Cut potatoes in half lengthwise. Cut each half in half lengthwise. Cut all 20 strips in half crosswise, for a total of 40 pieces. Scoop away most of potato, leaving thin layer on each skin.

Brush both sides with margarine. Sprinkle with seasoned salt. Place, skin-side up, on ungreased baking sheet. Bake in 400°F (205°C) oven for 10 to 15 minutes until crisp. Makes 40 appetizers.

*1 appetizer: 24 Calories; 1.1 g Total Fat (0.7 g Mono, 0.1 g Poly, 0.2 g Sat); 0 mg Cholesterol; 3 g Carbohydrate; trace Fibre; trace Protein; 15 mg Sodium*

Pictured below.

*These crisp, seasoned potato skins are always a hit.*

## serving suggestion

Serve with sour cream and chopped green onion on the side.

## variations

Omit seasoned salt. Sprinkle with 1/2 envelope of taco seasoning mix. Bake as directed.

Omit margarine and seasoned salt. Place potato wedges, skin-side down, on ungreased baking sheet. Sprinkle with 1 cup (250 mL) grated Cheddar cheese. Add either 1/3 cup (75 mL) cooked and crumbled bacon, 1/3 cup (75 mL) chopped green onion, or a combination of both. Bake as directed.

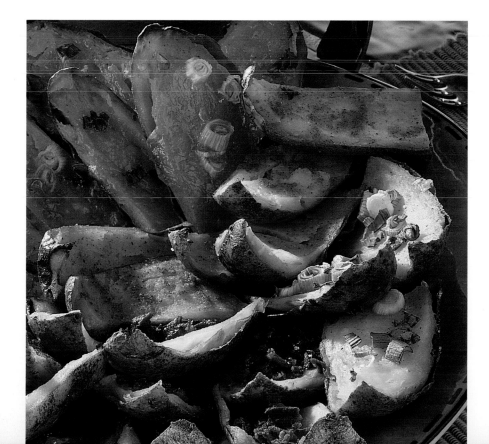

*Pronounced dohl-MAH-dehs, these are an eastern European delicacy.*

### note

Choose the best grapevine leaves for rolling and save the smaller or torn leaves for covering the sides and bottom of the casserole.

### serving suggestion

Serve at room temperature for a cocktail party or hot as a sit-down starter. Serve with a sprinkle of lemon juice if desired.

# Dolmades

| | | |
|---|---|---|
| Olive (or cooking) oil | 2 tbsp. | 30 mL |
| Finely chopped onion | 1 1/2 cups | 375 mL |
| Chopped pine nuts (or pecans) | 1/2 cup | 125 mL |
| Water | 2 cups | 500 mL |
| Basmati (or long grain white) rice | 1 cup | 250 mL |
| Dark raisins | 2/3 cup | 150 mL |
| Parsley flakes (or 1/4 cup, 60 mL, chopped fresh parsley) | 1 tbsp. | 15 mL |
| Medium tomato, seeded and chopped | 1 | 1 |
| Salt | 1 tsp. | 5 mL |
| Pepper | 1/8 tsp. | 0.5 mL |
| Ground cinnamon | 1/4 tsp. | 1 mL |
| Jar of grapevine leaves, drained (see Note, this page) | 17 oz. | 473 mL |
| Lemon juice | 1 1/2 tbsp. | 25 mL |
| Olive (or cooking) oil | 2 tbsp. | 30 mL |
| Water | 1 cup | 250 mL |

Heat first amount of olive oil in frying pan on medium. Add onion. Cook for 5 to 10 minutes until soft.

Add pine nuts. Cook for about 5 minutes until browned.

Add first amount of water, rice, raisins and parsley. Stir. Bring to a gentle boil on medium. Reduce heat to medium-low. Cover. Simmer for 15 to 20 minutes until rice is tender and liquid is absorbed.

Add tomato, salt, pepper and cinnamon. Stir. Cool enough to handle.

Rinse grapevine leaves under warm water. Blot dry. Place 2 1/2 tbsp. (37 mL) rice mixture on each of 32 grapevine leaves. Roll stem end over rice, tucking in sides as you roll up. Cover bottom and sides of greased 2 quart (2 L) casserole with some remaining grapevine leaves. Arrange rolls, seam-side down, close together over leaves.

Sprinkle with lemon juice and second amount of olive oil. Cover surface with any remaining grapevine leaves. Add second amount of water. Cover. Bake in 350°F (175°C) oven for 1 hour. Cool. Makes 32 dolmades.

*1 dolmade: 69 Calories; 3.2 g Total Fat (1.8 g Mono, 0.7 g Poly, 0.5 g Sat); 0 mg Cholesterol; 10 g Carbohydrate; 1 g Fibre; 2 g Protein; 186 mg Sodium*

Pictured on this page.

## Scallops With Bacon

| | | |
|---|---|---|
| Bacon slices, cut in half crosswise | 6 | 6 |
| Frozen sea (large) scallops | 12 | 12 |
| Boiling water, to cover | | |

Cook bacon in frying pan on medium until partially cooked. Do not cook too much or bacon will not be soft enough to roll when cooled. Remove to paper towels to drain. Cool.

Cook scallops in boiling water in medium saucepan for about 5 minutes until opaque. Drain. Cool. Roll 1 bacon piece around each scallop. Secure with wooden picks. Arrange in single layer on ungreased baking sheet. Bake in 425°F (220°C) oven for about 10 minutes until bacon is sizzling and scallops are heated through. Makes 12 appetizers.

*1 appetizer: 24 Calories; 1.6 g Total Fat (0.8 g Mono, 0.2 g Poly, 0.6 g Sat); 5 mg Cholesterol; trace Carbohydrate; 0 g Fibre; 2 g Protein; 60 mg Sodium*

Pictured above.

*This gourmet treat uses only two ingredients! It's so easy to make and it will disappear in no time.*

### time saver

To save some preparation and cleanup time, wrap uncooked bacon around cooked scallops. Broil for about 5 minutes per side until bacon is crisp.

### variation

If you feel daring, marinate the thawed, uncooked scallops in hot chili sauce for up to 1 hour.

*A great combination of flavours works its magic on these jumbo shrimp.*

## variation

Shrimp can also be grilled on an electric grill or gas barbecue. Preheat electric grill for 5 minutes or barbecue to medium. Cook shrimp on greased grill for about 2 minutes per side, brushing several times with boiled marinade, until pink. Do not overcook.

# Chili Lemon Shrimp

| | | |
|---|---|---|
| Olive (or cooking) oil | 2 tbsp. | 30 mL |
| Liquid honey | 3 tbsp. | 50 mL |
| Sweet (or regular) chili sauce | 1/4 cup | 60 mL |
| Finely grated lemon zest | 1 tsp. | 5 mL |
| Lemon juice | 1/4 cup | 60 mL |
| Chopped fresh parsley (or 1 1/2 tbsp., 25 mL, flakes) | 2/3 cup | 150 mL |
| Shallots (or green onions), finely chopped | 2 | 2 |
| Seasoned salt | 1 tsp. | 5 mL |
| Dried crushed chilies | 2 tsp. | 10 mL |
| Dry white (or alcohol-free) wine | 2/3 cup | 150 mL |
| Raw jumbo shrimp (about 25 to 30 with tails intact), peeled and deveined | 2 1/4 lbs. | 1 kg |
| Bamboo skewers (4 inch, 10 cm, length), soaked in water for 10 minutes | 25 – 30 | 25 – 30 |

Combine first 10 ingredients in large bowl.

Add shrimp. Stir until coated. Cover. Marinate in refrigerator for 3 hours, turning several times. Remove shrimp. Pour marinade into small saucepan. Bring to a boil. Boil for 5 minutes.

Thread 1 shrimp, starting at head end, lengthwise onto each skewer. Place on ungreased baking sheet. Broil on top rack for about 2 minutes per side, basting with marinade several times, until shrimp are pink. Makes 25 to 30 shrimp.

*1 shrimp: 72 Calories; 1.9 g Total Fat (0.9 g Mono, 0.4 g Poly, 0.3 g Sat); 61 mg Cholesterol; 4 g Carbohydrate; trace Fibre; 8 g Protein; 150 mg Sodium*

Pictured on page 65 and on front cover.

*One of the tastiest appetizers ever! Absolutely delectable.*

## note

Two 10 oz. (284 mL) cans of sliced mushrooms, drained and chopped, can be used in place of the fresh mushrooms.

## make ahead

To freeze unbaked, do not brush with egg. Freeze on baking sheet until firm. Transfer frozen turnovers to resealable freezer bag. Freeze for up to 6 months. Just before serving, arrange frozen turnovers in single layer on greased baking sheet. Brush with egg. Bake in 350°F (175°C) oven for 20 to 30 minutes until heated through and browned. If already baked, heat frozen turnovers in 325°F (160°C) oven for 15 to 20 minutes until hot.

## mushroom cups

Fill Toast Cups, page 31, with Mushroom Filling, this page. Heat in 400°F (205°C) oven for about 10 minutes until bubbly.

# Mushroom Turnovers

**CREAM CHEESE PASTRY**

| | | |
|---|---|---|
| Block of cream cheese, softened | 8 oz. | 250 g |
| Hard margarine (or butter), softened | 1/2 cup | 125 mL |
| All-purpose flour | 1 1/2 cups | 375 mL |

**MUSHROOM FILLING**

| | | |
|---|---|---|
| Hard margarine (or butter) | 3 tbsp. | 50 mL |
| Large onion, finely chopped | 1 | 1 |
| Fresh white mushrooms, chopped (see Note, this page) | 1/2 lb. | 225 g |
| All-purpose flour | 2 tbsp. | 30 mL |
| Salt | 1 tsp. | 5 mL |
| Pepper | 1/4 tsp. | 1 mL |
| Dried thyme | 1/4 tsp. | 1 mL |
| Sour cream | 1/4 cup | 60 mL |
| Large egg, fork-beaten | 1 | 1 |

**Cream Cheese Pastry:** Beat cream cheese and margarine in medium bowl until well mixed. Add flour. Mix well. Shape into ball. Chill for at least 1 hour.

**Mushroom Filling:** Melt margarine in frying pan on medium. Add onion and mushrooms. Cook for about 10 minutes, stirring often, until softened.

Add flour, salt, pepper and thyme. Stir. Add sour cream. Heat and stir until thickened. Remove from heat. Cool.

Roll out pastry on lightly floured surface to 1/8 inch (3 mm) thickness. Cut into 3 inch (7.5 cm) circles. Place 1 tsp. (5 mL) filling in centre of each circle. Dampen half of outer edge with egg. Fold over. Press edges together with fork or fingers to seal. Arrange in single layer on greased baking sheets. Cut tiny slits in top of each turnover. Brush tops with egg. Bake in 450°F (230°C) oven for about 10 minutes until golden brown. Makes 36 to 48 turnovers.

*1 turnover: 86 Calories; 6.5 g Total Fat (3.2 g Mono, 0.5 g Poly, 2.5 g Sat); 14 mg Cholesterol; 6 g Carbohydrate; trace Fibre; 2 g Protein; 132 mg Sodium*

Pictured on page 67 and on back cover.

*Tender, flaky phyllo pastry makes this delicious finger food even more tempting.*

## notes

There are two very different black bean sauce products available with the same name. What we refer to here is a thinner, smoother product that can be used as is. The concentrated version is paste-like and somewhat chunky. Both are found in the Asian section of the grocery store.

To toast sesame seeds, spread evenly in ungreased shallow pan. Bake in 350°F (175°C) oven for 5 to 10 minutes, stirring or shaking often, until desired doneness.

## make ahead

Assemble in morning and keep well-covered with damp tea towel until just before baking. Bake as directed.

# Beef Sprout Rolls

| | | |
|---|---|---|
| Cooking oil | 1 tbsp. | 15 mL |
| Finely chopped onion | 1/2 cup | 125 mL |
| Finely chopped celery | 1/2 cup | 125 mL |
| Coarsely chopped fresh bean sprouts | 1 1/2 cups | 375 mL |
| Grated carrot | 1/2 cup | 125 mL |
| Lean ground beef | 1/2 lb. | 225 g |
| Garlic clove, minced (or 1/4 tsp., 1 mL, powder) | 1 | 1 |
| Prepared black bean sauce (see Note, this page) | 2 tbsp. | 30 mL |
| Large eggs, fork-beaten | 2 | 2 |
| Salt | 1/8 tsp. | 0.5 mL |
| Coarsely ground pepper | 1/8 tsp. | 0.5 mL |
| Phyllo pastry sheets | 8 | 8 |
| Hard margarine (or butter), melted | 2 tbsp. | 30 mL |
| Sesame seeds, toasted (see Note, this page) | 1 tbsp. | 15 mL |

Heat frying pan on medium-high. Add cooking oil. Add onion, celery, bean sprouts and carrot. Stir-fry for 5 minutes. Transfer to medium bowl.

Scramble-fry ground beef and garlic in same frying pan until beef is no longer pink. Drain off fat.

Add vegetables to beef. Mix well. Add black bean sauce. Stir-fry for 2 minutes.

Reduce heat to medium-low. Add eggs, salt and pepper. Heat and stir until eggs just start to set. Cool. Mixture should be moist.

Layer 2 sheets of phyllo pastry together, spraying each with cooking spray. Cut in half lengthwise. Cut each half crosswise into 2 pieces. Repeat with remaining pastry sheets, for a total of 32 pieces, keeping pastry covered with damp tea towel to prevent drying out.

*(continued on next page)*

Place 2 tsp. (10 mL) beef mixture along 1 long side of each pastry piece. Roll up, tucking in ends. Roll will be thin. Brush with margarine. Sprinkle with sesame seeds. Place rolls on greased baking sheets. Bake in 375°F (190°C) oven for about 13 minutes until golden. Makes 32 rolls.

*1 roll: 47 Calories; 2.6 g Total Fat (1.3 g Mono, 0.5 g Poly, 0.6 g Sat); 17 mg Cholesterol; 4 g Carbohydrate; trace Fibre; 2 g Protein; 90 mg Sodium*

Pictured below.

Left: Beef Sprout Rolls, page 68
Right: Tortilla Roll-Ups, page 70

*These have become a favourite potluck appetizer. They're easy to make and the flavours of beef and pickle combine so well.*

## make ahead

Make the rolls the day before. Do not cut. Wrap tightly and chill. Just before serving, slice and secure with wooden picks.

## time saver

To save last-minute kitchen work, make rolls in the morning. Wrap and chill for 1 hour. Slice and secure with wooden picks. Arrange in single layer on serving platter. Cover and chill until ready to serve. Keep remaining slices chilled in a covered container, ready to refill platter as necessary.

## serving suggestion

Serve slightly chilled or at room temperature.

# Tortilla Roll-Ups

| | | |
|---|---|---|
| Block of light cream cheese, softened | 4 oz. | 125 g |
| Low-fat salad dressing (or mayonnaise) | 2 tbsp. | 30 mL |
| Dijon mustard | 2 tsp. | 10 mL |
| Finely chopped dill pickles, blotted dry | 1/4 cup | 60 mL |
| Flour tortillas (10 inch, 25 cm, diameter) | 3 | 3 |
| Shaved deli roast beef | 8 oz. | 225 g |

Combine cream cheese, salad dressing and mustard in small bowl until smooth. Add pickles. Mix well.

Divide and spread cream cheese mixture on each tortilla. Divide and layer beef on top. Roll up each tortilla very tightly. Wrap in plastic wrap. Chill for at least 1 hour. To serve, slice chilled rolls into 1 inch (2.5 cm) pieces. Secure with wooden picks. Makes 27 roll-ups.

*1 roll-up:* 46 Calories; 1.2 g Total Fat (0.7 g Mono, 0.2 g Poly, 0.7 g Sat); 9 mg Cholesterol; 3 g Carbohydrate; trace Fibre; 4 g Protein; 89 mg Sodium

Pictured on page 69.

# Crunchies

| | | |
|---|---|---|
| All-purpose flour | 1 1/2 cups | 375 mL |
| Grated sharp Cheddar cheese | 1 1/2 cups | 375 mL |
| Hard margarine (or butter), softened | 2/3 cup | 150 mL |
| Baking powder | 1 tsp. | 5 mL |
| Salt | 1/2 tsp. | 2 mL |
| Cayenne pepper | 1/4 tsp. | 1 mL |
| Crisp rice cereal | 1 cup | 250 mL |

*These delightful little morsels have the melt-in-your-mouth texture of shortbread and the crunch of a crisp rice cereal.*

Put first 6 ingredients into medium bowl. Mix well.

Add cereal. Mix with hands. Shape into 1 inch (2.5 cm) balls. Arrange in single layer on ungreased baking sheet. Bake in 375°F (190°C) oven for about 20 minutes until lightly browned. Makes 42 appetizers.

*1 appetizer:* 64 Calories; 4.5 g Total Fat (2.4 g Mono, 0.4 g Poly, 1.5 g Sat); 4 mg Cholesterol; 4 g Carbohydrate; trace Fibre; 2 g Protein; 107 mg Sodium

Pictured below.

*The delicious sauce coats each meatball generously.*

## meatball tips

To make uniform meatballs:

1. Pat meat mixture into 1 inch (2.5 cm) thick square on waxed paper. Cut into 1 inch (2.5 cm) cubes. Dip hands into water and gently roll cubes into balls.

2. Roll meat mixture into log. Cut into 2 inch (5 cm) sections. Roll each section into ball.

3. Use smallest size ice-cream scoop to measure equal amounts of meat mixture for appetizer meatballs. The scoops are generally available through restaurant supply outlets or kitchen specialty shops.

## make ahead

Arrange cooked meatballs in single layer on baking sheet. Freeze until firm. Transfer frozen meatballs to resealable freezer bag. Freeze for up to 3 months. Just before serving, reheat frozen meatballs on greased baking sheet with sides or in greased casserole in 350°F (175°C) oven for 15 to 20 minutes until heated through.

# Maple-Glazed Meatballs

| MEATBALLS | | |
|---|---|---|
| Lean ground beef | 1 1/2 lbs. | 680 g |
| Prepared horseradish | 2 tbsp. | 30 mL |
| Dry bread crumbs | 1 1/4 cups | 300 mL |
| Large eggs, fork-beaten | 2 | 2 |
| Skim evaporated milk | 1/2 cup | 125 mL |
| MAPLE SAUCE | | |
| Chili sauce | 1/2 cup | 125 mL |
| Corn (or cane) syrup | 1/2 cup | 125 mL |
| Soy sauce | 2 tbsp. | 30 mL |
| Dry mustard | 1/2 tsp. | 2 mL |
| Ground allspice | 1/2 tsp. | 2 mL |
| Cornstarch | 2 tsp. | 10 mL |
| Maple flavouring | 1 1/2 tsp. | 7 mL |

**Meatballs:** Put all 5 ingredients into medium bowl. Mix well. Shape into 3/4 inch (2 cm) balls. (See Meatball Tips, this page.) Arrange in single layer on greased baking sheet. Bake in 450°F (230°C) oven for about 10 minutes until browned and no longer pink inside.

**Maple Sauce:** Combine all 7 ingredients in medium saucepan. Bring to a boil on medium, stirring often. Makes 1 1/4 cups (300 mL) sauce. Add meatballs. Stir until heated through. Makes about 96 meatballs.

*1 meatball (with sauce):* 31 Calories; 1.3 g Total Fat (0.5 g Mono, 0.1 g Poly, 0.5 g Sat); 9 mg Cholesterol; 3 g Carbohydrate; trace Fibre; 2 g Protein; 65 mg Sodium

Pictured on page 73.

Top Left: Maple-Glazed Meatballs, above
Bottom Right: Spanish Meatballs, page 74

*Delightful meatballs with a savoury hint of wine and cloves.*

# Spanish Meatballs

**MEATBALLS**

| | | |
|---|---|---|
| Lean ground beef | 1 lb. | 454 g |
| Fresh whole wheat bread crumbs | 1 cup | 250 mL |
| Large egg, fork-beaten | 1 | 1 |
| Milk | 2 tbsp. | 30 mL |
| Garlic clove, minced (or 1/4 tsp., 1 mL, powder) | 1 | 1 |
| Salt | 1/4 tsp. | 1 mL |
| Pepper | 1/4 tsp. | 1 mL |

**SPANISH SAUCE**

| | | |
|---|---|---|
| Olive (or cooking) oil | 1 tbsp. | 15 mL |
| Medium onion, finely chopped | 1 | 1 |
| Garlic cloves, minced (or 1/2 tsp., 2 mL, powder) | 2 | 2 |
| Beef bouillon powder | 1/2 tsp. | 2 mL |
| Boiling water | 1/2 cup | 125 mL |
| Tomato paste | 1 tbsp. | 15 mL |
| Dry white (or alcohol-free) wine | 1/2 cup | 125 mL |
| Cornstarch | 2 tsp. | 10 mL |
| Brown sugar, packed | 1 tsp. | 5 mL |
| Pepper | 1/4 tsp. | 1 mL |
| Ground cloves | 1/8 tsp. | 0.5 mL |

**Meatballs:** Put all 7 ingredients into large bowl. Mix well. Shape into 1 inch (2.5 cm) balls. (See Meatball Tips, page 72.) Arrange in single layer on greased baking sheet. Bake in 350°F (175°C) oven for 10 minutes until browned. Meatballs may not be fully cooked. Drain. Set aside.

**Spanish Sauce:** Heat olive oil in medium saucepan on medium. Add onion and garlic. Cook for 2 to 3 minutes until onion is softened.

Dissolve bouillon powder in boiling water in small cup. Add to onion mixture. Stir. Add tomato paste. Stir.

Stir wine into cornstarch in same small cup until smooth. Gradually stir into tomato paste mixture. Heat and stir until boiling and thickened.

*(continued on next page)*

Add brown sugar, pepper and cloves. Stir. Makes about 1 1/4 cups (300 mL) sauce. Add meatballs. Heat on low for 25 to 30 minutes until meatballs are heated through and no longer pink inside. Makes about 36 meatballs.

*1 meatball (with sauce): 34 Calories; 1.6 g Total Fat (0.8 g Mono, 0.1 g Poly, 0.5 g Sat); 13 mg Cholesterol; 1 g Carbohydrate; trace Fibre; 3 g Protein; 42 mg Sodium*

Pictured on page 73.

# Wiener Bites

| Bacon slices | 12 | 12 |
|---|---|---|
| Wieners, cut into 6 pieces each | 8 | 8 |

Cook bacon in frying pan on medium until partially cooked. Do not cook too much or bacon will not be soft enough to roll when cooled. When cool enough to handle, cut each slice in half crosswise and then lengthwise. Wrap each bacon piece around each wiener piece. Secure with wooden picks. Arrange in single layer on ungreased baking sheet. Bake in 400°F (205°C) oven for about 5 minutes until sizzling hot and bacon is cooked. Makes 48 appetizers.

*1 appetizer: 32 Calories; 2.6 g Total Fat (1.3 g Mono, 0.3 g Poly, 1 g Sat); 5 mg Cholesterol; trace Carbohydrate; 0 g Fibre; 1 g Protein; 100 mg Sodium*

Pictured below.

*These are among the best. You'll have to make them in multiple quantities to keep the gang happy.*

## make ahead

Bake, drain and cool. Arrange in single layer on baking sheet. Freeze until firm. Transfer to resealable freezer bag. Reheat desired quantity as needed in 325°F (160°C) oven for 10 to 15 minutes until hot.

*These lip-smacking wings have a delicious sweet and sour coating.*

## chicken wing tips

To cut whole wings, cut off tips of each wing with sharp knife. Spread wing apart at joint until it separates somewhat. Cut apart at separation.

Freeze discarded wing tips to use in making chicken broth at a later date. Raw tips can be frozen for up to 9 months.

## make ahead

Arrange partially cooked drumettes in single layer on baking sheet. Freeze until firm. Transfer frozen drumettes to resealable freezer bag. Freeze for up to 1 month. Just before serving, arrange thawed drumettes in single layer on greased, foil-lined baking sheet with sides. Finish baking with sauce as directed in recipe.

# Bali Wings

| | | |
|---|---|---|
| Chicken drumettes (or whole chicken wings, split in half and tips discarded; see Chicken Wing Tips, this page) | 4 lbs. | 1.8 kg |
| BALI SAUCE | | |
| Brown sugar, packed | 1/2 cup | 125 mL |
| Granulated sugar | 1/4 cup | 60 mL |
| Cornstarch | 1/4 cup | 60 mL |
| Ground ginger | 1/2 tsp. | 2 mL |
| Salt | 1/2 tsp. | 2 mL |
| Pepper | 1/4 tsp. | 1 mL |
| Water | 1 cup | 250 mL |
| White vinegar | 1/2 cup | 125 mL |
| Soy sauce | 1/3 cup | 75 mL |

Arrange drumettes in single layer on greased foil-lined baking sheet with sides. Bake in 350°F (175°C) oven for 30 minutes.

**Bali Sauce:** Put first 6 ingredients into small saucepan. Stir well.

Add water, vinegar and soy sauce. Heat and stir on medium until boiling and thickened. Brush sauce over drumettes. Bake for 15 to 20 minutes, turning and brushing with sauce at least 2 more times, until tender and no longer pink inside. Makes about 32 drumettes or 48 wing pieces.

*1 drumette: 81 Calories; 3.9 g Total Fat (1.6 g Mono, 0.8 g Poly, 1.1 g Sat); 19 mg Cholesterol; 7 g Carbohydrate; trace Fibre; 5 g Protein; 237 mg Sodium*

Pictured on page 78.

# Buffalo Wings

| | | |
|---|---|---|
| Large eggs, fork-beaten | 2 | 2 |
| Milk | 1/4 cup | 60 mL |
| Hot pepper sauce | 1 tbsp. | 15 mL |
| All-purpose flour | 2/3 cup | 150 mL |
| Seasoned salt | 2 tsp. | 10 mL |
| Pepper | 1/2 tsp. | 2 mL |
| Chicken drumettes (or whole chicken wings, split in half and tips discarded; see Chicken Wing Tips, page 76) | 3 lbs. | 1.4 kg |
| Cooking oil, for deep-frying | | |
| Commercial Louisiana hot sauce (see Note, this page) | 1 – 4 tbsp. | 15 – 60 mL |

Combine eggs, milk and hot pepper sauce in small bowl.

Combine flour, seasoned salt and pepper in separate small bowl.

Dip each drumette into egg mixture. Dip into flour mixture until coated. Deep-fry, in batches, in hot (375°F, 190°C) cooking oil for 8 to 10 minutes until browned and crisp and no longer pink inside. Drain on paper towels. Put drumettes into large pail or bowl with cover.

Drizzle drumettes with hot sauce. Cover. Toss for 1 to 2 minutes until sauce is distributed evenly. Makes about 24 drumettes or 36 wing pieces.

*1 drumette: 96 Calories; 6.7 g Total Fat (3.1 g Mono, 1.6 g Poly, 1.4 g Sat); 37 mg Cholesterol; 3 g Carbohydrate; trace Fibre; 6 g Protein; 143 mg Sodium*

Pictured on page 78/79.

*A mouth-watering addition to any casual gathering.*

## note

Decide if you want hot wings or "suicide" hot wings by varying the amount of Louisiana hot sauce.

## make ahead

Arrange cooked drumettes in single layer on baking sheet. Freeze until firm. Transfer frozen drumettes to resealable freezer bag. Freeze for up to 1 month. Just before serving, reheat frozen drumettes on greased baking sheet with sides or in greased casserole in 350°F (175°C) oven for 15 to 20 minutes until heated through. Coat with sauce as directed in recipe.

## serving suggestion

For a quick dipping sauce, use preferred quantity of blue cheese creamy salad dressing.

Pictured on Next Page:
Top Left: Crusty Parmesan Wings, page 80
Top Right: Sweet And Sour Wings, page 81
Centre Left: Bali Wings, page 76
Centre Right: Buffalo Wings, this page
Bottom: Parmesan Chicken Wings, page 80

*Flavourful Parmesan cheese gives these wings a real lift.*

## make ahead

Arrange cooked drumettes in single layer on baking sheet. Freeze until firm. Transfer frozen drumettes to resealable freezer bag. Freeze for up to 1 month. Just before serving, reheat frozen drumettes on greased baking sheet with sides or in greased casserole in 350°F (175°C) oven for 15 to 20 minutes until heated through.

# Crusty Parmesan Wings

| | | |
|---|---|---|
| Golden Italian salad dressing | 3/4 cup | 175 mL |
| Grated Parmesan cheese | 1 cup | 250 mL |
| Fine dry bread crumbs | 1/2 cup | 125 mL |
| Paprika | 1 1/2 tsp. | 7 mL |
| Chicken drumettes (or whole chicken wings, split in half and tips discarded; see Chicken Wing Tips, page 76) | 3 lbs. | 1.4 kg |

Measure salad dressing into small bowl.

Put next 3 ingredients into separate small bowl. Mix well.

Dip each drumette into salad dressing. Dip into cheese mixture until coated. Arrange in single layer on greased foil-lined baking sheet with sides. Bake in 350°F (175°C) oven for about 45 minutes until tender and no longer pink inside. Makes about 24 drumettes or 36 wing pieces.

*1 drumette: 133 Calories; 10.8 g Total Fat (5 g Mono, 2.7 g Poly, 2.4 g Sat); 28 mg Cholesterol; 2 g Carbohydrate; trace Fibre; 7 g Protein; 243 mg Sodium*

Pictured on page 78.

*These wings will get the conversation going. Better make lots.*

## make ahead

Arrange cooked drumettes in single layer on baking sheet. Freeze until firm. Transfer frozen drumettes to resealable freezer bag. Freeze for up to 1 month. Just before serving, reheat frozen drumettes on greased baking sheet with sides or in greased casserole in 350°F (175°C) oven for 15 to 20 minutes until heated through.

# Parmesan Chicken Wings

| | | |
|---|---|---|
| Grated Parmesan cheese | 1 cup | 250 mL |
| Parsley flakes | 1 tsp. | 5 mL |
| Paprika | 1 tsp. | 5 mL |
| Salt | 1 tsp. | 5 mL |
| Pepper | 1/4 tsp. | 1 mL |
| Garlic powder | 1/4 tsp. | 1 mL |
| Chicken drumettes (or whole chicken wings, split in half and tips discarded; see Chicken Wing Tips, page 76) | 2 lbs. | 900 g |
| Hard margarine (or butter), melted | 1/2 cup | 125 mL |

*(continued on next page)*

Put first 6 ingredients into small bowl. Mix well.

Dip each drumette into margarine. Dip into cheese mixture until coated. Arrange in single layer on greased foil-lined baking sheet with sides. Bake in 350°F (175°C) oven for about 45 minutes until tender and no longer pink inside. Makes about 16 drumettes or 24 wing pieces.

*1 drumette: 166 Calories; 13.9 g Total Fat (6.8 g Mono, 1.9 g Poly, 4.2 g Sat); 33 mg Cholesterol; trace Carbohydrate; trace Fibre; 10 g Protein; 369 mg Sodium*

Pictured on page 78/79.

### variation

Adding about 1/4 cup (60 mL) fine bread crumbs to the cheese mixture will make it go further.

# Sweet And Sour Wings

*Destined to be the hit of the party.*

| | | |
|---|---|---|
| Chicken drumettes (or whole chicken wings, split in half and tips discarded; see Chicken Wing Tips, page 76) | 3 lbs. | 1.4 kg |
| Salt, sprinkle | | |
| Pepper, sprinkle | | |
| Brown sugar, packed | 1 cup | 250 mL |
| All-purpose flour | 1/4 cup | 60 mL |
| Water | 1/2 cup | 125 mL |
| White vinegar | 1/4 cup | 60 mL |
| Soy sauce | 1/4 cup | 60 mL |
| Ketchup | 1 tbsp. | 15 mL |

### make ahead

Arrange partially cooked drumettes in single layer on baking sheet. Freeze until firm. Transfer frozen drumettes to resealable freezer bag. Freeze for up to 1 month. Just before serving, arrange thawed drumettes on greased, foil-lined baking sheet with sides. Finish baking as directed in recipe.

Arrange drumettes in single layer on greased foil-lined baking sheet with sides. Sprinkle with salt and pepper. Bake in 350°F (175°C) oven for 30 minutes.

Put brown sugar and flour into small saucepan. Stir. Add water, vinegar, soy sauce and ketchup. Heat and stir on medium until boiling and thickened. Remove from heat. Brush drumettes liberally with sauce. Bake for about 20 minutes, turning and brushing with sauce at least 2 more times, until tender and no longer pink inside. Makes about 24 drumettes or 36 wing pieces.

*1 drumette: 126 Calories; 5.9 g Total Fat (2.3 g Mono, 7.5 g Poly, 1.7 g Sat); 28 mg Cholesterol; 11 g Carbohydrate; 1 g Fibre; 43 g Protein; 222 mg Sodium*

Pictured on page 78/79.

*These are so light and delicious—one will never be enough!*

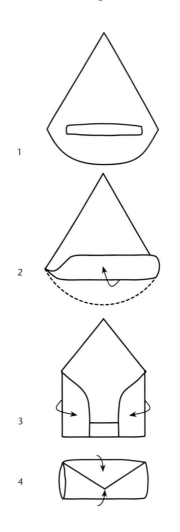

# Shrimp Salad Wraps

| | | |
|---|---|---|
| Short grain white rice | 3/4 cup | 175 mL |
| Water | 1 1/2 cups | 375 mL |
| Rice vinegar | 1 tbsp. | 15 mL |
| Salt | 1 tsp. | 5 mL |
| Water | 1/4 cup | 60 mL |
| Low-fat vegetable or chicken bouillon cube | 1/2 | 1/2 |
| Garlic clove, minced (or 1/4 tsp., 1 mL, powder) | 1 | 1 |
| Raw medium shrimp, peeled and deveined | 48 | 48 |
| Curry paste (available in Asian section of grocery store) | 2 tbsp. | 30 mL |
| Rice paper rounds (9 inch, 22 cm, diameter) | 12 | 12 |
| English cucumber (with peel), quartered lengthwise and cut julienne into 2 inch (5 cm) strips | 1/4 | 1/4 |
| Green onions, sliced lengthwise into 2 inch (5 cm) slivers | 2 | 2 |
| Medium carrot, cut julienne into 2 inch (5 cm) strips | 1 | 1 |

| CHILI DIPPING SAUCE | | |
|---|---|---|
| Chili sauce | 1/4 cup | 60 mL |
| Low-sodium soy sauce | 2 tbsp. | 30 mL |
| Rice vinegar | 2 tbsp. | 30 mL |
| Prepared horseradish | 1 tsp. | 5 mL |
| Liquid concentrated beef flavouring (such as Bovril) | 1 tsp. | 5 mL |

Dried crushed chilies, sprinkle

Combine first 4 ingredients in medium saucepan. Bring to a boil on medium. Reduce heat to medium-low. Cover. Simmer for 20 minutes until water is absorbed and rice is tender. Set aside to cool.

*(continued on next page)*

Heat second amount of water and partial bouillon cube in large frying pan on medium. Add garlic. Cook until garlic softened.

Add shrimp. Stir-fry for about 3 minutes until shrimp are pink. Do not drain any remaining broth. Remove shrimp to paper towels. Cool shrimp enough to handle. Slice in half lengthwise. Return to frying pan.

Add curry paste. Stir-fry for 1 minute.

Soak rice paper rounds, 1 at a time, in shallow pan of hot water for about 1 minute until soft. Cut into quarters. Divide cucumber, green onion and carrot evenly for 48 wraps. 1. Place vegetables crosswise along wide end of rice paper wedges. Spread 1 tbsp. (15 mL) rice on top of vegetables. Top each with 2 shrimp halves. 2. Fold rounded end up and over filling. 3. Bring two sides of wrapper over shrimp. 4. Roll up, starting at wide end.

**Chili Dipping Sauce:** Combine first 5 ingredients in small bowl.

Sprinkle with chilies. Makes about 6 tbsp. (100 mL) sauce. Serve with wraps. Makes 48 salad wraps.

*1 salad wrap with 1/2 tsp. (2 mL) sauce: 31 Calories; 0.6 g Total Fat (0.1 g Mono, 0.1 g Poly, trace Sat); 8 mg Cholesterol; 5 g Carbohydrate; trace Fibre; 2 g Protein; 158 mg Sodium*

Pictured below.

## serving suggestion

Serve chilled, at room temperature, or steamed over boiling water until warm.

*These are crispy on the outside and soft on the inside.*

## make ahead

Freeze unbaked rolls on baking sheet until firm. Transfer frozen rolls to resealable freezer bag. Just before serving, thaw and bake as directed. To bake from frozen state, add an additional 2 minutes to baking time.

## serving suggestion

Serve as is or with cocktail picks.

# Cheese Bites

| | | |
|---|---|---|
| Hard margarine (or butter), softened | 2 tbsp. | 30 mL |
| Light salad dressing (or mayonnaise) | 2 tbsp. | 30 mL |
| Grated sharp Cheddar cheese | 3/4 cup | 175 mL |
| Finely diced onion | 2 tbsp. | 30 mL |
| Finely chopped pimiento | 1 1/2 tsp. | 7 mL |
| Cayenne pepper, sprinkle | | |
| White sandwich bread slices, crusts removed | 8 | 8 |

Paprika, sprinkle (optional)

Put first 6 ingredients into small bowl. Mix well.

Flatten bread slices with rolling pin. Spread each bread slice with about 1 tbsp. (15 mL) cheese mixture. Roll up, jelly roll-style.

Sprinkle each roll with paprika. Place on ungreased baking sheet. Bake in 350°F (175°C) oven for about 10 minutes until toasted. Cut each roll into 4 pieces. Makes 32 appetizers.

*1 appetizer: 38 Calories; 2.1 g Total Fat (1 g Mono, 0.2 g Poly, 0.8 g Sat); 3 mg Cholesterol; 3 g Carbohydrate; trace Fibre; 1 g Protein; 65 mg Sodium*

Pictured below.

# Coconut Shrimp

| | | |
|---|---|---|
| Raw large shrimp (about 40 – 60 with tails intact), peeled and deveined | 2 1/4 lbs. | 1 kg |
| Large eggs | 3 | 3 |
| Water | 1 tbsp. | 15 mL |
| All-purpose flour | 1/2 cup | 125 mL |
| Medium unsweetened coconut | 3 1/2 cups | 875 mL |

Cooking oil, for deep-frying

Cut shrimp down back, almost but not through, to other side. Press to flatten slightly.

Beat eggs and water together with fork in small bowl. Dredge shrimp with flour. Dip shrimp into egg mixture. Dip into coconut.

Deep-fry, in batches, in hot (375°F, 190°C) cooking oil for 1 to 2 minutes until golden. Remove to paper towels to drain. Makes about 40 appetizers.

*1 appetizer: 107 Calories; 8.4 g Total Fat (1.8 g Mono, 0.9 g Poly, 5.1 g Sat); 45 mg Cholesterol; 4 g Carbohydrate; trace Fibre; 5 g Protein; 36 mg Sodium*

Pictured below.

*You'll earn rave reviews with these crunchy shrimp appetizers!*

**serving suggestion**

Serve with a sweet chili sauce.

*Crisp lettuce leaves encase a soft filling. This is an unusual but very delicious treat.*

# Lettuce Wraps

| | | |
|---|---|---|
| Cooking oil | 1 tsp. | 5 mL |
| Boneless, skinless chicken breast half (about 1), diced into 1/2 inch (12 mm) pieces | 4 oz. | 113 g |
| Grated carrot | 1/4 cup | 60 mL |
| Slivered onion | 1/4 cup | 60 mL |
| Slivered green pepper | 1 tbsp. | 15 mL |
| Slivered red pepper | 1 tbsp. | 15 mL |
| Slivered orange pepper | 1 tbsp. | 15 mL |
| Water | 1/4 cup | 60 mL |
| Package of instant noodles with chicken-flavoured packet, broken into 6 pieces and seasoning packet reserved | 3 1/2 oz. | 100 g |
| Unsalted peanuts | 1/4 cup | 60 mL |
| Reserved seasoning packet | 1/2 | 1/2 |
| Hoisin sauce | 1 tbsp. | 15 mL |
| Liquid honey | 1 tsp. | 5 mL |
| Pepper | 1/8 tsp. | 0.5 mL |
| Chili powder | 1/16 tsp. | 0.5 mL |
| Garlic powder | 1/16 tsp. | 0.5 mL |
| Hot pepper sauce | 1/4 tsp. | 1 mL |
| Leaf (or butter) lettuce leaves | 8 | 8 |

Heat cooking oil in large frying pan on medium. Add chicken. Scramble-fry until no longer pink.

Add carrot, onion and peppers. Stir-fry until vegetables are tender-crisp.

Add water and noodles. Stir. Cover. Simmer for about 2 minutes until noodles are softened.

Add next 8 ingredients. Stir until heated through. Transfer to small bowl.

Set bowl on platter and surround with lettuce leaves. Have each person spoon about 1/8 of chicken mixture onto lettuce leaf. Roll. Makes about 8 wraps.

*1 wrap: 103 Calories; 3.4 g Total Fat (1.6 g Mono, 1.1 g Poly, 0.5 g Sat); 8 mg Cholesterol; 12 g Carbohydrate; 1 g Fibre; 6 g Protein; 140 mg Sodium*

Pictured on page 87.

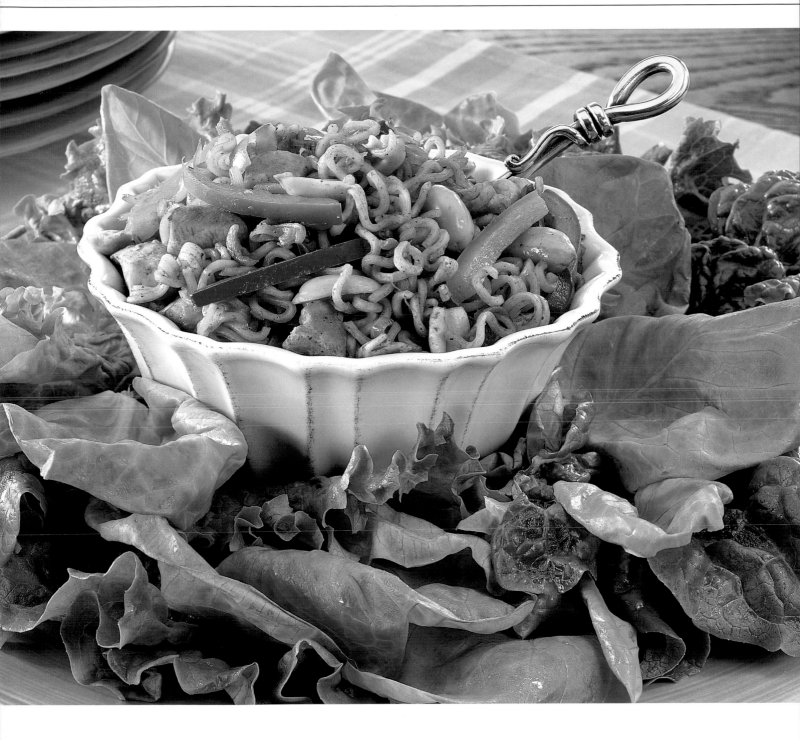

*A bit more time is needed to make these, but it's worth it. Once you get the hang of folding these, assembly will be faster.*

### serving suggestion

Serve with Spicy Dipping Sauce, page 16, or Soy Fire Dip, page 28.

# Spring Rolls

| | | |
|---|---|---|
| Lean ground chicken | 1/2 lb. | 225 g |
| Chopped fresh white mushrooms | 1 1/2 cups | 375 mL |
| Sesame (or cooking) oil | 2 tsp. | 10 mL |
| Salt | 1 tsp. | 5 mL |
| Granulated sugar | 1 tsp. | 5 mL |
| Ground ginger | 1 tsp. | 5 mL |
| Garlic powder | 1/4 tsp. | 1 mL |
| Chopped fresh bean sprouts | 3 cups | 750 mL |
| Grated carrot | 1/2 cup | 125 mL |
| Green onions, thinly sliced | 4 | 4 |
| Oyster sauce | 2 tbsp. | 30 mL |
| Dry sherry | 1 tbsp. | 15 mL |
| Egg roll wrappers | 25 | 25 |
| Cooking oil, for deep-frying | | |

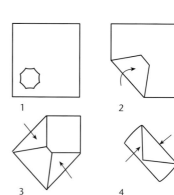

Scramble-fry ground chicken and mushrooms in sesame oil in frying pan until chicken is no longer pink and liquid is evaporated.

Add salt, sugar, ginger and garlic. Stir.

Add bean sprouts, carrot and green onion. Stir-fry on medium-high for about 5 minutes until liquid is evaporated.

Stir in oyster sauce and sherry. Stir-fry for 1 minute.

1. Place 2 tbsp. (30 mL) filling on each wrapper, diagonally off centre, closer to 1 corner. 2. Fold point up and over filling. Dampen open edges with water. 3. Fold side points in over filling. 4. Roll to opposite corner. Press to seal.

Deep-fry, in batches, in hot (375°F, 190°C) cooking oil for about 5 minutes until golden. Remove to paper towels to drain. Makes 25 spring rolls.

*1 spring roll: 85 Calories; 1.9 g Total Fat (0.9 g Mono, 0.5 g Poly, 0.2 g Sat); 8 mg Cholesterol; 12 g Carbohydrate; 1 g Fibre; 4 g Protein; 336 mg Sodium*

Pictured on page 89.

# Sesame Pork Balls

| | | |
|---|---|---|
| Lean ground pork | 1 lb. | 454 g |
| Large egg, fork-beaten | 1 | 1 |
| Fine dry bread crumbs | 1/2 cup | 125 mL |
| Garlic cloves, minced (or 1/2 tsp., 2 mL, powder) | 2 | 2 |
| Sliced green onion | 1/3 cup | 75 mL |
| Low-sodium soy sauce | 1 tbsp. | 15 mL |
| Cayenne pepper | 1/4 tsp. | 1 mL |
| Salt | 1/2 tsp. | 2 mL |
| Pepper, sprinkle | | |
| Sesame seeds | 1/2 cup | 125 mL |
| Bamboo skewers (4 inch, 10 cm, length), soaked in water for 10 minutes | 24 | 24 |

*This is a unique way to make pork balls. The sesame seeds are an attractive addition.*

## make ahead

Assemble pork balls in morning. Chill until ready to bake. Just before serving, bake as directed.

Combine first 9 ingredients in medium bowl until well mixed. Shape into 24 balls, about 1 inch (2.5 cm) in diameter.

Roll balls in sesame seeds.

Preheat lightly greased electric grill for 5 minutes. Push 1 ball onto each skewer. Cook for 10 to 15 minutes, turning often, until no longer pink inside. Makes 24 skewers.

*1 skewer:* 53 Calories; 3.1 g Total Fat (1.2 g Mono, 1 g Poly, 0.7 g Sat); 15 mg Cholesterol; 2 g Carbohydrate; trace Fibre; 4 g Protein; 111 mg Sodium

Pictured below.

Top Right: Spring Rolls, page 88
Bottom Left: Sesame Pork Balls, this page

*A great blend of flavours with a fresh Mediterranean feel.*

### make ahead

Make filling the day before and chill. Just before serving, spread on bread. Bake as directed.

# Bruschetta

| | | |
|---|---|---|
| Salad dressing (or mayonnaise) | 1/2 cup | 125 mL |
| Grated mozzarella cheese | 1 cup | 250 mL |
| Medium tomatoes, seeded and finely diced | 2 | 2 |
| Chopped pitted ripe olives | 1/4 cup | 60 mL |
| Grated fresh Parmesan cheese (or 2 tbsp., 30 mL, dry) | 1/4 cup | 60 mL |
| Dried whole oregano | 1 tsp. | 5 mL |
| Dried sweet basil | 1/4 tsp. | 1 mL |
| Pepper | 1/2 tsp. | 2 mL |
| Baguette bread loaf (about 24 – 27 inches, 60 – 67.5 cm, long) | 1 | 1 |
| Hard margarine (or butter), softened | 1/3 cup | 75 mL |

Combine first 8 ingredients in small bowl.

Cut baguette into 1 inch (2.5 cm) slices. Divide and spread margarine on 1 side of each slice. Place, buttered-side up, on ungreased baking sheet. Divide and spread tomato mixture on bread slices. Bake in 350°F (175°C) oven for about 15 minutes until hot and cheese is melted. Serve warm. Makes about 24 appetizers.

*1 appetizer: 99 Calories; 7.1 g Total Fat (3.8 g Mono, 1.2 g Poly, 1.7 g Sat); 6 mg Cholesterol; 6 g Carbohydrate; trace Fibre; 2 g Protein; 170 mg Sodium*

Pictured on page 91.

*This colourful flatbread is the perfect appetizer after a day of being outdoors. A crisp, golden crust is topped with a delicious mix of fresh ingredients. Enjoy!*

# Cornmeal Flatbread With Spinach And Onions

| | | |
|---|---|---|
| All-purpose flour | 1 1/3 cups | 325 mL |
| Yellow cornmeal | 2/3 cup | 150 mL |
| Instant yeast (1/4 oz., 8 g, envelope) | 2 1/4 tsp. | 11 mL |
| Salt | 1 tsp. | 5 mL |
| Granulated sugar | 1 tsp. | 5 mL |
| | | |
| Hot water | 3/4 cup | 175 mL |
| Olive (or cooking) oil | 1 tbsp. | 15 mL |
| | | |
| Olive (or cooking) oil | 1 tbsp. | 15 mL |
| Medium onions, thinly sliced | 2 | 2 |
| Garlic cloves, minced (or 1/2 tsp., 2 mL, powder) | 2 | 2 |
| Paprika | 1 tsp. | 5 mL |
| | | |
| Spinach leaves | 2 cups | 500 mL |
| Dark raisins | 1/3 cup | 75 mL |
| Slivered almonds | 1/3 cup | 75 mL |
| Balsamic (or red wine) vinegar | 1 tbsp. | 15 mL |
| Brown sugar, packed | 2 tsp. | 10 mL |
| Salt | 1/2 tsp. | 2 mL |
| | | |
| Yellow cornmeal | 1 1/2 tsp. | 7 mL |
| Crumbled feta cheese (about 1/2 cup, 125 mL) | 2 1/2 oz. | 70 g |

Combine first 5 ingredients in large bowl.

Add hot water and first amount of olive oil. Mix until stiff dough forms, adding more flour as needed. Turn out onto lightly floured surface. Knead for 1 to 2 minutes until well combined. Place dough on greased baking sheet. Cover with second greased baking sheet. Let stand in oven with light on and door closed for about 30 minutes until puffy.

Heat second amount of olive oil in large frying pan on medium-low. Add onion, garlic and paprika. Cook for about 15 minutes, stirring occasionally, until onion is very soft.

*(continued on next page)*

Add next 6 ingredients. Heat and stir for about 2 minutes until spinach is wilted. Drain any liquid from frying pan. Set aside.

Roll out dough on lightly floured surface to 10 x 15 inch (25 x 38 cm) rectangle. Sprinkle greased 11 x 17 inch (28 x 43 cm) baking sheet with second amount of cornmeal. Place rectangle on cornmeal. Fold edges of dough up about 1/2 inch (12 mm) to form rim. Spread spinach mixture evenly on dough. Sprinkle with feta cheese. Bake in 450°F (230°C) oven for about 25 minutes until bottom of crust is crisp and browned. Remove to wire rack to cool. Cuts into 12 pieces.

*1 piece: 175 Calories; 6.1 g Total Fat (3.4 g Mono, 0.8 g Poly, 1.6 g Sat); 6 mg Cholesterol; 26 g Carbohydrate; 2 g Fibre; 5 g Protein; 383 mg Sodium*

Pictured below.

*These are every bit as good as they look.*

### note

Beef is easier to slice when partially frozen.

### make ahead

Assemble and broil skewers until beef is medium-rare. Cool. Store in refrigerator until just before serving. Arrange in single layer on greased baking sheet. Bake in 400°F (205°C) oven for about 5 minutes until hot.

### serving suggestion

Serve with Red Sweet Sauce, page 95.

# Polynesian Satay

| | | |
|---|---|---|
| Soy sauce | 3/4 cup | 175 mL |
| Brown sugar, packed | 1/2 cup | 125 mL |
| Cooking oil | 2 tbsp. | 30 mL |
| Garlic clove, minced (or 1/4 tsp., 1 mL, powder) | 1 | 1 |
| Ground ginger | 1/2 tsp. | 2 mL |
| Thick sirloin steak, cut across grain into 1/8 inch (3 mm) thick slices (see Note, this page) | 1 1/2 lbs. | 680 g |
| Bamboo skewers (8 inch, 20 cm, length), soaked in water for 10 minutes | 12 | 12 |

Combine first 5 ingredients in medium bowl.

Add beef. Stir until coated. Cover. Marinate in refrigerator for at least 30 minutes. Drain and discard marinade.

Thread beef, accordion-style, onto skewers. Place on ungreased baking sheet. Broil on top rack for about 2 minutes per side until desired doneness. Serves 12.

*1 serving: 127 Calories; 6.2 g Total Fat (2.8 g Mono, 0.5 g Poly, 2.1 g Sat); 28 mg Cholesterol; 6 g Carbohydrate; 0 g Fibre; 12 g Protein; 578 mg Sodium*

Pictured on page 95.

# Red Sweet Sauce

| | | |
|---|---|---|
| Chili sauce | 1 cup | 250 mL |
| Fancy (mild) molasses | 1/4 cup | 60 mL |
| White vinegar | 1/4 cup | 60 mL |

Combine all 3 ingredients in small saucepan. Heat and stir on medium until heated through. Makes 1 1/2 cups (375 mL).

*1 tbsp. (15 mL): 22 Calories; 0.2 g Total Fat (trace Mono, 0 g Poly, trace Sat); 0 mg Cholesterol; 5 g Carbohydrate; 1 g Fibre; trace Protein; 156 mg Sodium*

Pictured below.

*This yummy sauce requires only three ingredients.*

## serving suggestion

Pour over hot Polynesian Satay, page 94, or beside as a dip.

Left: Red Sweet Sauce, this page
Right: Polynesian Satay, page 94

*The sauce is a perfect complement to the meatballs.*

# Meatballs With Chutney Sauce

| | | |
|---|---|---|
| Cooking oil | 2 tsp. | 10 mL |
| Chopped onion | 1/2 cup | 125 mL |
| Garlic cloves, minced (or 1/2 tsp., 2 mL, powder) | 2 | 2 |
| Finely grated peeled gingerroot | 1 tsp. | 5 mL |
| Lean ground chicken | 1 lb. | 454 g |
| Fresh bread crumbs (about 4 slices) | 1 1/2 cups | 375 mL |
| Large egg | 1 | 1 |
| Chopped fresh parsley (or 1 tbsp., 15 mL, flakes) | 1/4 cup | 60 mL |
| Hoisin sauce | 2 tbsp. | 30 mL |
| Salt | 1/2 tsp. | 2 mL |
| Cayenne pepper | 1/8 tsp. | 0.5 mL |
| Coarsely ground pepper | 1/16 tsp. | 0.5 mL |
| CHUTNEY SAUCE | | |
| Spicy mango (or other fruit) chutney | 1 cup | 250 mL |
| Water | 1/2 cup | 125 mL |
| Low-sodium soy sauce | 1/3 cup | 75 mL |
| Chili sauce | 1 tbsp. | 15 mL |
| Worcestershire sauce | 1 tsp. | 5 mL |
| Finely grated peeled gingerroot | 1 tsp. | 5 mL |

Heat cooking oil in small frying pan on medium. Add onion, garlic and ginger. Cook for about 5 minutes until onion is softened and golden. Transfer to medium bowl. Cool to room temperature.

Add next 8 ingredients to onion mixture. Mix well until mixture sticks together when squeezed. Shape into 1 inch (2.5 cm) balls. (See Meatball Tips, page 72.) Arrange in single layer on greased baking sheet. Bake on centre rack in 400°F (205°C) oven for about 10 minutes until no longer pink inside. Remove to paper towels to drain. Transfer to serving bowl. Makes about 45 meatballs.

**Chutney Sauce:** Process all 6 ingredients in food processor or blender until smooth. Transfer to medium saucepan. Bring to a boil on medium, stirring constantly. Reduce heat to medium-low. Simmer, uncovered, for 5 minutes. Makes 1 1/3 cups (325 mL) sauce. Pour over meatballs.

*1 meatball (with sauce): 48 Calories; 1.9 g Total Fat (0.2 g Mono, 0.1 g Poly, 0.1 g Sat); 5 mg Cholesterol; 5 g Carbohydrate; trace Fibre; 3 g Protein; 157 mg Sodium*

Pictured on this page.

# Baby Cheddar Tarts

**CREAM CHEESE PASTRY**

| | | |
|---|---|---|
| Hard margarine (or butter), softened | 1/2 cup | 125 mL |
| Block of cream cheese, softened | 4 oz. | 125 g |
| All-purpose flour | 1 cup | 250 mL |

**FILLING**

| | | |
|---|---|---|
| Grated medium Cheddar cheese | 1 cup | 250 mL |
| Large egg | 1 | 1 |
| Milk | 1/2 cup | 125 mL |
| Onion salt | 1/4 tsp. | 1 mL |
| Salt | 1/4 tsp. | 1 mL |

**Cream Cheese Pastry:** Beat margarine and cream cheese in medium bowl until smooth and light.

Add flour. Mix well. Roll into long thin log. Cut into 24 slices. Press into small tart pans to form shells.

**Filling:** Divide Cheddar cheese evenly among tart shells.

Beat egg in small bowl until frothy. Add milk, onion salt and salt. Mix well. Divide and spoon over cheese. Bake in 350°F (175°C) oven for 20 to 25 minutes until set. Makes 24 tarts.

*1 tart: 100 Calories; 7.8 g Total Fat (3.7 g Mono, 0.6 g Poly, 3.1 g Sat); 20 mg Cholesterol; 5 g Carbohydrate; trace Fibre; 3 g Protein; 136 mg Sodium*

Pictured on page 99 and on back cover.

*Your guests will not be able to resist these savoury snacks.*

## time saver

Measure all 5 filling ingredients (including the Cheddar cheese) into blender. Process until well combined. Pour into shells.

## make ahead

Freeze baked tarts in airtight container for up to 3 months. Just before serving, reheat thawed tarts in 325°F (160°C) oven for 15 to 20 minutes (or 30 to 40 minutes if frozen) until heated through.

## baby swiss tarts

Use grated Swiss cheese instead of Cheddar cheese.

*This hors d'oeuvre is a favourite! The creamy mushroom flavour is so timeless.*

## make ahead

Arrange uncut, unbaked rolls in single layer on baking sheet. Freeze until firm. Transfer frozen rolls to resealable freezer bag. Freeze for up to 1 month. Just before serving, cut partially thawed rolls into 3 pieces. Bake as directed.

## jiffy mushroom rolls

Divide and spread 1 can (10 oz., 284 mL) undiluted cream of mushroom soup on bread slices. Roll up. Cut into 3 pieces. Wrap each with 1/2 slice of half-cooked bacon. Secure with wooden pick. Broil for about 5 minutes, turning once at halftime, until bacon is crisp. Serve hot.

Pictured on page 99.

# Mushroom Rolls

| | | |
|---|---|---|
| Hard margarine (or butter) | 1/4 cup | 60 mL |
| Fresh white mushrooms, chopped | 1/2 lb. | 225 g |
| Chopped onion | 1/2 cup | 125 mL |
| Block of cream cheese, cut up | 8 oz. | 250 g |
| Worcestershire sauce | 1/2 tsp. | 2 mL |
| Salt | 1/2 tsp. | 2 mL |
| Pepper | 1/8 tsp. | 0.5 mL |
| Garlic powder | 1/8 tsp. | 0.5 mL |
| White sandwich bread loaf (sliced), crusts removed | 1 | 1 |
| Hard margarine (or butter), melted | 1/2 cup | 125 mL |

Melt first amount of margarine in frying pan on medium. Add mushrooms and onion. Cook for 5 to 10 minutes until onion is softened.

Add next 5 ingredients. Stir until cream cheese is melted. Cool.

Roll bread slices with rolling pin. Divide and spread mushroom mixture on each bread slice. Roll up. Brush with second amount of margarine. Cut each roll into 3 pieces. Arrange in single layer on ungreased baking sheet. Bake in 400°F (205°C) oven for 10 to 15 minutes until toasted. Makes about 48 rolls.

*1 roll:* 72 Calories; 5.4 g Total Fat (2.8 g Mono, 0.5 g Poly, 1.9 g Sat); 6 mg Cholesterol; 5 g Carbohydrate; trace Fibre; 1 g Protein; 125 mg Sodium

Pictured on page 99.

Top: Baby Cheddar Tarts, page 97
Centre Left: Jiffy Mushroom Rolls, this page
Bottom Right: Mushroom Rolls, above

*These soft, tasty meatballs are dressed up with an exceptionally good sauce.*

### make ahead

Transfer cooked meatballs with sauce to resealable freezer bag. Freeze for up to 3 months. Just before serving, reheat frozen meatballs and sauce in ungreased casserole in 350°F (175°C) oven for 15 to 20 minutes, stirring occasionally, until heated through.

# Cranberry Meatballs

| | | |
|---|---|---|
| Large eggs | 2 | 2 |
| Cornflake crumbs | 1 cup | 250 mL |
| Finely chopped onion | 1/2 cup | 125 mL |
| Soy sauce | 2 tbsp. | 30 mL |
| Parsley flakes | 1 tbsp. | 15 mL |
| Salt | 2 tsp. | 10 mL |
| Pepper | 1/2 tsp. | 2 mL |
| Garlic powder | 1/2 tsp. | 2 mL |
| Lean ground beef | 2 lbs. | 900 g |
| Can of cranberry sauce | 14 oz. | 398 mL |
| Chili sauce | 1/2 cup | 125 mL |
| Ketchup | 1/2 cup | 125 mL |
| Brown sugar, packed | 2 tbsp. | 30 mL |
| White vinegar | 1 tbsp. | 15 mL |

Beat eggs with fork in large bowl.

Add next 7 ingredients. Mix well.

Add ground beef. Mix well. Shape into 1 inch (2.5 cm) balls. (See Meatball Tips, page 72.) Put into ungreased 3 quart (3 L) casserole.

Combine remaining 5 ingredients in small bowl. Pour over meatballs. Bake, uncovered, in 350°F (175°C) oven for about 1 1/2 hours. Makes about 78 meatballs.

*1 meatball (with sauce): 47 Calories; 1.9 g Total Fat (0.8 g Mono, 0.1 g Poly, 0.7 g Sat); 12 mg Cholesterol; 5 g Carbohydrate; trace Fibre; 3 g Protein; 167 mg Sodium*

Pictured on page 101.

# Zucchini Treats

| Large eggs, fork-beaten | 4 | 4 |
| Finely chopped onion | 1/2 cup | 125 mL |
| Grated Parmesan cheese | 1/2 cup | 125 mL |
| Cooking oil | 1/2 cup | 125 mL |
| Parsley flakes | 1 tsp. | 5 mL |
| Salt | 1/2 tsp. | 2 mL |
| Celery salt | 1/2 tsp. | 2 mL |
| Dried whole oregano | 1/2 tsp. | 2 mL |
| Garlic powder | 1/4 tsp. | 1 mL |
| Biscuit mix | 1 cup | 250 mL |
| Thinly sliced zucchini (with peel) | 3 1/2 cups | 875 mL |
| Grated Parmesan cheese | 1/4 cup | 60 mL |

Put first 9 ingredients into medium bowl. Beat well.

Add biscuit mix and zucchini. Stir well. Turn into greased 9 × 13 inch (22 × 33 cm) pan.

Sprinkle with second amount of Parmesan cheese. Bake in 350°F (175°C) oven for about 30 minutes until browned. Cuts into 54 squares.

*1 square: 44 Calories; 3.3 g Total Fat (1.7 g Mono, 0.8 g Poly, 0.6 g Sat); 17 mg Cholesterol; 2 g Carbohydrate; trace Fibre; 1 g Protein; 103 mg Sodium*

Pictured below.

*You may cut these larger if you prefer. Parmesan cheese gives these little treats a delightful flavour.*

### make ahead

Bake ahead. Cool completely. Do not cut. Cover and chill for up to 24 hours or freeze for up to 6 months. Remove from refrigerator about 30 minutes before serving. Cut while still cold. Remove from freezer 1 to 2 hours before serving. Cut while still partially frozen.

Top Left: Cranberry Meatballs, page 100
Bottom Right: Zucchini Treats, this page

*The contrast between the dark beef and the orange cheese creates an attractive pinwheel effect.*

## make ahead

Make the rolls the day before. Do not cut. Wrap tightly and chill. Just before serving, slice and secure with wooden picks.

## serving suggestion

Serve slightly chilled or at room temperature.

*These scrumptious rolls are bursting with flavour. Watch out—they will be gone before you know it!*

## presentation idea

Cut on the diagonal into 1 1/2 inch (3.8 cm) slices. Secure with cocktail picks.

# Beefy Roll-Ups

| | | |
|---|---|---|
| Block of light cream cheese, softened | 4 oz. | 125 g |
| Sour cream | 1/4 cup | 60 mL |
| Chopped chives | 2 tsp. | 10 mL |
| Prepared horseradish | 1 1/2 tsp. | 7 mL |
| Prepared mustard | 1 tsp. | 5 mL |
| Flour tortillas (8 inch, 20 cm, diameter) | 4 | 4 |
| Shaved deli roast beef | 8 oz. | 225 g |
| Grated medium Cheddar cheese | 1 1/4 cups | 300 mL |

Mix first 5 ingredients well in small bowl.

Divide and spread cream cheese mixture on each tortilla. Lay beef over top. Sprinkle with Cheddar cheese. Roll up tightly. Wrap in plastic wrap. Chill for at least 1 hour. Trim ends. Cut each roll into 10 slices, for a total of 40 slices.

*1 slice: 46 Calories; 2.6 g Total Fat (0.8 g Mono, 0.2 g Poly, 1.4 g Sat); 10 mg Cholesterol; 2 g Carbohydrate; trace Fibre; 3 g Protein; 68 mg Sodium*

Pictured on page 103.

# Curried Chicken Rolls

| | | |
|---|---|---|
| Chili oil | 1 tsp. | 5 mL |
| Boneless, skinless chicken breast halves (about 4), cut lengthwise into long strips | 1 lb. | 454 g |
| Salt | 1/4 tsp. | 1 mL |
| Pepper | 1/8 tsp. | 0.5 mL |
| Curry paste (available in Asian section of grocery store) | 1 tbsp. | 15 mL |
| Mango chutney | 1 tbsp. | 15 mL |
| Worcestershire sauce | 1/4 tsp. | 1 mL |
| English cucumber (with peel) | 1 | 1 |
| Green onions, thinly sliced lengthwise | 4 | 4 |
| Flour tortillas (10 inch, 25 cm, diameter), warmed in oven | 4 | 4 |
| Chopped fresh cilantro (or fresh parsley) | 2 tbsp. | 30 mL |

*(continued on next page)*

Heat chili oil in frying pan on medium until hot. Add chicken. Sprinkle with salt and pepper. Stir-fry for about 3 minutes until browned.

Stir in curry paste, chutney and Worcestershire sauce. Cook for 10 minutes, stirring often, until chicken is no longer pink inside.

Slice cucumber in half lengthwise. Slice each half lengthwise into 4 strips. Divide and arrange cucumber, green onion and chicken mixture at bottom end of each tortilla.

Sprinkle with cilantro. Roll up tightly, jelly roll-style. Cut into 1 inch (2.5 cm) slices. Secure with wooden picks. Makes 40 chicken rolls.

*1 chicken roll:* 33 Calories; 0.5 g Total Fat (0.2 g Mono, 0.1 g Poly, 0.1 g Sat); 7 mg Cholesterol; 4 g Carbohydrate; trace Fibre; 3 g Protein; 45 mg Sodium

Pictured below and on back cover.

Left: Beefy Roll-Ups, page 102
Right: Curried Chicken Rolls, page 102

*This wonderful appetizer has an irresistible Asian flair.*

### notes

There are two very different black bean sauce products available with the same name. What we refer to here is a thinner, smoother product that can be used as is. The concentrated version is paste-like and somewhat chunky. Both are found in the Asian section of the grocery store.

To toast sesame seeds, spread evenly in ungreased shallow pan. Bake in 350°F (175°C) oven for 5 to 10 minutes, stirring or shaking often, until desired doneness.

### make ahead

Assemble in morning. Cover. Chill until ready to serve. Bake as directed.

# Beefy Pepper Dim Sum

| | | |
|---|---|---|
| Large green pepper | 1 | 1 |
| Large red pepper | 1 | 1 |
| Large yellow pepper | 1 | 1 |
| Lean ground beef | 1/2 lb. | 225 g |
| Garlic clove, minced (or 1/4 tsp., 1 mL, powder) | 1 | 1 |
| Salt | 1/2 tsp. | 2 mL |
| Chopped green onion | 1/4 cup | 60 mL |
| Finely diced water chestnuts | 1/4 cup | 60 mL |
| Prepared black bean sauce (see Note, this page) or soy sauce | 1 1/2 tbsp. | 25 mL |
| Large egg, fork-beaten | 1 | 1 |
| All-purpose flour | 1 tbsp. | 15 mL |
| Sesame seeds, toasted (see Note, this page) | 1 tbsp. | 15 mL |

Cut peppers in half crosswise. Remove seeds and white ribs. Cut each half into 4 pieces, for a total of 24 pieces.

Scramble-fry ground beef, garlic and salt in frying pan on medium-high for about 4 minutes until beef is no longer pink. Remove from heat.

Add next 5 ingredients. Mix well.

Arrange pepper pieces, skin-side down, on lightly greased baking sheet. Divide and spoon beef mixture into pepper pieces. Sprinkle with sesame seeds. Bake in 350°F (175°C) oven for 10 to 15 minutes until peppers are tender-crisp. Makes 24 appetizers.

*1 appetizer: 26 Calories; 1.3 g Total Fat (0.5 g Mono, 0.2 g Poly, 0.4 g Sat); 14 mg Cholesterol; 1 g Carbohydrate; trace Fibre; 2 g Protein; 88 mg Sodium*

Pictured on page 105 and on back cover.

*The savoury mushroom flavour of these tarts will warm you from the inside out.*

### make ahead

Prepare filling. Cool. Bake tart shells. Cool. Divide filling among tart shells. Freeze in airtight container for up to 3 months. Just before serving, reheat thawed tarts in 325°F (160°C) oven for 15 to 20 minutes (or 30 to 40 minutes if frozen) until heated through.

# Mushroom Tarts

| | | |
|---|---|---|
| Hard margarine (or butter) | 1 tbsp. | 15 mL |
| Chopped fresh mushrooms | 1 cup | 250 mL |
| Chopped green onion | 1 tbsp. | 15 mL |
| All-purpose flour | 2 tbsp. | 30 mL |
| Salt | 1/4 tsp. | 1 mL |
| Skim evaporated milk (or half-and-half cream) | 2/3 cup | 150 mL |
| Frozen mini-tart shells, thawed | 18 | 18 |

Melt margarine in medium saucepan. Add mushrooms and green onion. Cook for 5 to 10 minutes, stirring often, until mushrooms are golden.

Add flour and salt. Mix well.

Add evaporated milk. Heat and stir until boiling and thickened. Cool. Makes generous 1 cup (250 mL) filling.

Place unfilled tart shells on ungreased baking sheet. Bake in 400°F (205°C) oven for 10 to 13 minutes until lightly browned. Cool. Divide mushroom mixture evenly among tart shells. Bake for about 5 minutes until hot. Remove tarts from foil cups. Makes 18 tarts.

*1 tart: 53 Calories; 3 g Total Fat (1.6 g Mono, 0.6 g Poly, 0.7 g Sat); trace Cholesterol; 5 g Carbohydrate; trace Fibre; 1 g Protein; 100 mg Sodium*

Pictured on page 107.

*The wholesome flavour of the blue cheese and the sweetness of the dates are a perfect combination.*

# Date And Blue Cheese Tarts

Pastry for 2 crust pie, your own or a mix

| | | |
|---|---|---|
| Large eggs | 2 | 2 |
| Buttermilk (or reconstituted from powder) | 1/3 cup | 75 mL |
| Ground nutmeg | 1/2 tsp. | 2 mL |
| Finely chopped dates | 1/2 cup | 125 mL |
| Blue cheese, crumbled (about 1/3 cup, 75 mL) | 1 1/2 oz. | 43 g |

*(continued on next page)*

Roll out pastry on lightly floured surface to 1/4 inch (6 mm) thickness. Cut 24 circles with 3 1/4 inch (8.1 cm) cutter. Press circles into ungreased mini-muffin cups.

Beat eggs, buttermilk and nutmeg in medium bowl.

Add dates and blue cheese. Stir. Fill each tart shell with 2 tsp. (10 mL) date mixture. Bake in 375°F (190°C) oven for about 15 minutes until set. Makes 24 tarts.

*1 tart: 79 Calories; 4.5 g Total Fat (2 g Mono, 0.5 g Poly, 1.6 g Sat); 19 mg Cholesterol; 8 g Carbohydrate; trace Fibre; 2 g Protein; 103 mg Sodium*

Pictured below.

## make ahead

Freeze baked tarts in airtight container for up to 3 months. Just before serving, reheat thawed tarts in 325°F (160°C) oven for 15 to 20 minutes (or 30 to 40 minutes if frozen) until heated through.

## serving suggestion

Serve either warm or at room temperature.

Right: Date And Blue Cheese Tarts, page 106
Left: Mushroom Tarts, page 106

*These tasty wings have an unmistakable zip.*

### make ahead

Arrange partially cooked drumettes in single layer on baking sheet. Freeze until firm. Transfer frozen drumettes to resealable freezer bag. Freeze for up to 1 month. Just before serving, reheat frozen drumettes on greased baking sheet with sides or in greased casserole in 350°F (175°C) oven for 15 to 20 minutes until heated through.

# Glazed Wings

| Chicken drumettes (or whole chicken wings, split in half and tips discarded; see Chicken Wing Tips, page 76) | 3 lbs. | 1.4 kg |
|---|---|---|
| Apricot jam | 1 cup | 250 mL |
| Apple cider vinegar | 3 tbsp. | 50 mL |
| Soy sauce | 2 tsp. | 10 mL |
| Onion powder | 1/4 tsp. | 1 mL |
| Ground ginger | 1/4 tsp. | 1 mL |

Arrange drumettes in single layer on greased foil-lined baking sheet. Bake in 350°F (175°C) oven for 30 minutes.

Measure remaining 5 ingredients into small saucepan. Heat and stir on medium-low until simmering. Makes about 1 1/4 cups (300 mL) sauce. Brush over drumettes. Bake for 15 to 20 minutes, turning and brushing with sauce 2 or 3 times, until tender and no longer pink inside. Makes about 24 drumettes or 36 wing pieces.

*1 drumette (with sauce): 89 Calories; 3.9 g Total Fat (1.6 g Mono, 0.8 g Poly, 1.1 g Sat); 19 mg Cholesterol; 9 g Carbohydrate; 0 g Fibre; 5 g Protein; 53 mg Sodium*

Pictured on page 109.

*These first-rate chicken wings will marinate as they cook. Delicious!*

### make ahead

Freeze cooked drumettes, with liquid, for up to 1 month. Just before serving, reheat frozen drumettes in ungreased roaster or casserole in 350°F (175°C) oven for 15 to 20 minutes until heated through.

# Oriental Wings

| Chicken drumettes (or whole chicken wings, split in half and tips discarded; see Chicken Wing Tips, page 76) | 3 lbs. | 1.4 kg |
|---|---|---|
| Soy sauce | 1 cup | 250 mL |
| Water | 1/2 cup | 125 mL |
| Granulated sugar | 1/2 cup | 125 mL |
| Salt | 1/2 tsp. | 2 mL |
| Ground ginger | 1/4 tsp. | 1 mL |
| Garlic powder | 1/4 tsp. | 1 mL |

Place drumettes, meaty side down, in large ungreased baking pan or roaster.

*(continued on next page)*

Mix next 6 ingredients well in small bowl. Pour over drumettes. Bake, uncovered, in 350°F (175°C) oven for 1 1/2 to 2 hours, turning after 45 minutes, until tender and no longer pink inside. Makes about 24 drumettes or 36 wing pieces.

*1 drumette (with sauce):* 80 Calories; 3.9 g Total Fat (1.6 g Mono, 0.8 g Poly, 1.1 g Sat); 19 mg Cholesterol; 5 g Carbohydrate; 0 g Fibre; 6 g Protein; 793 mg Sodium

Pictured below.

### variation

Use an equal amount of liquid honey in place of the sugar.

Top Left: Oriental Wings, page 108
Centre Right: Glazed Wings, page 108
Bottom Left: Yakitori, page 110

*These little chicken kabobs are a unique and appealing appetizer. Make plenty.*

# Yakitori

| | | |
|---|---|---|
| Soy sauce | 3/4 cup | 175 mL |
| Granulated sugar | 1/4 cup | 60 mL |
| Cooking oil | 1 tbsp. | 15 mL |
| Garlic clove, minced (or 1/4 tsp., 1 mL, powder) | 1 | 1 |
| Ground ginger | 1/2 tsp. | 2 mL |
| Boneless, skinless chicken breast halves (about 2), cut into bite-size pieces | 8 oz. | 225 g |
| Green onions, cut into 1 inch (2.5 cm) pieces | 8 | 8 |
| Bamboo skewers (4 inch, 10 cm, length), soaked in water for 10 minutes | 24 | 24 |

Combine first 5 ingredients in medium bowl.

Add chicken and green onion. Cover. Marinate in refrigerator for about 30 minutes. Drain, reserving marinade.

Bring marinade to a boil in small saucepan. Boil for 5 minutes. Thread 2 pieces of chicken and 2 pieces of green onion alternately onto each skewer. Place on broiler rack. Broil on second rack from top for about 3 minutes per side, basting with marinade several times, until chicken is no longer pink inside. Makes 24 kabobs.

*1 kabob: 31 Calories; 0.7 g Total Fat (0.4 g Mono, 0.2 g Poly, 0.1 g Sat); 5 mg Cholesterol; 3 g Carbohydrate; trace Fibre; 3 g Protein; 546 mg Sodium*

Pictured on page 109.

# Quesadilla Starters

| Grated Monterey Jack cheese | 2 cups | 500 mL |
|---|---|---|
| Flour tortillas (8 inch, 20 cm, diameter) | 6 | 6 |
| Can of diced green chilies, drained | 4 oz. | 113 g |
| Medium avocado, chopped (optional) | 1 | 1 |
| Large tomato, finely diced | 1 | 1 |
| Finely chopped onion | 1/3 cup | 75 mL |
| Cooking oil (see Note, this page) | 2 tbsp. | 30 mL |

Scatter 1/3 cup (75 mL) cheese over half of each tortilla.

Divide green chilies, avocado, tomato and onion over cheese. Dampen tortilla edges with water. Fold tortilla over filled half. Press edges with fork to seal. Cover with damp tea towel to prevent drying out.

Heat 1 tbsp. (15 mL) cooking oil in frying pan on medium-low. Cook folded tortillas, in 2 or 3 batches, for about 3 minutes per side until browned and cheese is melted. Cut into 4 wedges each, for a total of 24 wedges.

*1 wedge: 92 Calories; 5.6 g Total Fat (2.4 g Mono, 0.7 g Poly, 2.2 g Sat); 9 mg Cholesterol; 7 g Carbohydrate; trace Fibre; 4 g Protein; 89 mg Sodium*

Pictured below.

*Here's an appetizer that won't crumble when you bite into it. Excellent served hot or cold.*

### note

You may prefer to lightly grease the frying pan with cooking spray and add only 1 tbsp. (15 mL) cooking oil.

### variation

Use cheese and veggies that you have on hand. Prepare, assemble and brown as directed.

*After one handful, you'll be hooked on these dark, caramel-flavoured nuts.*

**make ahead**

Store in covered container for up to 1 month or freeze for up to 6 months.

# Caramelized Nuts

| | | |
|---|---|---|
| Granulated sugar | 1 cup | 250 mL |
| Water | 1/2 cup | 125 mL |
| Nuts (your choice) | 2 cups | 500 mL |

Heat sugar in heavy frying pan on medium until melted and caramel in colour.

Stir in water. It will spatter furiously so be careful. Stir constantly until caramel melts and mixes with water. Sugar may lump, but continue stirring and heating until smooth.

Add nuts. Stir until coated. Spread evenly on greased baking sheet with sides. Bake in 300°F (150°C) oven for 30 minutes. Cool. Makes 2 cups (500 mL) nuts.

*1/4 cup (60 mL) nuts: 251 Calories; 14.8 g Total Fat (3.4 g Mono, 9.4 g Poly, 1.3 g Sat); 0 mg Cholesterol; 29 g Carbohydrate; 1 g Fibre; 3 g Protein; 3 mg Sodium*

Pictured on page 113.

*These delicious, crunchy nuts make the perfect gift for a friend or dinner host.*

**make ahead**

Store in covered container for up to 1 month or freeze for up to 6 months.

# Sugar-Coated Nuts

| | | |
|---|---|---|
| Mixture of pecan halves, walnut halves and whole blanched almonds | 4 cups | 1 L |
| Egg whites (large), room temperature | 2 | 2 |
| Granulated sugar | 1 cup | 250 mL |
| Salt | 1/16 tsp. | 0.5 mL |
| Hard margarine (or butter), melted | 2 tbsp. | 30 mL |

Spread nuts evenly in ungreased shallow baking pan. Bake in 350°F (175°C) oven for about 10 minutes, stirring or shaking often, until toasted. Cool. Reduce heat to 325°F (160°C).

Beat egg whites in medium bowl until soft peaks form. Gradually beat in sugar and salt until stiff. Fold in cooled nuts.

Grease baking sheet with sides with margarine. Spread nut mixture on baking sheet. Bake for about 30 minutes, stirring every 8 to 10 minutes, until toasted. Makes about 5 1/2 cups (1.4 L) nuts.

*1/4 cup (60 mL) nuts: 177 Calories; 14.4 g Total Fat (9 g Mono, 3.4 g Poly, 1.3 g Sat); 0 mg Cholesterol; 13 g Carbohydrate; 1 g Fibre; 2 g Protein; 23 mg Sodium*

Pictured on page 113.

Top Right: Sugar-Coated Nuts, above
Bottom Left: Caramelized Nuts, above

*A first-course classic!*

### note

If using small mushrooms, omit mozzarella cheese or place only a few shreds on each cap to prevent cheese from toppling off.

### make ahead

Stuff mushrooms in morning. Cover and chill. Just before serving, broil as directed.

# Favourite Mushrooms

| | | |
|---|---|---|
| Fresh large white mushrooms | 24 | 24 |
| Hard margarine (or butter) | 3 tbsp. | 50 mL |
| Finely chopped onion | 1 cup | 250 mL |
| Lean ground beef | 1/4 lb. | 113 g |
| Finely chopped celery | 2 tbsp. | 30 mL |
| Ketchup | 1/4 cup | 60 mL |
| Fine dry bread crumbs | 1/4 cup | 60 mL |
| Garlic powder | 1 tsp. | 5 mL |
| Salt | 1/2 tsp. | 2 mL |
| Pepper | 1/2 tsp. | 2 mL |
| Grated Parmesan cheese | 1/4 cup | 60 mL |
| Grated part-skim mozzarella cheese (see Note, this page) | 1/2 cup | 125 mL |

Remove stems from mushrooms. Chop stems finely. Set aside.

Melt margarine in medium frying pan on medium-high. Add onion, ground beef and celery. Scramble-fry until onion is softened and beef is no longer pink.

Add reserved mushroom stems and next 5 ingredients. Stir well. Remove from heat. Divide and stuff filling into mushroom caps. Arrange in single layer on ungreased baking sheet.

Sprinkle with Parmesan cheese and mozzarella cheese. Broil on second rack from top for about 5 minutes until heated through. Serve immediately. Makes 24 stuffed mushrooms.

*1 stuffed mushroom: 43 Calories; 2.7 g Total Fat (1.4 g Mono, 0.2 g Poly, 0.8 g Sat); 4 mg Cholesterol; 3 g Carbohydrate; trace Fibre; 2 g Protein; 134 mg Sodium*

Pictured on this page.

# Shrimp Cocktail

| | | |
|---|---|---|
| Shredded iceberg lettuce | 1 1/2 cups | 375 mL |
| Can of medium shrimp, rinsed and drained | 4 oz. | 113 g |
| Peeled and diced cooking apple (such as McIntosh) | 1/2 cup | 125 mL |
| Finely chopped celery | 1/4 cup | 60 mL |
| Chili sauce | 3/4 cup | 175 mL |
| Lemon juice | 2 tsp. | 10 mL |
| Worcestershire sauce | 1/4 – 1 tsp. | 1 – 5 mL |
| Onion powder | 1/2 tsp. | 2 mL |
| Salt | 1/4 tsp. | 1 mL |

Line sherbet glasses with lettuce. Divide shrimp over lettuce, saving a few for garnish if desired.

Combine remaining 7 ingredients in small bowl. Spoon sauce over shrimp. Makes 4 to 5 appetizers.

*1 appetizer: 101 Calories; 0.8 g Total Fat (0.1 g Mono, 0.2 g Poly, 0.2 g Sat); 43 mg Cholesterol; 17 g Carbohydrate; 4 g Fibre; 8 g Protein; 929 mg Sodium*

Pictured below.

*A very special beginning that is fit for a very special meal. This will become a family tradition at your holiday gatherings.*

## time saver

Use a frozen shrimp ring, thawed, for quick assembly and uniform-sized shrimp.

## variation

Omit apple. Double the amount of celery.

*Impress your friends and family with this easy Oriental appetizer.*

### serving suggestion

Serve with Spicy Dipping Sauce, page 16, or Soy Fire Dip, page 28.

# Green Onion Cakes

| | | |
|---|---|---|
| All-purpose flour | 2 cups | 500 mL |
| Salt | 1/2 tsp. | 2 mL |
| Very hot, but not boiling, water | 3/4 cup | 175 mL |
| Thinly sliced green onion | 3/4 cup | 175 mL |
| Cooking oil | 2 tbsp. | 30 mL |
| Salt, sprinkle | | |

Measure flour and salt into food processor.

With lid in place and machine running, pour hot water slowly into food chute until dough starts to form a ball. Turn dough out onto lightly floured surface. Knead for about 1 minute until smooth. Cover with plastic wrap. Let stand for at least 30 minutes. Shape into long roll. Divide into 12 portions.

Put green onion into shallow bowl. Flatten 1 piece of dough slightly between your palms. Press each side into green onion. Knead into dough. Shape into flattened circle. Roll out on lightly greased surface with greased rolling pin into 4 1/2 inch (11 cm) circle. Repeat with remaining dough, keeping onion cakes covered with plastic wrap to prevent drying out.

Heat 2 tsp. (10 mL) cooking oil in non-stick frying pan on medium-high. Arrange 4 onion cakes in single layer in frying pan. Cook on both sides, flattening down with lifter, until brown patches appear. Do not overcook. They should be soft, pliable and chewy. Remove to paper towels to drain. Sprinkle with salt. Repeat with remaining cooking oil and onion cakes. Cut into 2 or 4 pieces each. Makes 12 green onion cakes.

*1 green onion cake: 103 Calories; 2.5 g Total Fat (1.4 g Mono, 0.8 g Poly, 0.2 g Sat); 0 mg Cholesterol; 17 g Carbohydrate; 1 g Fibre; 2 g Protein; 115 mg Sodium*

Pictured on page 117.

Centre Left: Green Onion Cakes, above
Bottom Right: Pot Stickers, page 118

*Allow a little extra time to make these—they're worth it! They are visually impressive and so tasty. Your guests will love them.*

## serving suggestion

Serve with Spicy Dipping Sauce, page 16, or Soy Fire Dip, page 28.

# Pot Stickers

| | | |
|---|---|---|
| Grated cabbage | 3/4 cup | 175 mL |
| Lean ground pork | 6 oz. | 170 g |
| Cooked shrimp (about 5 oz., 140 g) | 3/4 cup | 175 mL |
| Finely chopped green onion | 3 tbsp. | 50 mL |
| Soy sauce | 1 tbsp. | 15 mL |
| Cornstarch | 1 tsp. | 5 mL |
| Ground ginger | 1/4 tsp. | 1 mL |
| Garlic powder | 1/4 tsp. | 1 mL |
| Salt | 1/4 tsp. | 1 mL |
| Dumpling wrappers | 36 | 36 |
| Boiling water | 12 cups | 3 L |
| Hard margarine (or butter) | 2 tsp. | 10 mL |

Put first 9 ingredients into medium bowl. Mix well.

Put 2 1/2 tsp. (12 mL) pork mixture onto centre of 1 dumpling wrapper. Dampen edge of wrapper with water. Fold over. Press to seal. Repeat with remaining pork mixture and dumpling wrappers, keeping rolled pot stickers covered with damp tea towel to prevent drying out.

Cook pot stickers, in 3 batches, in boiling water in large uncovered pot or Dutch oven on medium-high for 5 minutes. Remove with slotted spoon. Rinse with cold water.

Melt margarine in non-stick frying pan on medium. Arrange pot stickers close together in frying pan. Cook on 1 side only until well browned. Makes 36 pot stickers.

*1 pot sticker: 19 Calories; 0.5 g Total Fat (0.3 g Mono, 0.1 g Poly, 0.1 g Sat); 8 mg Cholesterol; 1 g Carbohydrate; trace Fibre; 2 g Protein; 70 mg Sodium*

Pictured on page 117.

# Green Chili Snacks

| | | |
|---|---|---|
| Creamed cottage cheese | 1 cup | 250 mL |
| Large eggs | 4 | 4 |
| All-purpose flour | 1/3 cup | 75 mL |
| Hard margarine (or butter), softened | 3 tbsp. | 50 mL |
| Baking powder | 1/2 tsp. | 2 mL |
| Baking soda | 1/2 tsp. | 2 mL |
| Salt | 1/2 tsp. | 2 mL |
| Grated sharp Cheddar cheese | 1 1/2 cups | 375 mL |
| Can of diced green chilies | 4 oz. | 113 g |

Put first 7 ingredients into medium bowl. Beat on medium until mixed.

Add cheese and green chilies. Stir. Turn into greased 8 × 8 inch (20 × 20 cm) baking dish. Bake in 350°F (175°C) oven for 45 to 55 minutes until set and lightly browned on top. Cuts into 25 pieces.

*1 piece: 68 Calories; 4.7 g Total Fat (1.9 g Mono, 0.3 g Poly, 2.1 g Sat); 42 mg Cholesterol; 2 g Carbohydrate; trace Fibre; 4 g Protein; 193 mg Sodium*

Pictured below.

*A simple, delicious recipe that's so easy to prepare.*

## make ahead

Bake ahead. Cool completely. Do not cut. Cover and chill for up to 24 hours or freeze for up to 6 months. Remove from refrigerator about 30 minutes before serving. Cut while still cold. Remove from freezer 1 to 2 hours before serving. Cut while still partially frozen.

## serving suggestion

As an alternative, reheat just before serving in 325°F (160°C) oven for 5 to 10 minutes. Serve warm.

*It takes extra time to get this dish into the refrigerator but it's ready to serve with barely any effort. The shrimp taste great as is—no dip is necessary.*

## serving suggestion

Serve with cocktail picks.

# Marinated Shrimp

| | | |
|---|---|---|
| Bay leaves | 3 | 3 |
| Dried crushed chilies | 2 tsp. | 10 mL |
| Whole allspice | 1 tsp. | 5 mL |
| Whole cloves | 1 tsp. | 5 mL |
| Mustard seed | 1 tsp. | 5 mL |
| Whole peppercorns | 1 tsp. | 5 mL |
| Boiling water | 10 cups | 2.5 L |
| Salt | 4 tsp. | 20 mL |
| Raw medium shrimp (about 70 – 80 with tails intact and not peeled) | 2 lbs. | 900 g |
| MARINADE | | |
| Water | 1/2 cup | 125 mL |
| Cooking oil | 1/4 cup | 60 mL |
| White vinegar | 1/3 cup | 75 mL |
| Worcestershire sauce | 2 tbsp. | 30 mL |
| Prepared mustard | 1 tsp. | 5 mL |
| Celery seed | 1 tsp. | 5 mL |
| Celery salt | 1/2 tsp. | 2 mL |
| Salt | 1/2 tsp. | 2 mL |
| Cayenne pepper | 1/8 tsp. | 0.5 mL |
| Large onion, thinly sliced | 1 | 1 |

Tie first 6 ingredients in double layer of cheesecloth.

Add to boiling water and salt in large pot or Dutch oven.

Add shrimp. Return to a boil. Boil, uncovered, for 2 to 3 minutes until shrimp are pink and curled. Drain. Cool. Peel and devein. Discard cheesecloth bag and contents.

**Marinade:** Combine first 9 ingredients in small bowl.

Layer 1/2 of shrimp in large bowl. Layer 1/2 of onion over shrimp. Layer with remaining shrimp and remaining onion. Pour marinade over all. Cover. Marinate in refrigerator for at least 24 hours. Transfer shrimp, onion and marinade to serving bowl or deep platter. Makes about 75 shrimp.

*1 shrimp (with marinade): 20 Calories; 0.9 g Total Fat (0.5 g Mono, 0.3 g Poly, 0.1 g Sat); 24 mg Cholesterol; trace Carbohydrate; trace Fibre; 3 g Protein; 56 mg Sodium*

Pictured on page 121.

*These succulent meatballs will be a hit every time! Dip in Apricot Sauce.*

### make ahead

Meatballs can be frozen and heated in 350°F (175°C) oven for 15 to 20 minutes until hot.

### apricot sauce

In a small bowl combine 1 cup (250 mL) apricot jam, 3 tbsp. (50 mL) cider vinegar and 1/4 tsp. (1 mL) paprika. Stir well, pour into a pretty bowl and dip in.

*These are very striking, and they taste even better than they look!*

### make ahead

Freeze baked tarts (in foil cups) in airtight container for up to 3 months. Just before serving, reheat thawed tarts in 325°F (160°C) oven for 15 to 20 minutes (or 30 to 40 minutes if frozen) until heated through. Remove from foil cups.

# Polynesian Meatballs

| Lean ground beef | 2 lbs. | 900 g |
|---|---|---|
| Can of water chestnuts, drained and finely chopped | 10 oz. | 284 mL |
| Soy sauce | 3 tbsp. | 50 mL |
| Brown (or granulated) sugar, packed | 1 tbsp. | 15 mL |
| Garlic cloves, minced | 2 | 2 |
| Parsley flakes | 1 tsp. | 5 mL |
| Onion powder | 1/2 tsp. | 2 mL |

Put all 7 ingredients into large bowl. Mix well. Shape into 1 inch (2.5 cm) balls. (See Meatball Tips, page 72.) Place on ungreased baking sheet with sides. Bake in 375°F (190°C) oven for about 15 minutes until meatballs are no longer pink inside. Makes about 78 meatballs.

*1 meatball: 20 Calories; 1 g Total Fat (0.4 g Mono, trace Poly, 0.4 g Sat); 6 mg Cholesterol; 1 g Carbohydrate; trace Fibre; 2 g Protein; 45 mg Sodium*

Pictured on page 123.

# Crab Tartlets

| Large eggs | 2 | 2 |
|---|---|---|
| All-purpose flour | 2 tbsp. | 30 mL |
| Salad dressing (or mayonnaise) | 1/2 cup | 125 mL |
| Milk | 1/2 cup | 125 mL |
| Green onions, finely chopped | 3 | 3 |
| Can of crabmeat, drained and cartilage removed, flaked | 4 1/4 oz. | 120 g |
| Grated Swiss cheese | 2 cups | 500 mL |
| Frozen mini-tart shells, thawed | 60 | 60 |

Beat eggs in medium bowl until frothy. Add flour, salad dressing and milk. Stir well. Add green onion, crab and cheese. Stir to combine well.

Place tart shells on ungreased baking sheet. Divide cheese mixture evenly among tart shells. Bake on lowest rack in 350°F (175°C) oven for about 40 minutes until set. Makes 60 tarts.

*1 tart: 45 Calories; 3.5 g Total Fat (1.5 g Mono, 0.7 g Poly, 1.1 g Sat); 12 mg Cholesterol; 2 g Carbohydrate; trace Fibre; 2 g Protein; 50 mg Sodium*

Pictured on page 123.

Top: Polynesian Meatballs, above
Bottom: Crab Tartlets, above

Throughout this book measurements are given in Conventional and Metric measure. To compensate for differences between the two measurements due to rounding, a full metric measure is not always used. The cup used is the standard 8 fluid ounce. Temperature is given in degrees Fahrenheit and Celsius. Baking pan measurements are in inches and centimetres as well as quarts and litres. An exact metric conversion is given on this page as well as the working equivalent (Metric Standard Measure).

## Pans

| Conventional – Inches | Metric – Centimetres |
|---|---|
| 8 × 8 inch | 20 × 20 cm |
| 9 × 9 inch | 22 × 22 cm |
| 9 × 13 inch | 22 × 33 cm |
| 10 × 15 inch | 25 × 38 cm |
| 11 × 17 inch | 28 × 43 cm |
| 8 × 2 inch round | 20 × 5 cm |
| 9 × 2 inch round | 22 × 5 cm |
| 10 × 4 1/2 inch tube | 25 × 11 cm |
| 8 × 4 × 3 inch loaf | 20 × 10 × 7.5 cm |
| 9 × 5 × 3 inch loaf | 22 × 12.5 × 7.5 cm |

## Oven Temperatures

| Fahrenheit (°F) | Celsius (°C) | Fahrenheit (°F) | Celsius (°C) |
|---|---|---|---|
| 175° | 80° | 350° | 175° |
| 200° | 95° | 375° | 190° |
| 225° | 110° | 400° | 205° |
| 250° | 120° | 425° | 220° |
| 275° | 140° | 450° | 230° |
| 300° | 150° | 475° | 240° |
| 325° | 160° | 500° | 260° |

## Spoons

| Conventional Measure | Metric Exact Conversion Millilitre (mL) | Metric Standard Measure Millilitre (mL) |
|---|---|---|
| 1/8 teaspoon (tsp.) | 0.6 mL | 0.5 mL |
| 1/4 teaspoon (tsp.) | 1.2 mL | 1 mL |
| 1/2 teaspoon (tsp.) | 2.4 mL | 2 mL |
| 1 teaspoon (tsp.) | 4.7 mL | 5 mL |
| 2 teaspoons (tsp.) | 9.4 mL | 10 mL |
| 1 tablespoon (tbsp.) | 14.2 mL | 15 mL |

## Cups

| | | |
|---|---|---|
| 1/4 cup (4 tbsp.) | 56.8 mL | 60 mL |
| 1/3 cup (5 1/3 tbsp.) | 75.6 mL | 75 mL |
| 1/2 cup (8 tbsp.) | 113.7 mL | 125 mL |
| 2/3 cup (10 2/3 tbsp.) | 151.2 mL | 150 mL |
| 3/4 cup (12 tbsp.) | 170.5 mL | 175 mL |
| 1 cup (16 tbsp.) | 227.3 mL | 250 mL |
| 4 1/2 cups | 1022.9 mL | 1000 mL(1 L) |

## Dry Measurements

| Conventional Measure Ounces (oz.) | Metric Exact Conversion Grams (g) | Metric Standard Measure Grams (g) |
|---|---|---|
| 1 oz. | 28.3 g | 28 g |
| 2 oz. | 56.7 g | 57 g |
| 3 oz. | 85.0 g | 85 g |
| 4 oz. | 113.4 g | 125 g |
| 5 oz. | 141.7 g | 140 g |
| 6 oz. | 170.1 g | 170 g |
| 7 oz. | 198.4 g | 200 g |
| 8 oz. | 226.8 g | 250 g |
| 16 oz. | 453.6 g | 500 g |
| 32 oz. | 907.2 g | 1000 g (1 kg) |

## Casseroles

### Canada & Britain

| Standard Size Casserole | Exact Metric Measure |
|---|---|
| 1 qt. (5 cups) | 1.13 L |
| 1 1/2 qts. (7 1/2 cups) | 1.69 L |
| 2 qts. (10 cups) | 2.25 L |
| 2 1/2 qts. (12 1/2 cups) | 2.81 L |
| 3 qts. (15 cups) | 3.38 L |
| 4 qts. (20 cups) | 4.5 L |
| 5 qts. (25 cups) | 5.63 L |

### United States

| Standard Size Casserole | Exact Metric Measure |
|---|---|
| 1 qt. (4 cups) | 900 mL |
| 1 1/2 qts. (6 cups) | 1.35 L |
| 2 qts. (8 cups) | 1.8 L |
| 2 1/2 qts. (10 cups) | 2.25 L |
| 3 qts. (12 cups) | 2.7 L |
| 4 qts. (16 cups) | 3.6 L |
| 5 qts. (20 cups) | 4.5 L |

# tip index

Almonds – to toast . . . . . . . . . . . . . . 28

Beef – to slice easily . . . . . . . . . . . . . 94

Black bean sauce – to differentiate
between products . . . . . . . . . 68, 104

Chicken wings
– to freeze . . . . . . . 76, 77, 80, 81, 108
– to make ahead . . 76, 77, 80, 81, 108
– to separate whole wings . . . . . . . . 76

Cilantro – to substitute parsley for . . . . 36

Citrus stripper – to create 'stripes' . . . . 14

Corned beef – to substitute for canned . 30

Crinkle cutter – to make ruffled edges . 14

Drumettes, see Chicken wings

Eggs
– to make perfect hard-boiled . . . . . . 59
– to slice hard-boiled easily . . . . . . . . 59

Freezing
– chicken wings . . . 76, 77, 80, 81, 108
– meatballs. . . . . . 72, 74, 96,100, 122
– tarts. . . . . . . . . . . . . .56, 97,106, 107

Hard-boiled eggs
– to make perfect. . . . . . . . . . . . . . . 59
– to slice easily . . . . . . . . . . . . . . . . 59

Hot peppers – to chop safely . . . . . 36, 48

Meatballs
– to freeze . . . . . . 72, 74, 96, 100, 122
– to make ahead . . . . . 72, 74, 96, 100
– to make uniform size. . . . . . . . . . . 72

Mushrooms – to substitute canned. . . . 66

Nuts
– to make ahead . . . . . . . . . . . . . . 112
– to toast . . . . . . . . . . . . . . . . . . . . 28

Parsley – as substitute for cilantro . . . . . 36

Peppers, hot – to chop safely . . . . . 36, 48

Sauce, black bean – to
differentiate between
products . . . . . . . . . . . . . . . . 68, 104

Sesame seeds – to toast . . 18, 28, 68, 104

Shrimp – to substitute for canned. . . .6, 30

Slicing
– beef. . . . . . . . . . . . . . . . . . . . . . . 94
– hard-boiled eggs. . . . . . . . . . . . . . 59

Tarts
– to freeze . . . . . 56, 97,106, 107, 122
– to make ahead  56, 97,106, 107, 122

Toasting nuts and seeds . . 18, 28, 68, 104

Wings, see Chicken wings

# recipe index

*A*

Apricot Sauce . . . . . . . . . . . . . . 122
Antipasto . . . . . . . . . . . . . . . . . . 46
Artichoke Dip . . . . . . . . . . . . . . . 28

*B*

Baby Cheddar Tarts . . . . . . . . . . . 97
Baby Swiss Tarts . . . . . . . . . . . . . 97
Bacon
    Jiffy Mushroom Rolls. . . . . . . . 98
    Scallops With . . . . . . . . . . . . 63
    Spinach Dip #1 . . . . . . . . . . . 26
    Wiener Bites . . . . . . . . . . . . . 75
Bali Sauce. . . . . . . . . . . . . . . . . . 76
Bali Wings. . . . . . . . . . . . . . . . . . 76
Bean Sprouts
    Beef Sprout Rolls. . . . . . . . . . 68
    Spring Rolls. . . . . . . . . . . . . . 88
Beans
    Black Bean Dip . . . . . . . . . . . . 8
    Devil's Dip . . . . . . . . . . . . . . 12
    Double Devil's Dip . . . . . . . . 12
    Fruity Salsa . . . . . . . . . . . . . . 36
    Kidney Bean Dip. . . . . . . . . . . 8
    Mexican Snackies . . . . . . . . . 54
    Polynesian Meatballs. . . . . . . 122
    Refried Bean Dip. . . . . . . . . . 52
    Spreading Forest Fire . . . . . . 38
Beef
    Beefy Pepper Dim Sum. . . . . 104
    Beefy Roll-Ups. . . . . . . . . . . 102
    Cheesy Meat Canapés . . . . . . 58
    Corned Beef Mousse. . . . . . . . 30
    Cranberry Meatballs . . . . . . . 100
    Favourite Mushrooms . . . . . . 114
    Maple-Glazed Meatballs . . . . . 72
    Mexican Snackies . . . . . . . . . 54
    Polynesian Meatballs. . . . . . . 122
    Polynesian Satay . . . . . . . . . . 94
    Refried Bean Dip. . . . . . . . . . 52
    Spanish Meatballs. . . . . . . . . 74
    Tortilla Roll-Ups . . . . . . . . . . 70
Beef Sprout Rolls. . . . . . . . . . . . . 68
Beefy Pepper Dim Sum. . . . . . . . 104
Beefy Roll-Ups. . . . . . . . . . . . . . 102

**Most Loved**

**Most Loved Treats**

by Jean Paré

*most loved recipe collection*

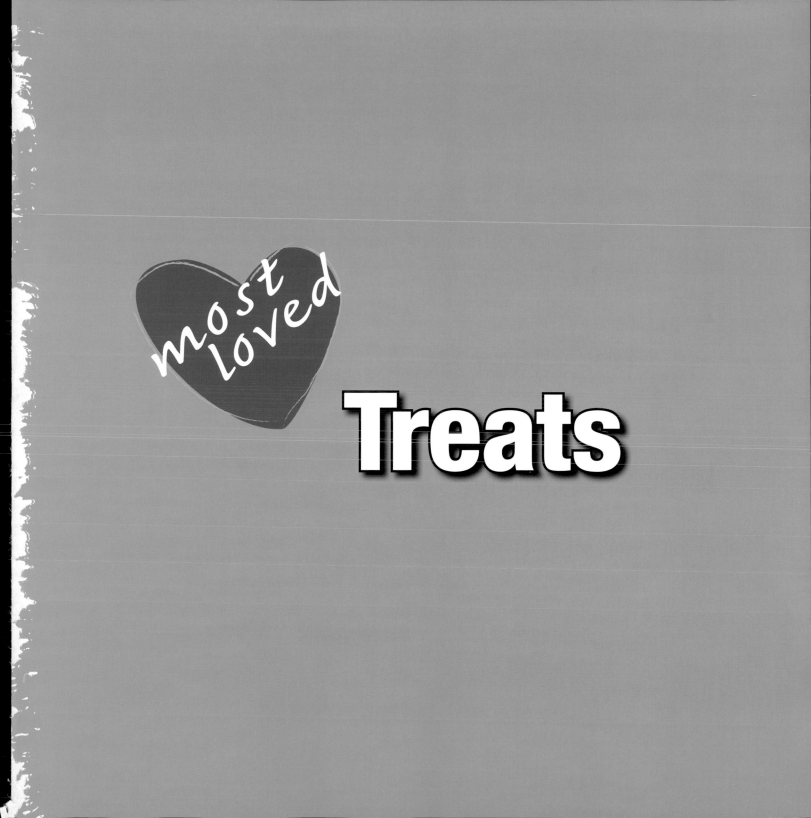

most loved

Treats

**Divider Photo:**
Candy Bar Squares, page 92

*We gratefully acknowledge the following suppliers for their generous support of our Test and Photography Kitchens:*

*Corelle®*
*Hamilton Beach® Canada*
*Lagostina®*
*Proctor Silex® Canada*
*Tupperware®*

*Our special thanks to the following businesses for providing props for photography:*

*Anchor Hocking Canada*
*Canhome Global*
*Casa Bugatti*
*Cherison Enterprises Inc.*
*Danesco Inc.*
*Island Pottery Inc.*
*Klass Works*
*Linens 'N Things*
*Micheals The Arts And Crafts Store*
*Mikasa Home Store*
*Pfaltzgraff Canada*
*Pier 1 Imports*
*Stokes*
*The Royal Doulton Store*
*Zellers*

**Pictured from left:** Chocolate Orange Cake, page 6; Swedish Tea Cakes, page 34; Nanaimo Bars, page 72; Mars Bars Squares, page 74; Bocconne Dolce, page 52.

## table of contents

# the Company's Coming story

*"never share a recipe you wouldn't use yourself"*

Jean Paré (pronounced "jeen PAIR-ee") grew up understanding that the combination of family, friends and home cooking is the best recipe for a good life. From her mother, she learned to appreciate good cooking, while her father praised even her earliest attempts in the kitchen. When Jean left home, she took with her a love of cooking, many family recipes and an intriguing desire to read cookbooks as if they were novels!

In 1963, when her four children had all reached school age, Jean volunteered to cater the 50th Anniversary of the Vermilion School of Agriculture, now Lakeland College, in Alberta, Canada. Working out of her home, Jean prepared a dinner for more than 1,000 people, which launched a flourishing catering operation that continued for over 18 years. During that time, she had countless opportunities to test new ideas with immediate feedback—resulting in empty plates and contented customers! Whether preparing cocktail sandwiches for a house party or serving a hot meal for 1,500 people, Jean Paré earned a reputation for good food, courteous service and reasonable prices.

As requests for her recipes mounted, Jean was often asked the question, "Why don't you write a cookbook?" Jean responded by teaming up with her son, Grant Lovig, in the fall of 1980 to form Company's Coming Publishing Limited. The publication of *150 Delicious Squares* on April 14, 1981 marked the debut of what would soon become one of the world's most popular cookbook series.

The company has grown since those early days when Jean worked from a spare bedroom in her home. Today, she continues to write recipes while working closely with the staff of the Recipe Factory, as the Company's Coming test kitchen is affectionately known. There she fills the role of mentor, assisting with the development of recipes people most want to use for everyday cooking and easy entertaining. Every Company's Coming recipe is *kitchen-tested* before it's approved for publication.

Jean's daughter, Gail Lovig, is responsible for marketing and distribution, leading a team that includes sales personnel located in major cities across Canada. In addition, Company's Coming cookbooks are published and distributed under licence in the United States, Australia and other world markets. Bestsellers many times over in English, Company's Coming cookbooks have also been published in French and Spanish.

Familiar and trusted in home kitchens around the world, Company's Coming cookbooks are offered in a variety of formats. Highly regarded as kitchen workbooks, the softcover Original Series, with its lay-flat plastic comb binding, is still a favourite among readers.

Jean Paré's approach to cooking has always called for *quick and easy recipes* using *everyday ingredients.* That view has served her well. The recipient of many awards, including the Queen Elizabeth Golden Jubilee medal, Jean was appointed a Member of the Order of Canada, her country's highest lifetime achievement honour.

Jean continues to gain new supporters by adhering to what she calls The Golden Rule of Cooking: *"Never share a recipe you wouldn't use yourself."* It's an approach that works— *millions of times over!*

# foreword

*Most Loved Treats* is the third volume in our Most Loved Recipe Collection and is especially compiled to satisfy your sweet tooth. Whether you crave something quick and delicious to top off your supper or something slow and sweet to linger over with coffee or tea, you're sure to find the perfect treat among these time-honoured favourites. Every recipe is easy to follow and uses common ingredients you most likely have on hand, but results in extraordinary treats you didn't know you could make at home. Try it! You'll find you can almost taste that first bite with your eyes!

Dessert is the grand finale at mealtime. I usually follow a heavier meal with a light dessert, but I go all out with dessert if the meal is lighter. To help you choose just the right treat for the occasion, we've organized the recipes in this book into five convenient sections. You'll find every recipe photographed in scrumptious colour. When you have some extra time to spend in the kitchen, select something from the Cakes & Cheesecakes section to show off your culinary skills. When you have the urge to bake something soft, chocolate or nutty for snacking, Cookies has just what you need. Looking for a more substantial treat? Try any one of our delightful Desserts. The section on Squares, Bars & Brownies is stacked full of bite-size bliss, and Sweet Snacks is filled with those oh-so-tempting favourites you just can't do without.

Want something extra special to complete the tasty treat you've just made? Why not display it to full advantage on a brightly coloured serving plate or on delicate china? Add fruit garnishes or chocolate curls and you're all set for company! And remember, the next treat you make could become your newest family tradition—because the best part of making something sweet is sharing it with those you love.

With this superb collection of *Most Loved Treats*, you'll never be at a loss when company's coming, even if it's only a company of one—you!

*Jean Paré*

## nutrition information

Each recipe has been analyzed using the most up-to-date version of the Canadian Nutrient File from Health Canada, which is based on the United States Department of Agriculture (USDA) Nutrient Data Base. If more than one ingredient is listed (such as "hard margarine or butter"), or a range is given (1 – 2 tsp., 5 – 10 mL) then the first ingredient or amount is used in the analysis. Where an ingredient reads "sprinkle," "optional," or "for garnish," it is not included as part of the nutrition information. Milk, unless stated otherwise, is 1% and cooking oil, unless stated otherwise, is canola.

Margaret Ng, B.Sc. (Hon), M.A.
Registered Dietitian

*Milk chocolate flavour with a splash of orange. A delicious dessert to serve any time.*

**note**

To make sour milk, measure 1 tbsp. (15 mL) white vinegar or lemon juice into 1 cup (250 mL) liquid measure. Add milk to make 3/4 cup (175 mL). Stir. Let stand for 1 minute.

# Chocolate Orange Cake

| | | |
|---|---|---|
| Hard margarine (or butter), softened | 1/2 cup | 125 mL |
| Granulated sugar | 3/4 cup | 175 mL |
| Large eggs | 2 | 2 |
| Orange flavouring | 2 tsp. | 10 mL |
| Semi-sweet chocolate baking squares (1 oz., 28 g, each), chopped | 3 | 3 |
| Sour milk (see Note) | 3/4 cup | 175 mL |
| All-purpose flour | 2 cups | 500 mL |
| Baking soda | 1 tsp. | 5 mL |
| Salt | 1/2 tsp. | 2 mL |
| **CHOCOLATE ORANGE ICING** | | |
| Icing (confectioner's) sugar | 4 cups | 1 L |
| Block of cream cheese, softened | 8 oz. | 250 g |
| Cocoa, sifted if lumpy | 1/2 cup | 125 mL |
| Hard margarine (or butter), softened | 1/4 cup | 60 mL |
| Orange flavouring | 2 tsp. | 10 mL |

Cream margarine and sugar in large bowl. Add eggs, 1 at a time, beating well after each addition. Add orange flavouring. Beat well.

Heat and stir chocolate and sour milk in heavy medium saucepan on medium-low until chocolate is melted. Mixture will look curdled. Remove from heat. Let stand for 5 minutes.

Combine flour, baking soda and salt in medium bowl. Add to margarine mixture in 3 additions, alternating with chocolate mixture in 2 additions, beginning and ending with flour mixture. Divide and spread evenly in 2 greased 8 inch (20 cm) round pans. Bake in 350°F (175°C) oven for about 25 minutes until wooden pick inserted in centre comes out clean. Let stand in pans for 5 minutes before inverting onto wire racks to cool completely.

**Chocolate Orange Icing:** Beat all 5 ingredients in medium bowl until smooth. Makes about 3 cups (750 mL) icing. Place 1 cake layer on serving plate. Spread with 3/4 cup (175 mL) icing. Place second layer on top. Spread top and side with remaining icing. Cuts into 12 wedges.

*1 wedge: 538 Calories; 23.3 g Total Fat (11.2 g Mono, 1.8 g Poly, 9 g Sat); 59 mg Cholesterol; 80 g Carbohydrate; 2 g Fibre; 7 g Protein; 430 mg Sodium*

Pictured on page 7.

*A recipe this old and this good lasts through the years and stands the test of time. You can omit the topping and use as a shortcake.*

# Lazy Daisy Cake

| | | |
|---|---|---|
| Large eggs | 2 | 2 |
| Granulated sugar | 1 cup | 250 mL |
| Vanilla | 1 tsp. | 5 mL |
| All-purpose flour | 1 cup | 250 mL |
| Baking powder | 1 tsp. | 5 mL |
| Salt | 1/2 tsp. | 2 mL |
| Milk | 1/2 cup | 125 mL |
| Hard margarine (or butter) | 1 tbsp. | 15 mL |
| **COCONUT TOPPING** | | |
| Hard margarine (or butter) | 3 tbsp. | 50 mL |
| Brown sugar, packed | 1/2 cup | 125 mL |
| Half-and-half cream (or milk) | 2 tbsp. | 30 mL |
| Flake coconut | 1/2 cup | 125 mL |

Beat eggs in medium bowl until frothy. Add sugar, 2 tbsp. (30 mL) at a time while beating, until thickened. Add vanilla. Beat well.

Combine flour, baking powder and salt in small bowl. Add to egg mixture. Stir.

Heat and stir milk and margarine in small heavy saucepan on medium until margarine is melted. Add to flour mixture. Stir well. Spread batter evenly in greased 9 x 9 inch (22 x 22 cm) pan. Bake in 350°F (175°C) oven for 25 to 30 minutes until wooden pick inserted in centre comes out clean.

**Coconut Topping:** Measure margarine, brown sugar and cream into medium saucepan. Bring to a rolling boil on medium-high, stirring occasionally. Remove from heat.

Add coconut. Stir. Spread evenly over warm cake. Return to oven for about 3 minutes until top is bubbling. Let stand in pan on wire rack until cool. Cuts into 12 pieces.

*1 piece: 226 Calories; 7.7 g Total Fat (3.1 g Mono, 0.6 g Poly, 3.6 g Sat); 37 mg Cholesterol; 37 g Carbohydrate; 1 g Fibre; 3 g Protein; 198 mg Sodium*

Pictured on page 9.

*Very pretty, moist cake with a tangy lime bite. Serve with Juicy Berries for an extra-special treat.*

### juicy berries

Combine 2 cups (500 mL) whole fresh berries (such as blackberries, blueberries or raspberries) and sliced strawberries in medium bowl. Add 1 cup (250 mL) white grape juice and 1/2 cup (125 mL) white corn syrup. Stir gently until coated. Chill for 1 hour to blend flavours. Serve with Lime Poppy Seed Cake.

### juicy berries variation

Ice wine is a slightly more expensive, but delightful way to flavour berries. Omit white grape juice and corn syrup. Add 1/2 to 3/4 cup (125 to 175 mL) ice wine to 1 1/2 to 3 cups (375 to 750 mL) berries. Stir gently. A sweet dessert wine may be used instead of ice wine.

# Lime Poppy Seed Cake

| | | |
|---|---|---|
| Milk | 1 cup | 250 mL |
| Poppy seeds | 3 tbsp. | 50 mL |
| Egg whites (large), room temperature | 3 | 3 |
| Almond flavouring | 1 tsp. | 5 mL |
| Hard margarine (or butter), softened | 1 cup | 250 mL |
| Granulated sugar | 1 1/4 cups | 300 mL |
| Egg yolks (large) | 3 | 3 |
| Finely grated lime zest | 1 tbsp. | 15 mL |
| All-purpose flour | 2 cups | 500 mL |
| Baking powder | 1 tbsp. | 15 mL |
| Salt | 1/2 tsp. | 2 mL |
| Hot water | 2 tbsp. | 30 mL |
| Icing (confectioner's) sugar | 3/4 cup | 175 mL |
| Lime juice | 6 tbsp. | 100 mL |

Heat and stir milk and poppy seeds in small saucepan on medium until very hot, but not boiling. Remove from heat. Let stand until room temperature.

Beat egg whites and flavouring in medium bowl until stiff peaks form. Set aside.

Cream margarine and granulated sugar in large bowl. Add egg yolks, lime zest and milk mixture. Beat well.

Combine flour, baking powder and salt in small bowl. Add to margarine mixture. Beat well. Fold egg white mixture into flour mixture until no white streaks remain. Spread evenly in greased 10 inch (25 cm) angel food tube pan or 10 inch (25 cm) springform pan. Bake in 325°F (160°C) oven for about 1 hour until wooden pick inserted in centre of cake comes out clean. Let stand in pan for 10 minutes before removing to serving plate.

Stir hot water into icing sugar in small bowl until smooth. Add lime juice. Stir. Drizzle over hot cake, allowing syrup to soak in. Cool. Cuts into 12 wedges.

*1 wedge: 384 Calories; 18.8 g Total Fat (11.2 g Mono, 2.6 g Poly, 4 g Sat); 55 mg Cholesterol; 50 g Carbohydrate; 1 g Fibre; 5 g Protein; 408 mg Sodium*

Pictured on page 11.

*Rich and delicious. Very moist. Freezes well.*

# Date Cake

| | | |
|---|---|---|
| Chopped pitted dates | 1 1/2 cups | 375 mL |
| Baking soda | 1 1/2 tsp. | 7 mL |
| Boiling water | 1 1/2 cups | 375 mL |
| Hard margarine (or butter), softened | 3/4 cup | 175 mL |
| Brown sugar, packed | 1 cup | 250 mL |
| Granulated sugar | 1/2 cup | 125 mL |
| Large eggs | 2 | 2 |
| Vanilla | 1 tsp. | 5 mL |
| All-purpose flour | 2 1/2 cups | 625 mL |
| Baking powder | 1 1/2 tsp. | 7 mL |
| Salt | 1/2 tsp. | 2 mL |
| Hard margarine (or butter) | 1/3 cup | 75 mL |
| Brown sugar, packed | 1 cup | 250 mL |
| Half-and-half cream (or milk) | 3 tbsp. | 50 mL |
| Fine coconut | 1 cup | 250 mL |

Place dates in medium bowl. Sprinkle with baking soda. Pour boiling water over top. Set aside until cool. Stir.

Cream next 3 ingredients in large bowl. Add eggs, 1 at a time, beating well after each addition. Add vanilla. Beat.

Combine flour, baking powder and salt in small bowl. Add to margarine mixture in 3 additions, alternating with date mixture in 2 additions, beginning and ending with flour mixture. Spread evenly in greased 9 x 13 inch (22 x 33 cm) pan. Bake in 325°F (160°C) oven for 40 to 50 minutes until wooden pick inserted in centre comes out clean.

Measure next 3 ingredients into medium saucepan. Bring to a rolling boil on medium-high, stirring occasionally. Remove from heat.

Add coconut. Stir. Spread evenly over warm cake. Return to oven for about 3 minutes until top is bubbling. Let stand in pan on wire rack until cool. Cuts into 18 pieces.

*1 piece:* 365 Calories; 15.4 g Total Fat (7.7 g Mono, 1.3 g Poly, 5.5 g Sat); 24 mg Cholesterol; 56 g Carbohydrate; 2 g Fibre; 3 g Protein; 347 mg Sodium

Pictured on page 13.

*A warm and comforting dessert on a chilly winter evening.*

# Sticky Ginger Fig Cake

| | | |
|---|---|---|
| Chopped figs | 1 1/3 cups | 325 mL |
| Baking soda | 1 tsp. | 5 mL |
| Boiling water | 1 1/3 cups | 325 mL |
| Hard margarine (or butter), softened | 1/3 cup | 75 mL |
| Brown sugar, packed | 2/3 cup | 150 mL |
| Large eggs | 2 | 2 |
| All-purpose flour | 1 cup | 250 mL |
| Baking powder | 2 tsp. | 10 mL |
| Minced crystallized ginger | 1/4 cup | 60 mL |
| **CINNAMON BRANDY SAUCE** | | |
| Hard margarine (or butter), cut up | 1/2 cup | 125 mL |
| Brown sugar, packed | 1/2 cup | 125 mL |
| Whipping cream | 1/2 cup | 125 mL |
| Brandy | 2 tbsp. | 30 mL |
| Ground cinnamon | 1/2 tsp. | 2 mL |

Place figs in medium bowl. Sprinkle with baking soda. Pour boiling water over top. Let stand for 10 minutes. Process (with liquid) in blender or food processor until almost smooth (see Safety Tip).

Cream margarine and brown sugar in large bowl. Add eggs, 1 at a time, beating well after each addition.

Combine flour, baking powder and ginger in small bowl. Add to margarine mixture. Stir well. Add fig mixture. Stir. Line bottom and side of greased 8 inch (20 cm) springform pan with parchment (not waxed) paper. Spread batter evenly in pan. Bake in 350°F (175°C) oven for about 50 minutes until wooden pick inserted in centre of cake comes out clean. Let stand in pan for 10 minutes before removing to wire rack to cool.

**Cinnamon Brandy Sauce:** Heat and stir all 5 ingredients in medium saucepan on medium until boiling. Boil for about 5 minutes, without stirring, until slightly thickened. Let stand for 5 minutes. Makes 1 cup (250 mL) sauce. Drizzle over individual servings of warm cake. Cuts into 8 wedges.

*1 wedge: 545 Calories; 27 g Total Fat (15.2 g Mono, 2.6 g Poly, 7.8 g Sat); 72 mg Cholesterol; 73 g Carbohydrate; 4 g Fibre; 5 g Protein; 530 mg Sodium*

Pictured on page 15.

**Safety Tip:** Follow blender manufacturer's instructions for processing hot liquids. If in doubt, we recommend using a hand blender.

*Simple and delicious. Dust with icing sugar instead of the icing for a less sweet dessert.*

# White Chocolate Pound Cake

| | | |
|---|---|---|
| White chocolate baking squares (1 oz., 28 g, each), chopped | 4 | 4 |
| Evaporated milk | 1 cup | 250 mL |
| Hard margarine (or butter), softened | 1 cup | 250 mL |
| Granulated sugar | 1 2/3 cups | 400 mL |
| Large eggs | 5 | 5 |
| All-purpose flour | 2 3/4 cups | 675 mL |
| Baking soda | 1/2 tsp. | 2 mL |
| Salt | 1/2 tsp. | 2 mL |
| WHITE CHOCOLATE ICING | | |
| Hard margarine (or butter) | 1/4 cup | 60 mL |
| White chocolate baking squares (1 oz., 28 g, each), chopped | 3 | 3 |
| Icing (confectioner's) sugar | 2 cups | 500 mL |
| Milk | 1 tbsp. | 15 mL |
| Vanilla | 1/2 tsp. | 2 mL |

Heat and stir chocolate and evaporated milk in heavy medium saucepan on medium-low until chocolate is melted. Remove from heat. Let stand for 5 minutes.

Cream margarine and sugar in large bowl. Add eggs, 1 at a time, beating well after each addition.

Combine flour, baking soda and salt in medium bowl. Add to margarine mixture in 3 additions, alternating with chocolate mixture in 2 additions, beginning and ending with flour mixture. Spread evenly in greased 12 cup (3 L) bundt pan. Bake in 325°F (160°C) oven for about 1 hour until wooden pick inserted in centre of cake comes out clean. Let stand in pan for 20 minutes before inverting onto wire rack to cool completely.

**White Chocolate Icing:** Heat margarine and chocolate in small heavy saucepan on lowest heat, stirring often, until chocolate is almost melted. Do not overheat. Remove from heat. Stir until smooth.

Add icing sugar, milk and vanilla. Beat until smooth. Add more milk if necessary until barely pourable consistency. Drizzle over cake. Cuts into 16 wedges.

*1 wedge: 467 Calories; 20.7 g Total Fat (11.7 g Mono, 1.9 g Poly, 5.8 g Sat); 71 mg Cholesterol; 65 g Carbohydrate; 1 g Fibre; 7 g Protein; 343 mg Sodium*

Pictured on page 17.

*A pretty contrast—amber pumpkin on dark gingersnap crust. Tastes as good as it looks. Make a day ahead. Freezes well.*

# Pumpkin Cheesecake

**GINGERSNAP CRUMB CRUST**

| | | |
|---|---|---|
| Hard margarine (or butter) | 1/4 cup | 60 mL |
| Finely crushed gingersnap cookies | 1 1/4 cups | 300 mL |

**FILLING**

| | | |
|---|---|---|
| Blocks of cream cheese (8 oz., 250 g, each), softened | 2 | 2 |
| Granulated sugar | 2/3 cup | 150 mL |
| Large eggs | 2 | 2 |
| Can of pure pumpkin (no spices) | 14 oz. | 398 mL |
| Ground cinnamon | 1/2 tsp. | 2 mL |
| Ground nutmeg | 1/2 tsp. | 2 mL |
| Ground ginger | 1/2 tsp. | 2 mL |
| Salt | 1/2 tsp. | 2 mL |

**Gingersnap Crumb Crust:** Melt margarine in medium saucepan. Remove from heat. Add crushed gingersnaps. Stir well. Press firmly in ungreased 9 inch (22 cm) springform pan. Bake in 350°F (175°C) oven for 10 minutes. Let stand until cool.

**Filling:** Beat cream cheese and sugar in large bowl until smooth. Add eggs, 1 at a time, beating after each addition until just combined.

Add remaining 5 ingredients. Beat well. Spread evenly over crust. Bake for 50 to 60 minutes until centre is almost set. Run knife around inside edge of pan to allow cheesecake to settle evenly. Let stand in pan on wire rack until cooled completely. Chill overnight. Cuts into 12 wedges.

*1 wedge: 302 Calories; 20.7 g Total Fat (7.8 g Mono, 1.2 g Poly, 10.5 g Sat); 82 mg Cholesterol; 25 g Carbohydrate; 1 g Fibre; 5 g Protein; 360 mg Sodium*

Pictured on page 19.

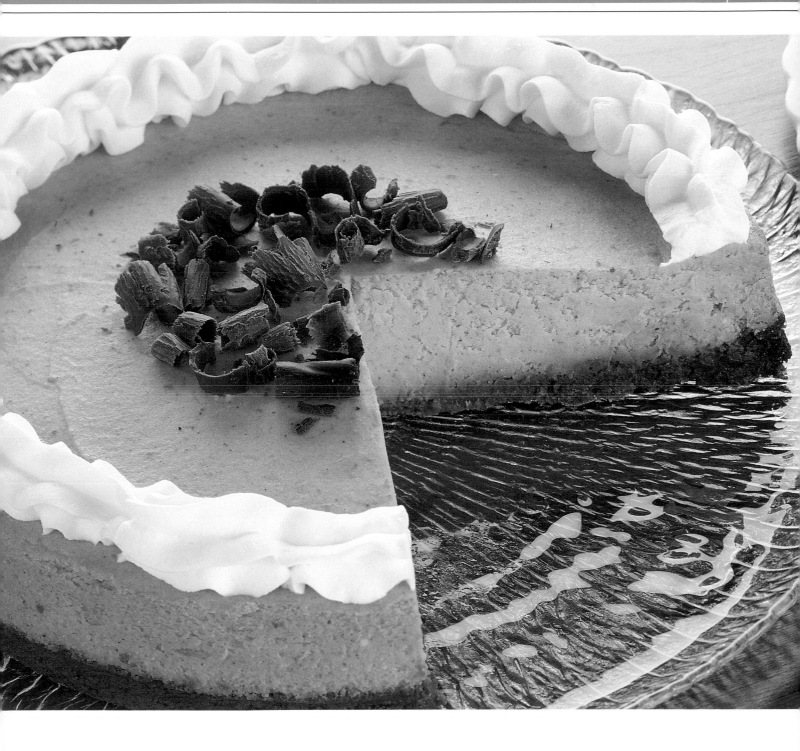

*Garnish with whipped topping and whole cookies for an extra-special look that's sure to make the kids smile.*

# Cookie Cheesecake

**COOKIE CRUMB CRUST**

| | | |
|---|---|---|
| Hard margarine (or butter) | 2 tbsp. | 30 mL |
| Finely crushed cream-filled chocolate cookies | 1 1/2 cups | 375 mL |

**FILLING**

| | | |
|---|---|---|
| Blocks of light cream cheese (8 oz., 250 g, each), softened | 3 | 3 |
| Granulated sugar | 1 cup | 250 mL |
| Vanilla | 1 1/2 tsp. | 7 mL |
| Whipping cream | 1 cup | 250 mL |
| Large eggs | 3 | 3 |
| Coarsely chopped cream-filled chocolate cookies | 1 cup | 250 mL |

**Cookie Crumb Crust:** Melt margarine in medium saucepan. Remove from heat. Add crushed cookies. Stir well. Press firmly in bottom and 1/2 inch (12 mm) up side of greased 10 inch (25 cm) springform pan.

**Filling:** Beat cream cheese, sugar and vanilla in large bowl until smooth. Add whipping cream. Beat. Add eggs, 1 at a time, beating after each addition until just combined.

Fold in chopped cookies until evenly distributed. Spread evenly over crust. Bake in 325°F (160°C) oven for about 1 1/4 hours until centre is almost set. Run knife around inside edge of pan to allow cheesecake to settle evenly. Let stand in pan on wire rack until cooled completely. Chill overnight. Cuts into 16 wedges.

*1 wedge: 318 Calories; 20.2 g Total Fat (7.7 g Mono, 1.2 g Poly, 9.7 g Sat); 88 mg Cholesterol; 28 g Carbohydrate; trace Fibre; 7 g Protein; 452 mg Sodium*

Pictured on page 21.

*Mint and chocolate make a refreshing after-dinner dessert. Made using a microwave oven. Serve with a hot cup of coffee or a cool glass of milk.*

# Crème de Menthe Cheesecake

| CHOCOLATE CRUMB CRUST | | |
|---|---|---|
| Hard margarine (or butter) | 1/4 cup | 60 mL |
| Chocolate wafer crumbs | 1 1/4 cups | 300 mL |
| Granulated sugar (optional) | 2 tbsp. | 30 mL |
| **FILLING** | | |
| Blocks of cream cheese (4 oz., 125 g, each), softened | 3 | 3 |
| Granulated sugar | 1/2 cup | 125 mL |
| Large eggs | 2 | 2 |
| Mint-flavoured liqueur (such as green Crème de Menthe) | 1/3 cup | 75 mL |
| **CHOCOLATE SOUR CREAM TOPPING** | | |
| Semi-sweet chocolate chips | 1/2 cup | 125 mL |
| Sour cream | 1/2 cup | 125 mL |

**Chocolate Crumb Crust:** Place margarine in microwave-safe medium bowl. Microwave, uncovered, on high (100%) for about 35 seconds until melted. Add wafer crumbs and sugar. Stir well. Press firmly in bottom and up side of 9 inch (22 cm) microwave-safe pie plate. Microwave, uncovered, on high (100%) for 2 minutes. Set aside.

**Filling:** Beat cream cheese and sugar in large bowl until smooth. Add eggs, 1 at a time, beating after each addition until just combined. Add liqueur. Beat well. Spread evenly in crust. Cover with waxed paper. Microwave on medium (50%) for about 10 minutes, turning dish halfway through baking time if microwave doesn't have turntable, until centre is set. Let stand for 5 minutes.

**Chocolate Sour Cream Topping:** Place chips in 1 cup (250 mL) liquid measure. Microwave, uncovered, on medium (50%) for about 2 minutes until almost melted. Do not overheat. Stir until smooth. Add sour cream. Stir well. Spread evenly over filling. Chill for 3 to 4 hours until set. Cuts into 8 wedges.

*1 wedge:* 486 Calories; 31.6 g Total Fat (12.1 g Mono, 1.9 g Poly, 15.8 g Sat); 111 mg Cholesterol; 41 g Carbohydrate; 1 g Fibre; 7 g Protein; 340 mg Sodium

Pictured on page 23.

*An attractive, rosy-coloured dessert. Cream cheese and cherries are always a favourite.*

# Cherry Chilled Cheesecake

**GRAHAM CRUMB CRUST**

| | | |
|---|---|---|
| Hard margarine (or butter) | 1/3 cup | 75 mL |
| Graham cracker crumbs | 1 1/4 cups | 300 mL |
| Brown sugar, packed | 2 tbsp. | 30 mL |

**FILLING**

| | | |
|---|---|---|
| Block of cream cheese, softened | 8 oz. | 250 g |
| Icing (confectioner's) sugar | 1 1/2 cups | 375 mL |
| Vanilla | 1/2 tsp. | 2 mL |
| Can of cherry pie filling | 19 oz. | 540 mL |
| Frozen whipped topping, thawed (or whipped cream) | 2 cups | 500 mL |

**Graham Crumb Crust:** Melt margarine in medium saucepan. Remove from heat. Add graham crumbs and brown sugar. Stir well. Reserve 3 tbsp. (50 mL) crumb mixture in small cup. Press remaining mixture firmly in ungreased 9 x 9 inch (22 x 22 cm) pan. Bake in 350°F (175°C) oven for 10 minutes. Let stand in pan on wire rack until cooled completely.

**Filling:** Beat cream cheese, icing sugar and vanilla in medium bowl until smooth. Add pie filling. Stir well. Spread evenly over crust.

Spread whipped topping evenly over filling. Sprinkle reserved crumb mixture over top. Chill overnight. Cuts into 12 pieces.

*1 piece: 329 Calories; 17 g Total Fat (6.2 g Mono, 1 g Poly, 8.8 g Sat); 23 mg Cholesterol; 43 g Carbohydrate; 1 g Fibre; 3 g Protein; 189 mg Sodium*

Pictured on page 27.

# Mini-Chip Cheesecakes

| | | |
|---|---|---|
| Chocolate wafers | 12 | 12 |
| Blocks of light cream cheese (8 oz., 250 g, each), softened | 2 | 2 |
| Granulated sugar | 3/4 cup | 175 mL |
| Large eggs | 2 | 2 |
| Vanilla | 1 tsp. | 5 mL |
| Mini semi-sweet chocolate chips | 1/2 cup | 125 mL |
| Mini semi-sweet chocolate chips | 1/2 cup | 125 mL |

*This make-ahead dessert is a favourite with young and old. Garnish with whipped topping and chocolate curls.*

Line 12 ungreased muffin cups with large paper liners. Place 1 wafer in bottom of each liner.

Beat cream cheese and sugar in medium bowl until smooth. Add eggs, 1 at a time, beating after each addition until just combined. Add vanilla. Beat.

Heat first amount of chips in small heavy saucepan on lowest heat, stirring often, until chocolate is almost melted. Do not overheat. Remove from heat. Stir until smooth. Add to cream cheese mixture. Stir.

Fold second amount of chips into cream cheese mixture until evenly distributed. Divide and spoon over wafers. Bake in 325°F (160°C) oven for 25 to 30 minutes until set. Let stand in pan on wire rack until cool. Chill for 2 to 3 hours. Makes 12 mini-cheesecakes.

*1 mini-cheesecake: 255 Calories; 14.2 g Total Fat (4.8 g Mono, 0.6 g Poly, 7.8 g Sat); 62 mg Cholesterol; 29 g Carbohydrate; 1 g Fibre; 6 g Protein; 338 mg Sodium*

Pictured on page 27.

*This treat has a built-in topping—no icing required.*

# Cheesy Cupcakes

| | | |
|---|---|---|
| Block of light cream cheese, softened | 8 oz. | 250 g |
| Granulated sugar | 1/2 cup | 125 mL |
| Large egg | 1 | 1 |
| Semi-sweet chocolate chips | 1 cup | 250 mL |
| All-purpose flour | 1 1/2 cups | 375 mL |
| Granulated sugar | 1 cup | 250 mL |
| Cocoa, sifted if lumpy | 1/3 cup | 75 mL |
| Baking soda | 1 tsp. | 5 mL |
| Salt | 1/2 tsp. | 2 mL |
| Hard margarine (or butter), softened | 6 tbsp. | 100 mL |
| Warm water | 1 cup | 250 mL |
| Vanilla | 1 tsp. | 5 mL |

Beat cream cheese, first amount of sugar and egg in small bowl until smooth. Add chips. Stir. Set aside.

Combine next 5 ingredients in large bowl. Make a well in centre.

Add margarine, warm water and vanilla to well. Beat for about 2 minutes until smooth. Line 20 ungreased muffin cups with large paper liners. Divide and spoon batter into each cup. Divide and spoon cream cheese mixture over batter. Bake in 350°F (175°C) oven for 30 to 35 minutes until wooden pick inserted in centre of cupcake comes out clean. Makes 20 cupcakes.

*1 cupcake: 207 Calories; 9.1 g Total Fat (4.1 g Mono, 0.6 g Poly, 3.9 g Sat); 19 mg Cholesterol; 30 g Carbohydrate; 1 g Fibre; 3 g Protein; 256 mg Sodium*

Pictured on page 27.

Top Right: Cheesy Cupcakes, above
Centre Left: Mini-Chip Cheesecakes, page 25
Bottom Right: Cherry Chilled Cheesecake, page 24

*A wonderful blend of flavours in a sweet, chewy macaroon! Almost too pretty to eat—but not quite!*

# Cherry Coconut Macaroons

| | | |
|---|---|---|
| Flake coconut | 2 cups | 500 mL |
| Maraschino cherries, blotted dry and chopped | 3/4 cup | 175 mL |
| Sliced almonds, toasted (see Note) | 1/2 cup | 125 mL |
| All-purpose flour | 1/2 cup | 125 mL |
| Salt | 1/4 tsp. | 1 mL |
| Egg whites (large) | 4 | 4 |
| Almond flavouring | 1/2 tsp. | 2 mL |
| Granulated sugar | 1/2 cup | 125 mL |

Combine first 5 ingredients in medium bowl.

Beat egg whites and flavouring on medium in large bowl until frothy. Add sugar, 1 tbsp. (15 mL) at a time while beating, until soft peaks form. Fold coconut mixture into egg white mixture until just moistened. Drop, using 2 tbsp. (30 mL) for each, about 2 inches (5 cm) apart, onto greased cookie sheets. Bake in 325°F (160°C) oven for about 15 minutes until edges are golden. Let stand on cookie sheets for 5 minutes before removing to wire racks to cool. Makes about 2 1/2 dozen (30) macaroons.

*1 macaroon: 85 Calories; 5.1 g Total Fat (0.8 g Mono, 0.3 g Poly, 3.7 g Sat); 0 mg Cholesterol; 9 g Carbohydrate; 1 g Fibre; 2 g Protein; 30 mg Sodium*

Pictured on page 29.

Top Right: Cherry Coconut Macaroons, above
Centre Left: Cranberry Chip Cookies, page 30
Bottom: Pecan Caramel Kisses, page 31

*Festive, flavourful cookies that will satisfy any sweet craving!*

# Cranberry Chip Cookies

| | | |
|---|---|---|
| Large eggs | 2 | 2 |
| Brown sugar, packed | 1 2/3 cups | 400 mL |
| Vanilla | 1 tsp. | 5 mL |
| All-purpose flour | 1 3/4 cups | 425 mL |
| Baking powder | 1 tsp. | 5 mL |
| Baking soda | 1/2 tsp. | 2 mL |
| Cooking oil | 1/2 cup | 125 mL |
| Dried cranberries | 1/2 cup | 125 mL |
| Unsalted peanuts | 1/2 cup | 125 mL |
| White chocolate chips | 1/2 cup | 125 mL |

Beat eggs, brown sugar and vanilla in large bowl until light and creamy.

Combine flour, baking powder and soda in small bowl. Add to egg mixture. Stir well.

Add remaining 4 ingredients. Stir until evenly distributed. Cover. Chill for 1 hour. Roll dough into balls, using 1 tbsp. (15 mL) for each. Arrange balls, about 2 inches (5 cm) apart, on greased cookie sheets. Bake in 350°F (175°C) oven for about 15 minutes until golden. Let stand on cookie sheets for 5 minutes before removing to wire racks to cool. Makes about 3 1/2 dozen (42) cookies.

*1 cookie: 107 Calories; 4.6 g Total Fat (2.4 g Mono, 1.2 g Poly, 0.8 g Sat); 11 mg Cholesterol; 16 g Carbohydrate; 1 g Fibre; 1 g Protein; 33 mg Sodium*

Pictured on page 29.

# Pecan Caramel Kisses

| | | |
|---|---|---|
| Egg whites (large), room temperature | 2 | 2 |
| Cream of tartar | 1/8 tsp. | 0.5 mL |
| Maple flavouring | 1/4 tsp. | 1 mL |
| Icing (confectioner's) sugar | 1 cup | 250 mL |
| Chopped pecans, toasted (see Note) | 1/3 cup | 75 mL |
| Caramels | 10 | 10 |
| Milk | 2 tsp. | 10 mL |

Beat egg whites, cream of tartar and flavouring in medium bowl until stiff peaks form. Add icing sugar, 2 tbsp. (30 mL) at a time while beating, until very glossy and stiff.

Fold pecans into egg white mixture until evenly distributed. Drop, using 1 tbsp. (15 mL) for each, about 2 inches (5 cm) apart, onto greased parchment (not waxed) paper-lined cookie sheets. Bake in 275°F (140°C) oven for about 30 minutes until dry and edges are golden. Let stand on cookie sheets for 5 minutes before removing to wire racks to cool.

Heat and stir caramels and milk in small saucepan on medium-low until smooth. Remove from heat. Let stand for 5 minutes. Drizzle over meringues. Makes about 2 1/2 dozen (30) meringues.

*1 meringue: 37 Calories; 1.2 g Total Fat (0.6 g Mono, 0.2 g Poly, 0.3 g Sat); 0 mg Cholesterol; 7 g Carbohydrate; trace Fibre; 0 g Protein; 10 mg Sodium*

Pictured on page 29.

*Light and crispy meringues drizzled with sticky caramel sauce. Crunchy toasted pecans make this an immensely satisfying sweet treat.*

### note

To toast nuts, place in single layer in ungreased shallow pan. Bake in 350°F (175°C) oven for 5 to 8 minutes, stirring or shaking often, until desired doneness.

*These often don't make it from the cookie sheet to the cookie jar! A little expensive to make, but simply irresistible.*

## variation

For smaller cookies, roll dough into 1 1/2 inch (3.8 cm) balls. Arrange balls, about 2 inches (5 cm) apart, on greased cookie sheets. Flatten cookies slightly with flat-bottomed glass dipped in second amount of granulated sugar. Bake in 375°F (190°C) oven for 8 to 10 minutes until golden. Let stand on cookie sheets for 5 minutes before removing to wire racks to cool. Makes about 5 dozen (60) cookies.

# Giant Candy Bar Cookies

| | | |
|---|---|---|
| Hard margarine (or butter), softened | 1 cup | 250 mL |
| Granulated sugar | 1 cup | 250 mL |
| Brown sugar, packed | 1 cup | 250 mL |
| Large eggs | 2 | 2 |
| Vanilla | 2 tsp. | 10 mL |
| All-purpose flour | 2 cups | 500 mL |
| Baking powder | 1 tsp. | 5 mL |
| Baking soda | 1 tsp. | 5 mL |
| Salt | 1/2 tsp. | 2 mL |
| Quick-cooking rolled oats (not instant) | 2 1/3 cups | 575 mL |
| Chocolate-covered crispy toffee bars (such as Skor or Heath), 1 1/2 oz. (39 g) each, chopped | 8 | 8 |
| Granulated sugar | 1/4 cup | 60 mL |

Cream margarine, first amount of granulated sugar and brown sugar in large bowl. Add eggs, 1 at a time, beating well after each addition. Add vanilla. Beat.

Combine next 4 ingredients in small bowl. Add to margarine mixture. Stir until just moistened.

Add rolled oats and chocolate bar pieces. Stir well. Roll into 2 inch (5 cm) balls. Arrange 4 to 6 balls, about 4 inches (10 cm) apart, on greased cookie sheet.

Dip flat-bottomed glass into second amount of granulated sugar. Flatten cookies to 1/2 inch (12 mm) thickness, dipping glass in sugar as necessary. Bake in 375°F (190°C) oven for about 11 minutes until golden. Let stand on cookie sheet for 5 minutes before removing to wire rack to cool. Repeat with remaining dough. Makes about 3 dozen (36) cookies.

*1 cookie: 204 Calories; 9.2 g Total Fat (3.8 g Mono, 0.8 g Poly, 1.3 g Sat); 17 mg Cholesterol; 29 g Carbohydrate; 1 g Fibre; 3 g Protein; 168 mg Sodium*

Pictured on page 33.

*Also known as Swedish Pastry and Thumbprints. So good, you'll need to make more!*

# Swedish Tea Cakes

| | | |
|---|---|---|
| Hard margarine (or butter), softened | 1/2 cup | 125 mL |
| Brown sugar, packed | 1/4 cup | 60 mL |
| Egg yolk (large) | 1 | 1 |
| All-purpose flour | 1 cup | 250 mL |
| Baking powder | 1/2 tsp. | 2 mL |
| Salt | 1/8 tsp. | 0.5 mL |
| Egg white (large), fork-beaten | 1 | 1 |
| Finely chopped nuts (your favourite), for coating | 2/3 cup | 150 mL |
| Jam or jelly (red is best), your favourite | 6 tbsp. | 100 mL |

Cream margarine and brown sugar in large bowl. Add egg yolk. Beat well.

Combine flour, baking powder and salt in small bowl. Add to margarine mixture. Stir until stiff dough forms. Roll dough into balls, using 2 tsp. (10 mL) for each.

Dip balls into egg white. Roll in nuts. Arrange balls, about 2 inches (5 cm) apart, on greased cookie sheets. Dent each with thumb. Bake in 325°F (160°C) oven for 5 minutes. Remove from oven. Press dents again. Bake for 10 to 15 minutes until golden. Let stand on cookie sheets for 5 minutes before removing to wire racks.

Fill each dent with 1 tsp. (5 mL) jam. (Unfilled tea cakes may be stored in airtight container and filled with jam just before serving.) Makes about 20 tea cakes.

*1 tea cake: 125 Calories; 7.7 g Total Fat (3.8 g Mono, 2.2 g Poly, 1.2 g Sat); 11 mg Cholesterol; 13 g Carbohydrate; 1 g Fibre; 2 g Protein; 88 mg Sodium*

Pictured on page 35.

*These are definitely more impressive than regular cookies but still easy enough for kids to make! A tasty one-bite snack that will make you popular with kids and grown-ups alike.*

## cookie pizza

Press 3 cups (750 mL) cookie dough evenly in greased 12 inch (30 cm) pizza pan. Sprinkle with semi-sweet chocolate chips, butterscotch chips, candy-coated chocolate candies (such as Smarties or M & M's), cereal flakes, coconut, peanuts or any other favourites. Bake in 375°F (190°C) oven for 12 to 15 minutes until puffy and golden. Serve warm or cold. Cuts into 16 wedges.

# Peanut Butter Hide-Aways

| | | |
|---|---|---|
| Hard margarine (or butter), softened | 1/2 cup | 125 mL |
| Smooth peanut butter | 1/2 cup | 125 mL |
| Granulated sugar | 1/3 cup | 75 mL |
| Brown sugar, packed | 1/3 cup | 75 mL |
| Large egg | 1 | 1 |
| All-purpose flour | 1 1/3 cups | 325 mL |
| Baking powder | 1 tsp. | 5 mL |
| Baking soda | 1/2 tsp. | 2 mL |
| Salt | 1/4 tsp. | 1 mL |
| Miniature peanut butter cups | 36 | 36 |

Beat first 4 ingredients in large bowl until light and creamy. Add egg. Beat well.

Combine next 4 ingredients in small bowl. Add to margarine mixture. Stir until just moistened. Dough will be stiff. Roll into 36 balls, using 1 tbsp. (15 mL) for each. Place 1 ball in each of 36 ungreased mini-muffin cups. Bake in 375°F (190°C) oven for about 10 minutes until puffy and golden. Remove from oven.

Remove and discard foil cup from peanut butter cups. Press 1 peanut butter cup into each hot cookie. Loosen edges of cookies with tip of knife. Chill for 20 minutes before removing from pan. If cookies are difficult to remove, tap bottom of pan several times on hard surface or let stand until cookies are room temperature. Makes 3 dozen (36) cookies.

*1 cookie: 120 Calories; 7.3 g Total Fat (3.5 g Mono, 1.1 g Poly, 2.1 g Sat); 7 mg Cholesterol; 12 g Carbohydrate; 1 g Fibre; 3 g Protein; 119 mg Sodium*

Pictured on page 39.

# Oatmeal Chip Cookies

| | | |
|---|---|---|
| Hard margarine (or butter), softened | 1 cup | 250 mL |
| Brown sugar, packed | 2 cups | 500 mL |
| Large eggs | 2 | 2 |
| Vanilla | 1 tsp. | 5 mL |
| All-purpose flour | 2 cups | 500 mL |
| Baking powder | 1 tsp. | 5 mL |
| Baking soda | 1/2 tsp. | 2 mL |
| Quick-cooking rolled oats (not instant) | 2 cups | 500 mL |
| Semi-sweet chocolate chips | 2 cups | 500 mL |
| Medium unsweetened coconut | 3/4 cup | 175 mL |

Beat margarine and sugar in large bowl until light and creamy. Add eggs, 1 at a time, beating well after each addition. Add vanilla. Beat.

Combine flour, baking powder and soda in small bowl. Add to margarine mixture. Stir well.

Add remaining 3 ingredients. Stir until well distributed. Drop, using 2 tbsp. (30 mL) for each, about 2 inches (5 cm) apart, onto greased cookie sheets. Bake in 350°F (175°C) oven for 8 to 10 minutes until golden. Let stand on cookie sheets for 5 minutes before removing to wire racks to cool. Makes about 5 dozen (60) cookies.

*1 cookie: 126 Calories; 6.2 g Total Fat (2.9 g Mono, 0.5 g Poly, 2.5 g Sat); 7 mg Cholesterol; 17 g Carbohydrate; 1 g Fibre; 2 g Protein; 61 mg Sodium*

Pictured below.

*Chocolate and oatmeal make the ultimate cookie. A great favourite.*

## oatmeal chip pizza

Press 3 cups (750 mL) cookie dough evenly in greased 12 inch (30 cm) pizza pan. Sprinkle with semi-sweet chocolate chips, butterscotch chips, candy-coated chocolate candies (such as Smarties or M & M's), cereal flakes, coconut, peanuts or any other favourites. Bake in 350°F (175°C) oven for 12 to 15 minutes until golden. Cuts into 16 wedges.

*These delicious cookies contain no flour. Soft and chewy. Makes a huge batch. Use an extra-large bowl, plastic tub or roaster to mix these.*

## rainbow chip pizza

Press 3 cups (750 mL) cookie dough evenly in greased 12 inch (30 cm) pizza pan. Sprinkle with semi-sweet chocolate chips, butterscotch chips, candy-coated chocolate candies (such as Smarties or M & M's), cereal flakes, coconut, peanuts or any other favourites. Bake in 350°F (175°C) oven for 12 to 15 minutes until golden. Cuts into 16 wedges.

# Rainbow Chip Cookies

| | | |
|---|---|---|
| Smooth peanut butter | 6 cups | 1.5 L |
| Brown sugar, packed | 6 cups | 1.5 L |
| Granulated sugar | 4 cups | 1 L |
| Hard margarine (or butter), softened | 2 cups | 500 mL |
| Large eggs | 12 | 12 |
| Vanilla | 1 tbsp. | 15 mL |
| Golden corn syrup | 1 tbsp. | 15 mL |
| Quick-cooking rolled oats (not instant) | 18 cups | 4.5 L |
| Semi-sweet chocolate chips | 2 cups | 500 mL |
| Candy-coated chocolate candies (such as Smarties or M & M's) | 2 cups | 500 mL |
| Baking soda | 8 tsp. | 40 mL |

Beat first 4 ingredients in extra-large bowl until light and creamy. Add eggs, 2 at a time, beating well after each addition. Add vanilla and corn syrup. Beat.

Add remaining 4 ingredients. Stir well. Roll into balls, using 2 tbsp. (30 mL) for each. Arrange balls, about 2 inches (5 cm) apart, on greased cookie sheets. Flatten slightly. Bake in 350°F (175°C) oven for 7 to 8 minutes until golden. Overbaking will make them hard. Let stand on cookie sheets for 5 minutes before removing to wire racks to cool. Makes about 26 dozen (312) cookies.

*1 cookie: 108 Calories; 5.2 g Total Fat (2.4 g Mono, 1 g Poly, 1.1 g Sat); 8 mg Cholesterol; 14 g Carbohydrate; 1 g Fibre; 3 g Protein; 78 mg Sodium*

Pictured on page 39.

Top Left: Rainbow Chip Cookies, above
Bottom Right: Peanut Butter Hide-Aways, page 36

*Pretty, 3-layered cookie. Freezes well before, or after, baking.*

# Icebox Ribbons

| | | |
|---|---|---|
| Hard margarine (or butter), softened | 1 cup | 250 mL |
| Granulated sugar | 1 cup | 250 mL |
| Large egg | 1 | 1 |
| Vanilla | 1 tsp. | 5 mL |
| All-purpose flour | 2 1/2 cups | 625 mL |
| Baking powder | 1 tsp. | 5 mL |
| Salt | 1/4 tsp. | 1 mL |
| Red liquid (or paste) food colouring | | |
| Chopped red glazed cherries | 1/4 cup | 60 mL |
| Medium unsweetened coconut | 1/3 cup | 75 mL |
| Semi-sweet chocolate chips | 1/3 cup | 75 mL |
| Chopped nuts (your favourite) | 1/3 cup | 75 mL |

Cream margarine and sugar in large bowl. Add egg and vanilla. Beat well.

Combine flour, baking powder and salt in medium bowl. Add to margarine mixture. Stir until stiff dough forms. Divide dough into 3 equal portions.

Knead enough red food colouring into 1 portion of dough until pink. Add cherries. Knead until evenly distributed. Press in foil-lined 8 × 4 × 3 inch (20 × 10 × 7.5 cm) loaf pan.

Add coconut to second portion of dough. Knead until evenly distributed. Press evenly over pink layer.

Heat chips in small heavy saucepan on lowest heat, stirring often, until almost melted. Do not overheat. Remove from heat. Stir until smooth. Add chocolate and nuts to third portion of dough. Knead until no streaks remain. Press evenly over coconut layer. Cover with plastic wrap. Chill overnight. Remove from pan. Remove and discard foil. Cut into 1/4 inch (6 mm) thick slices. Cut each slice into 3 pieces. Arrange slices, about 2 inches (5 cm) apart, on greased cookie sheets. Bake in 350°F (175°C) oven for 10 to 12 minutes until edges are golden. Let stand on cookie sheets for 5 minutes before removing to wire racks to cool. Makes about 5 1/2 dozen (66) cookies.

*1 cookie:* 72 Calories; 4 g Total Fat (2.1 g Mono, 0.6 g Poly, 1.1 g Sat); 3 mg Cholesterol; 8 g Carbohydrate; trace Fibre; 1 g Protein; 50 mg Sodium

Pictured on page 43.

# Noodle Power

| | | |
|---|---|---|
| Semi-sweet chocolate chips | 1 cup | 250 mL |
| Butterscotch chips | 1 cup | 250 mL |
| Hard margarine (or butter) | 1/4 cup | 60 mL |
| Smooth peanut butter | 1/4 cup | 60 mL |
| Dry chow mein noodles | 2 cups | 500 mL |
| Unsalted peanuts | 1 cup | 250 mL |

Heat first 4 ingredients in large heavy saucepan on lowest heat, stirring often, until chips are almost melted. Do not overheat. Remove from heat. Stir until smooth.

Add noodles and peanuts. Stir until coated. Mixture will be soft. Drop, using 2 tsp. (10 mL) for each, onto waxed paper-lined cookie sheets. Let stand until set. May be chilled to hasten setting. Makes 2 1/2 dozen (30) cookies.

*1 cookie: 123 Calories; 8.3 g Total Fat (3.7 g Mono, 1.9 g Poly, 2.2 g Sat); 0 mg Cholesterol; 12 g Carbohydrate; 1 g Fibre; 2 g Protein; 47 mg Sodium*

Pictured on page 42.

*These little stacks are shiny and ever so good. They are softer to bite into than other similar cookies.*

# Coconut Peaks

| | | |
|---|---|---|
| Flake coconut | 3 cups | 750 mL |
| Icing (confectioner's) sugar | 2 cups | 500 mL |
| Hard margarine (or butter), melted | 1/4 cup | 60 mL |
| Half-and-half cream (or milk) | 2 tbsp. | 30 mL |
| Semi-sweet chocolate chips | 1 cup | 250 mL |
| Hard margarine (or butter) | 1 tbsp. | 15 mL |

Combine first 4 ingredients in large bowl. Roll into balls, using 1/2 tbsp. (7 mL) for each. Squeeze tops to form peaks that resemble haystacks. Arrange on waxed paper-lined cookie sheet. Chill, uncovered, overnight.

Heat chips and second amount of margarine in small heavy saucepan on lowest heat, stirring often, until chips are almost melted. Do not overheat. Remove from heat. Stir until smooth. Dip peaks of cookies into chocolate mixture. Let stand until chocolate is set. Makes 2 1/2 dozen (30) cookies.

*1 cookie: 143 Calories; 10 g Total Fat (2.2 g Mono, 0.3 g Poly, 7 g Sat); 0 mg Cholesterol; 15 g Carbohydrate; 1 g Fibre; 1 g Protein; 28 mg Sodium*

Pictured on page 42.

*These will take the spotlight on any plate of cookies! A no-bake treat that freezes well.*

**Photo Legend next page**
1. Noodle Power, this page
2. Coconut Rum Diagonals, page 44
3. Icebox Ribbons, page 40
4. Coconut Peaks, this page

*Pretty diamond-shaped cookies with an awesome flavour combination.*

### coconut diagonals

Omit the rum flavouring. Use same amount of vanilla.

## Coconut Rum Diagonals

| | | |
|---|---|---|
| Hard margarine (or butter), softened | 1/2 cup | 125 mL |
| Granulated sugar | 1/4 cup | 60 mL |
| Vanilla | 1 tsp. | 5 mL |
| Salt | 1/8 tsp. | 0.5 mL |
| All-purpose flour | 1 cup | 250 mL |
| Flake coconut | 1 cup | 250 mL |
| Baking powder | 1/2 tsp. | 2 mL |
| RUM ICING | | |
| Icing (confectioner's) sugar | 1 cup | 250 mL |
| Water | 1 1/2 tbsp. | 25 mL |
| Rum flavouring | 1/2 tsp. | 2 mL |

Beat first 4 ingredients in large bowl until light and creamy.

Combine flour, coconut and baking powder in small bowl. Add to margarine mixture. Stir well. Divide dough into 6 equal portions. Roll each portion into 9 inch (22 cm) rope. Arrange ropes, about 2 inches (5 cm) apart, on greased cookie sheets. Bake in 350°F (175°C) oven for 18 to 22 minutes until golden. Let stand on cookie sheets on wire racks for 5 minutes.

**Rum Icing:** Stir all 3 ingredients in small bowl, adding more water or icing sugar if necessary until spreading consistency. Ice ropes while still warm. Cut each rope into 1 inch (2.5 cm) diagonals, for a total of 4 1/2 dozen (54) cookies.

*1 diagonal: 50 Calories; 3 g Total Fat (1.2 g Mono, 0.2 g Poly, 1.4 g Sat); 0 mg Cholesterol; 6 g Carbohydrate; trace Fibre; 0 g Protein; 31 mg Sodium*

Pictured on page 43.

*These melt in your mouth! Garnish with your favourite Christmas candy.*

## Whipped Shortbread

| | | |
|---|---|---|
| Butter (not margarine), softened | 1 cup | 250 mL |
| Granulated sugar | 1/2 cup | 125 mL |
| All-purpose flour | 1 1/2 cups | 375 mL |
| Cornstarch | 1/4 cup | 60 mL |

Beat butter and sugar in medium bowl until light and creamy.

*(continued on next page)*

Combine flour and cornstarch in small bowl. Add to butter mixture, 2 tbsp.
(30 mL) at a time while beating, until smooth. Pipe 1 1/2 inch (3.8 cm) rosettes,
about 2 inches (5 cm) apart, onto ungreased cookie sheets. Bake in 375°F
(190°C) oven for 12 to 14 minutes until just golden. Let stand on cookie
sheets for 5 minutes before removing to wire racks to cool. Makes 2 1/2 dozen
(30) cookies.

*1 cookie: 99 Calories; 6.6 g Total Fat (1.9 g Mono, 0.3 g Poly, 4.1 g Sat); 18 mg Cholesterol;
10 g Carbohydrate; trace Fibre; 1 g Protein; 66 mg Sodium*

Pictured on page 47.

## Candy Cane Cookies

*A fun cookie for the whole family to make together.*

| | | |
|---|---|---|
| Hard margarine (or butter), softened | 1 cup | 250 mL |
| Icing (confectioner's) sugar | 1 cup | 250 mL |
| Large egg | 1 | 1 |
| Almond flavouring | 1 tsp. | 5 mL |
| Vanilla | 1 tsp. | 5 mL |
| Peppermint flavouring | 1/4 tsp. | 1 mL |
| All-purpose flour | 2 1/2 cups | 625 mL |
| Baking powder | 1 tsp. | 5 mL |
| Salt | 1 tsp. | 5 mL |
| Red liquid food colouring | 1/2 tsp. | 2 mL |

Beat first 6 ingredients in large bowl until light and creamy.

Combine flour, baking powder and salt in medium bowl. Add to margarine
mixture. Stir until stiff dough forms. Divide dough into 2 equal portions.

Knead food colouring into 1 portion of dough until evenly tinted. Roll about
1 tsp. (5 mL) of each colour dough into 5 1/2 inch (14 cm) rope. Lay side by
side. Pinch ends together. Twist and form into candy cane shape. Repeat with
remaining dough. Arrange, about 2 inches (5 cm) apart, on greased cookie
sheets. Bake in 350°F (175°C) oven for about 10 minutes until just golden. Let
stand on cookie sheets for 5 minutes before removing to wire racks to cool.
Makes about 4 1/2 dozen (54) cookies.

*1 cookie: 65 Calories; 3.7 g Total Fat (2.4 g Mono, 0.4 g Poly, 0.8 g Sat); 4 mg Cholesterol;
7 g Carbohydrate; trace Fibre; 1 g Protein; 94 mg Sodium*

Pictured on page 47.

*These freeze well—a great way to get a head start on your holiday baking.*

# Sugar Cookies

| | | |
|---|---|---|
| Hard margarine (or butter), softened | 3/4 cup | 175 mL |
| Granulated sugar | 3/4 cup | 175 mL |
| Large egg | 1 | 1 |
| Vanilla | 1 tsp. | 5 mL |
| All-purpose flour | 2 cups | 500 mL |
| Baking soda | 1 tsp. | 5 mL |
| Cream of tartar | 1 tsp. | 5 mL |
| Ground cardamom (optional) | 1/4 tsp. | 1 mL |
| Salt | 1/4 tsp. | 1 mL |

Cream margarine and sugar in large bowl. Add egg and vanilla. Beat well.

Combine remaining 5 ingredients in medium bowl. Add to margarine mixture. Stir until stiff dough forms. Roll dough out to 1/8 inch (3 mm) thickness on lightly floured surface. Cut out dough using lightly floured cookie cutters. Arrange cookies, about 2 inches (5 cm) apart, on greased cookie sheets. Bake in 350°F (175°C) oven for about 10 minutes until golden. Let stand on cookie sheets for 5 minutes before removing to wire racks to cool. Makes 7 dozen (84) cookies.

*1 cookie: 35 Calories; 1.8 g Total Fat (1.2 g Mono, 0.2 g Poly, 0.4 g Sat); 3 mg Cholesterol; 4 g Carbohydrate; trace Fibre; 0 g Protein; 43 mg Sodium*

Pictured on page 47.

# Easy Glaze

| | | |
|---|---|---|
| Water | 2 tsp. | 10 mL |
| Icing (confectioner's) sugar | 1/2 cup | 125 mL |
| Liquid (or paste) food colouring | | |

Stir water into icing sugar in small bowl, adding more water or icing sugar if necessary until spreading consistency. Add food colouring, 1 drop at a time, stirring well after each addition until desired colour is reached. Makes about 6 tbsp. (100 mL).

*6 tbsp. (100 mL) glaze: 247 Calories; 0.1 g Total Fat (0 g Mono, 0 g Poly, 0 g Sat); 0 mg Cholesterol; 63 g Carbohydrate; 0 g Fibre; 0 g Protein; 1 mg Sodium*

Pictured on page 47 (on Sugar Cookies).

Top Left: Candy Cane Cookies, page 45
Top Right: Whipped Shortbread, page 44
Bottom Left: Sugar Cookies, this page

*Tell the kids they can have cookies for breakfast—they'll love it!*

# Nutri-Cookies

| | | |
|---|---|---|
| Hard margarine (or butter), softened | 1/2 cup | 125 mL |
| Smooth peanut butter | 1/2 cup | 125 mL |
| Liquid honey | 1 cup | 250 mL |
| Large eggs | 2 | 2 |
| Vanilla | 1 tsp. | 5 mL |
| Quick-cooking rolled oats (not instant) | 3 cups | 750 mL |
| All-purpose flour | 1 1/2 cups | 375 mL |
| Unsweetened medium coconut | 1 cup | 250 mL |
| Sultana raisins | 1 cup | 250 mL |
| Natural wheat bran | 3/4 cup | 175 mL |
| Shelled sunflower seeds | 1/2 cup | 125 mL |
| Chopped walnuts (or your favourite) | 1/2 cup | 125 mL |
| Baking soda | 1 tsp. | 5 mL |
| Salt | 1 tsp. | 5 mL |

Cream margarine and peanut butter in large bowl. Add honey, eggs and vanilla. Beat well.

Add remaining 9 ingredients. Stir well. Roll dough into balls, using 1 tbsp. (15 mL) for each. Flatten slightly. Arrange cookies, about 2 inches (5 cm) apart, on ungreased cookie sheets. Bake in 375°F (190°C) oven for about 12 minutes until golden. Let stand on cookie sheets for 5 minutes before removing to wire racks to cool. Makes 8 dozen (96) cookies.

*1 cookie: 74 Calories; 3.5 g Total Fat (1.3 g Mono, 0.9 g Poly, 1.1 g Sat); 4 mg Cholesterol; 10 g Carbohydrate; 1 g Fibre; 2 g Protein; 59 mg Sodium*

Pictured on page 49.

## Soft Molasses Drops

*An old-time recipe. Moist and spicy.*

| All-purpose flour | 3 1/2 cups | 875 mL |
| Granulated sugar | 3/4 cup | 175 mL |
| Ground ginger | 1 tsp. | 5 mL |
| Ground cinnamon | 1 tsp. | 5 mL |
| Salt | 1/2 tsp. | 2 mL |
| Fancy (mild) molasses | 3/4 cup | 175 mL |
| Hard margarine (or butter), softened | 3/4 cup | 175 mL |
| Large egg | 1 | 1 |
| Baking soda | 1 1/2 tsp. | 7 mL |
| Hot prepared strong coffee (or hot milk) | 1/2 cup | 125 mL |

Measure first 8 ingredients, in order given, into large bowl. Stir.

Stir baking soda into hot coffee. Add to flour mixture. Beat well. Drop, using 1 tbsp. (15 mL) for each, about 2 inches (5 cm) apart, onto greased cookie sheets. Bake in 375°F (190°C) oven for 10 to 12 minutes until dry but soft. Let stand on cookie sheets for 5 minutes before removing to wire racks to cool. Makes 5 dozen (60) cookies.

*1 cookie: 73 Calories; 2.6 g Total Fat (1.6 g Mono, 0.3 g Poly, 0.5 g Sat); 4 mg Cholesterol; 12 g Carbohydrate; trace Fibre; 1 g Protein; 83 mg Sodium*

Pictured below.

Left and Top Centre: Soft Molasses Drops, this page
Bottom Centre: Nutri-Cookies, page 48
Right: Hermits, page 50

*One of the best known—and best loved—drop cookies! Our cookie jar was always filled with these.*

# Hermits

| Hard margarine (or butter), softened | 1 cup | 250 mL |
| Brown sugar, packed | 1 1/2 cups | 375 mL |
| Large eggs | 3 | 3 |
| Vanilla | 1 tsp. | 5 mL |
| All-purpose flour | 3 cups | 750 mL |
| Sultana raisins | 1 cup | 250 mL |
| Chopped pitted dates | 1 cup | 250 mL |
| Chopped walnuts (or your favourite) | 2/3 cup | 150 mL |
| Baking powder | 1 tsp. | 5 mL |
| Baking soda | 1 tsp. | 5 mL |
| Ground cinnamon | 1 tsp. | 5 mL |
| Ground nutmeg | 1/2 tsp. | 2 mL |
| Salt | 1/2 tsp. | 2 mL |
| Ground allspice | 1/4 tsp. | 1 mL |

Cream margarine and sugar in large bowl. Add eggs, 1 at a time, beating well after each addition. Add vanilla. Beat.

Add remaining 10 ingredients. Stir until well distributed. Drop, using 1 tbsp. (15 mL) for each, about 2 inches (5 cm) apart, onto greased cookie sheets. Bake in 375°F (190°C) oven for 6 to 8 minutes until golden. Let stand on cookie sheets for 5 minutes before removing to wire racks to cool. Makes 4 1/2 dozen (54) cookies.

*1 cookie: 117 Calories; 4.9 g Total Fat (2.7 g Mono, 1 g Poly, 0.9 g Sat); 12 mg Cholesterol; 17 g Carbohydrate; 1 g Fibre; 2 g Protein; 101 mg Sodium*

Pictured on page 49.

# Butterscotch Cookies

| | | |
|---|---|---|
| Smooth peanut butter | 3 tbsp. | 50 mL |
| Butterscotch chips | 1 cup | 250 mL |
| Cornflakes cereal | 3 cups | 750 mL |
| Chopped pecans (or walnuts) | 1/2 cup | 125 mL |

*These no-bake cookies are golden and crunchy. Sweet, with a mild peanut butter flavour!*

Heat peanut butter and chips in large heavy saucepan on lowest heat, stirring often, until chips are almost melted. Do not overheat. Remove from heat. Stir until smooth.

Add cereal and pecans. Stir until coated. Drop, using 2 tbsp. (30 mL) for each, onto waxed paper-lined cookie sheets. Let stand until set. Makes about 2 1/2 dozen (30) cookies.

*1 cookie: 53 Calories; 2.4 g Total Fat (1.3 g Mono, 0.6 g Poly, 0.3 g Sat); 0 mg Cholesterol; 8 g Carbohydrate; trace Fibre; 1 g Protein; 36 mg Sodium*

Pictured below.

*An Italian favourite. This dessert (boh-KOHN-nee DOHL-chay) has meringue layers smothered with chocolate, strawberries and cream.*

## strawberry meringue shortcake

Trace ten 4 inch (10 cm) circles as directed in recipe. Divide and spoon egg white mixture into circles. Spread evenly to edges, forming raised sides. Bake as directed for about 30 minutes. To serve, fill with sweetened strawberries and top with whipped cream.

# Bocconne Dolce

| MERINGUE | | |
|---|---|---|
| Egg whites (large), room temperature | 6 | 6 |
| Cream of tartar | 1/4 tsp. | 1 mL |
| Granulated sugar | 1 1/2 cups | 375 mL |
| **FILLING** | | |
| Semi-sweet chocolate chips | 1 cup | 250 mL |
| Water | 3 tbsp. | 50 mL |
| Whipping cream | 3 cups | 750 mL |
| Granulated sugar | 1/3 cup | 75 mL |
| Vanilla | 2 tsp. | 10 mL |
| Fresh strawberries, sliced lengthwise | 3 cups | 750 mL |

Fresh whole strawberries, for garnish
Chocolate curls (see Note, page 57),
    for garnish

**Meringue:** Beat egg whites and cream of tartar in medium bowl until soft peaks form. Add sugar, 1 tbsp. (15 mL) at a time while beating, until stiff peaks form and sugar is dissolved. Line bottoms of 2 baking sheets with parchment (not waxed) paper. Trace two 8 inch (20 cm) circles about 1 1/2 inches (3.8 cm) apart on first paper, and one 8 inch (20 cm) circle on second paper. Turn papers over (or use foil with circles marked on top). Divide and spoon meringue onto circles. Spread evenly to edge of each. Bake in 250°F (120°C) oven for about 45 minutes until dry. Turn oven off. Let stand in oven with door ajar until cool. Remove meringues to wire racks and discard parchment paper.

**Filling:** Heat chips and water in small heavy saucepan on lowest heat, stirring often, until chips are almost melted. Do not overheat. Remove from heat. Stir until smooth. Divide and spread over 2 meringues.

Beat whipping cream, sugar and vanilla in large bowl until stiff peaks form. Divide and spread over all 3 meringues.

Carefully place 1 meringue with chocolate on serving plate. Spoon 1/2 of sliced strawberries evenly over whipped cream. Place second meringue with chocolate on top. Spoon remaining strawberries evenly over whipped cream. Place third meringue on top.

Garnish with strawberries and chocolate curls. Chill for 4 to 5 hours before serving. Serves 8.

*1 serving: 612 Calories; 37.2 g Total Fat (11.1 g Mono, 1.3 g Poly, 22.9 g Sat); 110 mg Cholesterol; 70 g Carbohydrate; 3 g Fibre; 6 g Protein; 78 mg Sodium*

Pictured on page 53.

*Also known as Death By Chocolate, this is a wonderful crowd-pleaser. Recipe can be cut in half for a smaller group.*

## Truffle Trifle

| | | |
|---|---|---|
| Box of chocolate cake mix (2 layer size) | 1 | 1 |
| Coffee-flavoured liqueur (such as Kahlúa) or 1/2 cup (125 mL) cold prepared strong coffee | 2/3 cup | 150 mL |
| Boxes of instant chocolate pudding powder (4 serving size, each) | 2 | 2 |
| Milk | 4 cups | 1 L |
| Frozen whipped topping, thawed | 4 cups | 1 L |
| Chocolate-covered crispy toffee bars (such as Heath or Skor), 1 1/2 oz. (39 g) each, crushed | 6 | 6 |
| Chocolate curls (see Note, page 57), for garnish | | |

Prepare cake mix according to package directions. Divide and spread evenly in 2 greased 8 inch (20 cm) round pans. Bake as directed. Let stand in pans for 5 minutes before inverting onto wire racks to cool completely.

Transfer first cake layer to cutting board. Drizzle with 1/2 of liqueur. Cut into 1 inch (2.5 cm) cubes. Transfer to 6 quart (6 L) glass trifle bowl. Transfer second cake layer to cutting board. Drizzle with remaining liqueur. Cut into 1 inch (2.5 cm) cubes. Set aside.

Beat pudding powder and milk in medium bowl until slightly thickened. Pour 1/2 of pudding over cake in bowl.

Spread 1/2 of whipped topping evenly over pudding. Sprinkle 1/2 of crushed toffee bars over whipped topping. Repeat layering with remaining cake cubes, pudding, whipped topping and crushed toffee bars.

Garnish with chocolate curls. Chill for 1 hour. Serves 20.

*1 serving: 303 Calories; 11.2 g Total Fat (1.7 g Mono, 0.4 g Poly, 4.6 g Sat); 9 mg Cholesterol; 45 g Carbohydrate; 0 g Fibre; 4 g Protein; 434 mg Sodium*

Pictured on page 55.

Left: Mango Raspberry Trifles, page 56
Right: Truffle Trifle, above

*Mango and fresh raspberries make this a very colourful dessert. Assemble in individual wine glasses and serve after a special meal.*

# Mango Raspberry Trifles

| | | |
|---|---|---|
| Orange-flavoured liqueur (such as Grand Marnier) | 2 tbsp. | 30 mL |
| Orange juice | 1/4 cup | 60 mL |
| Mascarpone cheese | 1 1/3 cups | 325 mL |
| Icing (confectioner's) sugar | 1/3 cup | 75 mL |
| Giant ladyfingers | 8 | 8 |
| Cans of sliced mango with syrup (14 oz., 398 mL, each), drained and sliced diagonally | 2 | 2 |
| Fresh raspberries | 1 1/3 cups | 325 mL |

Combine liqueur and orange juice in small bowl.

Beat mascarpone cheese and icing sugar in separate small bowl until smooth.

Break each ladyfinger in half, for a total of 16 pieces. Dip 8 pieces into orange juice mixture. Place 2 pieces in each of 4 serving glasses. Divide and spoon 1/2 of mango over ladyfingers. Divide and spoon 1/2 of cheese mixture over mango. Divide and spoon 1/2 of raspberries over cheese mixture. Dip remaining ladyfinger pieces in orange juice mixture. Repeat layering with remaining ladyfinger pieces, mango and cheese mixture. Garnish with remaining raspberries. Chill. Serves 4.

*1 serving: 560 Calories; 32.1 g Total Fat (9.3 g Mono, 1.7 g Poly, 19 g Sat); 210 mg Cholesterol; 57 g Carbohydrate; 4 g Fibre; 11 g Protein; 293 mg Sodium*

Pictured on page 55.

*Pure bliss. Soft and creamy. Do not freeze.*

# Chocolate Mousse

| | | |
|---|---|---|
| Semi-sweet chocolate chips | 1 cup | 250 mL |
| Egg yolks (large) | 4 | 4 |
| Vanilla | 1/2 tsp. | 2 mL |
| Egg whites (large), room temperature (see Safety Tip) | 4 | 4 |
| Icing (confectioner's) sugar | 1/4 cup | 60 mL |
| Whipping cream (or 1 envelope of dessert topping) | 1 cup | 250 mL |

*(continued on next page)*

**Whipped cream, for garnish**
**Chocolate filigrees (see Note), for garnish**
**Chocolate curls (see Note), for garnish**

Heat chips in heavy medium saucepan on lowest heat, stirring often, until chips are almost melted. Do not overheat. Remove from heat. Stir until smooth. Add egg yolks and vanilla. Stir well. Transfer to large bowl.

Beat egg whites in medium bowl until soft peaks form. Add icing sugar, 1 tbsp. (15 mL) at a time while beating, until stiff peaks form.

Using same beaters, beat first amount of whipping cream in small bowl until stiff peaks form or prepare dessert topping according to package directions.

Fold 2 tbsp. (30 mL) egg white mixture into chocolate mixture to lighten. Fold in remaining egg white mixture until no white streaks remain. Fold in whipped cream until well combined. Divide and spoon into 8 individual bowls or goblets. Chill for at least 6 hours. Garnish with whipped cream, chocolate filigrees and chocolate curls. Makes 4 3/4 cups (1.2 L) mousse. Serves 8.

*1 serving: 255 Calories; 19.3 g Total Fat (6.1 g Mono, 0.9 g Poly, 11 g Sat); 144 mg Cholesterol; 19 g Carbohydrate; 1 g Fibre; 5 g Protein; 45 mg Sodium*

Pictured below.

**Safety Tip:** This recipe uses uncooked eggs. Make sure to use fresh, clean Grade A eggs. Keep chilled and consume the same day it is prepared. Always discard leftovers. Pregnant women, young children or the elderly are not advised to eat anything containing raw egg.

### note

To make chocolate filigrees, tape parchment (or waxed) paper onto rolling pin. Drizzle melted chocolate back and forth over curve of rolling pin in desired designs. Let stand until set. Carefully peel paper from chocolate design.

### note

To make chocolate curls, peel room temperature chocolate firmly along its length with sharp vegetable peeler. For narrower curls, use flat underside of peeler.

*This creamy dish somehow became known as Sex In A Pan—no doubt miscopied from Six in a Pan. Garnish with shaved chocolate.*

## Six Layer Dessert

### CRUST

| | | |
|---|---|---|
| Hard margarine (or butter) | 1/2 cup | 125 mL |
| All-purpose flour | 1 cup | 250 mL |
| Finely chopped nuts (your favourite), optional | 1/2 cup | 125 mL |
| Granulated sugar | 2 tbsp. | 30 mL |

### LAYERS

| | | |
|---|---|---|
| Block of cream cheese, softened | 8 oz. | 250 g |
| Icing (confectioner's) sugar | 1 cup | 250 mL |
| Whipping cream (or 1 envelope of dessert topping) | 1 cup | 250 mL |
| Box of instant chocolate pudding powder (4 serving size) | 1 | 1 |
| Milk | 1 1/2 cups | 375 mL |
| Box of instant vanilla pudding powder (4 serving size) | 1 | 1 |
| Milk | 1 1/2 cups | 375 mL |

**Crust:** Melt margarine in medium saucepan. Remove from heat. Add flour, nuts and sugar. Stir well. Press firmly in ungreased 9 × 13 inch (22 × 33 cm) pan. Bake in 325°F (160°C) oven for about 15 minutes until golden. Let stand in pan on wire rack until cooled completely.

**Layers:** Beat cream cheese and icing sugar in medium bowl until smooth. Spread evenly over crust.

Beat whipping cream in small bowl until stiff peaks form. Spread 1/2 of whipped cream evenly over cream cheese layer.

Beat chocolate pudding powder and first amount of milk in medium bowl for about 2 minutes until slightly thickened. Spread evenly over whipped cream layer. Let stand until set.

Beat vanilla pudding powder and second amount of milk in medium bowl for about 2 minutes until slightly thickened. Spread evenly over chocolate pudding layer. Let stand until set. Spread remaining whipped cream evenly over vanilla pudding layer. Chill overnight. Cuts into 15 pieces.

*1 piece: 309 Calories; 18.4 g Total Fat (7.6 g Mono, 1.1 g Poly, 8.8 g Sat); 40 mg Cholesterol; 33 g Carbohydrate; trace Fibre; 4 g Protein; 352 mg Sodium*

Pictured on page 59.

Top: Raspberry Dessert, page 60
Centre: Six Layer Dessert, above
Bottom: Glimmering Slice, page 61

*Mix and match various combinations of strawberry or raspberry jelly powder and frozen strawberries or raspberries. All are delicious!*

# Raspberry Dessert

**GRAHAM CRUMB CRUST**

| | | |
|---|---|---|
| Hard margarine (or butter), melted | 1/2 cup | 125 mL |
| Graham cracker crumbs | 2 cups | 500 mL |
| Brown sugar, packed | 1/4 cup | 60 mL |

**SECOND LAYER**

| | | |
|---|---|---|
| Block of cream cheese, softened | 8 oz. | 250 g |
| Icing (confectioner's) sugar | 1/2 cup | 125 mL |
| Vanilla | 1 tsp. | 5 mL |
| Salt | 1/2 tsp. | 2 mL |

**THIRD LAYER**

| | | |
|---|---|---|
| Boiling water | 1 1/4 cups | 300 mL |
| Boxes of strawberry-flavoured jelly powder (gelatin), 3 oz. (85 g) each | 2 | 2 |
| Granulated sugar | 1/4 cup | 60 mL |
| Package of frozen raspberries in syrup, thawed | 15 oz. | 425 g |
| Lemon juice | 1 tsp. | 5 mL |

**TOP LAYER**

| | | |
|---|---|---|
| Whipping cream | 2 cups | 500 mL |
| Icing (confectioner's) sugar | 1/4 cup | 60 mL |
| Vanilla | 1 tsp. | 5 mL |

**Graham Crumb Crust:** Combine margarine, graham crumbs and brown sugar in medium bowl. Stir well. Reserve 1/2 cup (125 mL) crumb mixture for garnish. Press remaining crumb mixture firmly in ungreased 9 × 13 inch (22 × 33 cm) pan. Bake in 350°F (175°C) oven for 10 minutes. Let stand in pan on wire rack until cooled completely.

**Second Layer:** Beat all 4 ingredients in small bowl until smooth. Spread evenly over graham crust.

**Third Layer:** Pour boiling water into separate small bowl. Add jelly powder and sugar. Stir until dissolved.

Add raspberries with syrup and lemon juice. Stir. Chill, stirring and scraping side of bowl every 10 minutes, until jelly mixture starts to thicken. Spread evenly over cream cheese layer. Chill until set.

**Top Layer:** Beat all 3 ingredients in small bowl until stiff peaks form. Spread evenly over jelly layer. Sprinkle with reserved crumbs. Chill. Cuts into 15 pieces.

*(continued on next page)*

*1 piece: 395 Calories; 24.3 g Total Fat (9.6 g Mono, 1.4 g Poly, 12 g Sat); 57 mg Cholesterol; 42 g Carbohydrate; 2 g Fibre; 4 g Protein; 318 mg Sodium*

Pictured on page 59.

# Glimmering Slice

*This looks as spectacular as it tastes!*

**GRAHAM CRUMB CRUST**

| | | |
|---|---|---|
| Hard margarine (or butter), melted | 1/2 cup | 125 mL |
| Graham cracker crumbs | 2 cups | 500 mL |
| Brown sugar, packed | 1/4 cup | 60 mL |

**SECOND LAYER**

| | | |
|---|---|---|
| Envelope of unflavoured gelatin (1 tbsp., 15 mL) | 1 | 1 |
| Cold water | 1/4 cup | 60 mL |
| Cold water | 1/2 cup | 125 mL |
| Lemon juice | 1/2 cup | 125 mL |
| Can of sweetened condensed milk | 11 oz. | 300 mL |

**THIRD LAYER**

| | | |
|---|---|---|
| Boiling water | 3 cups | 750 mL |
| Boxes of raspberry-flavoured jelly powder (gelatin), 3 oz. (85 g) each | 2 | 2 |

**Graham Crumb Crust:** Combine margarine, graham crumbs and brown sugar in medium bowl. Stir well. Press firmly in ungreased 9 x 13 inch (22 x 33 cm) pan. Bake in 350°F (175°C) oven for 10 minutes. Let stand in pan on wire rack until cooled completely.

**Second Layer:** Sprinkle gelatin over first amount of cold water in small saucepan. Let stand for 1 minute. Heat and stir on low until gelatin is dissolved. Remove from heat.

Combine second amount of cold water, lemon juice and condensed milk in small bowl. Add gelatin mixture. Beat well. Spread evenly over graham crust.

**Third Layer:** Pour boiling water into separate small bowl. Add jelly powder. Stir until jelly powder is dissolved. Chill, stirring and scraping side of bowl every 10 minutes, until jelly mixture starts to thicken. Spread evenly over lemon mixture. Chill until set. Cuts into 15 pieces.

*1 piece: 254 Calories; 9.9 g Total Fat (5.4 g Mono, 0.9 g Poly, 3 g Sat); 9 mg Cholesterol; 39 g Carbohydrate; trace Fibre; 4 g Protein; 212 mg Sodium*

Pictured on page 59.

*Top with your favourite fruit to create a colourful presentation.*

# Fruit Pizza

## CRUST

| | | |
|---|---|---|
| All-purpose flour | 1 1/4 cups | 300 mL |
| Brown sugar, packed | 1/3 cup | 75 mL |
| Icing (confectioner's) sugar | 3 tbsp. | 50 mL |
| Hard margarine (or butter), cut up | 2/3 cup | 150 mL |

## TOPPING

| | | |
|---|---|---|
| Blocks of cream cheese (4 oz., 125 g, each), softened | 3 | 3 |
| Granulated sugar | 1/2 cup | 125 mL |
| Vanilla | 1 tsp. | 5 mL |
| Variety of fresh fruit (such as strawberries, kiwifruit, peaches and blueberries), sliced | | |

## APRICOT GLAZE

| | | |
|---|---|---|
| Apricot jam (or orange marmalade) | 1/4 cup | 60 mL |
| Water | 1 tbsp. | 15 mL |

**Crust:** Combine flour, brown sugar and icing sugar in medium bowl. Cut in margarine until mixture resembles fine crumbs. Press mixture together to form smooth ball. Press firmly in ungreased 12 inch (30 cm) pizza pan. Bake in 350°F (175°C) oven for 10 to 15 minutes until golden. Let stand in pan on wire rack until cooled completely.

**Topping:** Beat cream cheese, sugar and vanilla in large bowl until smooth. Spread evenly over crust. Arrange fruit in attractive pattern over cream cheese mixture.

**Apricot Glaze:** Combine apricot jam and water in small bowl. Press through sieve into separate small bowl. Brush lightly over fruit. Chill. Cuts into 12 wedges.

*1 wedge: 359 Calories; 22 g Total Fat (10.1 g Mono, 1.5 g Poly, 9.1 g Sat); 34 mg Cholesterol; 38 g Carbohydrate; 2 g Fibre; 4 g Protein; 225 mg Sodium*

Pictured on page 63.

*This scrumptious dessert will catch everyone's attention when you bring it out of the freezer!*

# Peanut Ice Cream Treat

| | | |
|---|---|---|
| Butterscotch (or caramel) ice cream topping | 1/3 cup | 75 mL |
| Chocolate (or fudge) ice cream topping | 1/3 cup | 75 mL |
| Commercial chocolate crumb crust (9 inch, 22 cm, diameter) | 1 | 1 |
| Vanilla (or butterscotch ripple) ice cream, softened | 4 cups | 1 L |
| Roasted unsalted peanuts, chopped | 1/2 cup | 125 mL |
| Butterscotch (or caramel) ice cream topping, for garnish | | |
| Chocolate (or fudge) ice cream topping, for garnish | | |

Spoon alternating teaspoonfuls (using 1 tsp., 5 mL, for each) of first amounts of butterscotch and chocolate toppings over crust. Freeze for 20 minutes.

Spread ice cream evenly over crust.

Sprinkle peanuts over ice cream. Cover with plastic wrap. Freeze for at least 8 hours or overnight until firm.

Drizzle second amounts of butterscotch and chocolate toppings over peanuts. Freeze until firm. Cuts into 8 wedges.

*1 wedge: 425 Calories; 23.1 g Total Fat (9.2 g Mono, 4.4 g Poly, 8.1 g Sat); 33 mg Cholesterol; 52 g Carbohydrate; 1 g Fibre; 7 g Protein; 313 mg Sodium*

Pictured on page 65 and on back cover.

*Can it get any better than this for banana split lovers?*

## chocolate dips

Heat and stir 2 semi-sweet chocolate baking squares (1 oz., 28 g, each) in small heavy saucepan on lowest heat until chocolate is almost melted. Do not overheat. Remove from heat. Stir until smooth. Dip bottom half of each of 18 banana chips in chocolate, allowing excess to drip back into saucepan. Place chips on parchment paper-lined baking sheet. Chill until set. Makes 18 dips.

# Banana Macadamia Sundaes

**CARAMEL SAUCE**

| | | |
|---|---|---|
| Brown sugar, packed | 1/2 cup | 125 mL |
| Hard margarine (or butter) | 1/3 cup | 75 mL |
| Whipping cream | 1/3 cup | 75 mL |
| Vanilla | 1/2 tsp. | 2 mL |

**CHOCOLATE FUDGE SAUCE**

| | | |
|---|---|---|
| Whipping cream | 1/2 cup | 125 mL |
| Semi-sweet chocolate bar (3 1/2 oz., 100 g), chopped | 1 | 1 |
| Large marshmallows, chopped | 6 | 6 |
| Chocolate ice cream, approximately | 3 cups | 750 mL |
| Medium bananas | 6 | 6 |
| Whipped cream | 1 1/2 cups | 375 mL |
| Coarsely chopped macadamia nuts, toasted (see Note) | 3/4 cup | 175 mL |
| Chocolate Dips, for garnish | 18 | 18 |

**Caramel Sauce:** Heat and stir all 4 ingredients in medium saucepan on medium until boiling. Boil, without stirring, for about 5 minutes until smooth and slightly thickened. Remove from heat. Makes about 2/3 cup (150 mL) Caramel Sauce.

**Chocolate Fudge Sauce:** Heat and stir whipping cream, chocolate and marshmallow in medium saucepan on medium until smooth. Makes about 1 cup (250 mL) fudge sauce.

In each of six 1 1/2 cup (375 mL) float glasses or wine goblets, layer as follows:

1. 1 scoop ice cream (1/4 cup, 60 mL)
2. 1/2 banana, sliced
3. 1 1/2 tbsp. (25 mL) Caramel Sauce
4. 2 tbsp. (30 mL) whipped cream
5. 1 tbsp. (15 mL) macadamia nuts
6. 1 scoop ice cream (1/4 cup, 60 mL)
7. 1/2 banana, sliced
8. 2 1/2 tbsp. (37 mL) Chocolate Fudge Sauce
9. 2 tbsp. (30 mL) whipped cream
10. 1 tbsp. (15 mL) macadamia nuts

Garnish each with 3 Chocolate Dips. Makes 6 sundaes.

*1 sundae: 832 Calories; 56 g Total Fat (25.6 g Mono, 2.4 g Poly, 25 g Sat); 101 mg Cholesterol; 86 g Carbohydrate; 4 g Fibre; 7 g Protein; 217 mg Sodium*

Pictured on page 67 and on back cover.

*Pears poached in maple syrup and port wine, with a hint of cinnamon and cloves. The perfect treat on a cold day.*

# Poached Maple Pears

| **Fresh firm medium pears** | 4 | 4 |
|---|---|---|
| **Port wine** | 1 cup | 250 mL |
| **Orange juice** | 1/2 cup | 125 mL |
| **Maple (or maple-flavoured) syrup** | 1/3 cup | 75 mL |
| **Cinnamon stick (4 inch, 10 cm, length)** | 1 | 1 |
| **Whole cloves** | 6 | 6 |

**Fresh mint leaves, for garnish**

Carefully remove cores from pears using apple corer, leaving pear whole. Peel pears.

Combine next 5 ingredients in medium saucepan. Lay pears on sides in wine mixture. Bring to a boil on medium. Reduce heat to medium-low. Simmer, uncovered, for 15 to 20 minutes, turning pears occasionally, until softened and evenly coloured. Remove pears using slotted spoon. Cover to keep warm. Remove and discard cinnamon stick and cloves. Bring wine mixture to a boil on medium. Boil, uncovered, for 10 to 15 minutes until reduced to about 3/4 cup (175 mL).

Slice pears evenly, making 6 or 7 cuts from large end of pear to within 1/2 inch (12 mm) of small end. Place 1 pear, large end down, on each of 4 dessert plates. Fan pear slices out slightly. Drizzle with wine mixture. Garnish with mint leaves. Serves 4.

*1 serving: 177 Calories; 0.2 g Total Fat (0 g Mono, 0 g Poly, 0 g Sat); 0 mg Cholesterol; 35 g Carbohydrate; 3 g Fibre; 1 g Protein; 9 mg Sodium*

Pictured on page 69.

Top Left: Brandied Peaches, page 70
Top Right: Baked Apples, page 70
Centre: Poached Maple Pears, above

*Make as many or as few as needed. Good with a scoop of ice cream.*

**variations**

Add 1 tsp. (5 mL) ground cinnamon to brown sugar. Stir well. Proceed as directed.

Remove apples from oven about halfway through baking time. Spoon mincemeat into cavities. Bake as directed.

# Baked Apples

| | | |
|---|---|---|
| Medium cooking apples (such as McIntosh) 4 | | 4 |
| Brown sugar, packed | 1 cup | 250 mL |
| Hard margarine (or butter), softened | 2 tsp. | 10 mL |

Carefully remove cores from apples using apple corer, leaving apples whole (with peel). Arrange in ungreased 8 × 8 inch (20 × 20 cm) pan. Divide and pack brown sugar into centre of each apple. Spoon 1/2 tsp. (2 mL) margarine over brown sugar. Bake in 350°F (175°C) oven for 25 to 35 minutes until apples are tender. Transfer 1 apple to each of 4 individual bowls. Spoon sauce from pan over apples. Serves 4.

*1 serving: 317 Calories; 2.4 g Total Fat (1.3 g Mono, 0.3 g Poly, 0.5 g Sat); 0 mg Cholesterol; 78 g Carbohydrate; 3 g Fibre; 0 g Protein; 45 mg Sodium*

Pictured on page 69.

*A dessert solution that fits all occasions.*

**variation**

Use only 2 tbsp. (30 mL) reserved juice and substitute Grand Marnier (orange-flavoured liqueur) for the brandy.

# Brandied Peaches

| | | |
|---|---|---|
| Cans of peach halves in pear juice (14 oz., 398 mL, each) | 2 | 2 |
| Brown sugar, packed | 2/3 cup | 150 mL |
| Hard margarine (or butter) | 2 tbsp. | 30 mL |
| Ground cinnamon | 1/4 tsp. | 1 mL |
| Lemon juice | 1 tsp. | 5 mL |
| Brandy flavouring (or 1/4 cup, 60 mL, brandy) | 1 tsp. | 5 mL |
| Almond flavouring (optional) | 1/4 tsp. | 1 mL |
| Vanilla ice cream | 6 cups | 1.5 L |

Drain peaches, reserving juice. Chop peaches. Transfer to medium saucepan. Add reserved juice. Add next 6 ingredients. Bring to a boil on medium. Reduce heat to medium-low. Simmer, uncovered, for 5 minutes, stirring occasionally.

Scoop 1/2 cup (125 mL) ice cream into each of 12 individual dishes. Divide and spoon brandied peaches over top. Serves 12.

*1 serving: 237 Calories; 9.6 g Total Fat (3.5 g Mono, 0.5 g Poly, 5.1 g Sat); 31 mg Cholesterol; 37 g Carbohydrate; 1 g Fibre; 3 g Protein; 86 mg Sodium*

Pictured on page 69.

# Brown Betty

| | | |
|---|---|---|
| Peeled, cored and sliced cooking apples (such as McIntosh) | 6 cups | 1.5 L |
| Granulated sugar | 3/4 cup | 175 mL |
| **STREUSEL TOPPING** | | |
| All-purpose flour | 1 1/4 cups | 300 mL |
| Brown sugar, packed | 3/4 cup | 175 mL |
| Salt | 1/2 tsp. | 2 mL |
| Hard margarine (or butter), cut up | 1/2 cup | 125 mL |

Place apple slices in ungreased shallow 3 quart (3 L) casserole. Sprinkle sugar over top.

**Streusel Topping:** Combine flour, brown sugar and salt in medium bowl. Cut in margarine until mixture resembles coarse crumbs. Scatter evenly over apple. Press down lightly. Bake, uncovered, in 375°F (190°C) oven for about 40 minutes until apple is tender. Serves 8.

*1 serving: 392 Calories; 12.5 g Total Fat (7.9 g Mono, 1.4 g Poly, 2.6 g Sat); 0 mg Cholesterol; 70 g Carbohydrate; 2 g Fibre; 2 g Protein; 299 mg Sodium*

Pictured below.

*An all-time favourite. Good hot or cold. Even better served with ice cream.*

### rhubarb betty

Omit apple and use same amount of sliced fresh or frozen rhubarb, adding 1/2 cup (125 mL) more sugar. Better yet, add a few raisins and omit the extra sugar. Bake as directed.

### fresh fruit betty

Omit apple and use fresh peaches, peeled and sliced, or fresh apricots, quartered. Bake as directed.

*A treat everyone looks forward to! Freezes well.*

# Nanaimo Bars

| BOTTOM LAYER | | |
|---|---|---|
| Hard margarine (or butter) | 1/2 cup | 125 mL |
| Cocoa, sifted if lumpy | 1/3 cup | 75 mL |
| Granulated sugar | 1/4 cup | 60 mL |
| Large egg, fork-beaten | 1 | 1 |
| | | |
| Graham cracker crumbs | 1 3/4 cups | 425 mL |
| Fine (or medium unsweetened) coconut | 3/4 cup | 175 mL |
| Finely chopped walnuts | 1/2 cup | 125 mL |
| MIDDLE LAYER | | |
| Icing (confectioner's) sugar | 2 cups | 500 mL |
| Hard margarine (or butter), softened | 1/2 cup | 125 mL |
| Milk | 3 tbsp. | 50 mL |
| Vanilla custard powder | 2 tbsp. | 30 mL |
| TOP LAYER | | |
| Semi-sweet chocolate chips | 2/3 cup | 150 mL |
| Hard margarine (or butter) | 2 tbsp. | 30 mL |

**Bottom Layer:** Heat and stir margarine, cocoa and sugar in heavy medium saucepan on medium-low until smooth. Add egg. Stir until thickened. Remove from heat.

Add graham crumbs, coconut and walnuts. Stir well. Press firmly in ungreased 9 x 9 inch (22 x 22 cm) pan.

**Middle Layer:** Beat all 4 ingredients in medium bowl until smooth. Spread evenly over bottom layer.

**Top Layer:** Heat chips and margarine in small heavy saucepan on lowest heat, stirring often, until chips are almost melted. Do not overheat. Remove from heat. Stir until smooth. Cool slightly. Spread evenly over middle layer. Chill until top layer is set. Cuts into 36 squares.

*1 square: 153 Calories; 10.1 g Total Fat (4.9 g Mono, 1.4 g Poly, 3.3 g Sat); 9 mg Cholesterol; 16 g Carbohydrate; 1 g Fibre; 2 g Protein; 106 mg Sodium*

Pictured on page 73.

Top Left: Mars Bars Squares, page 74
Top Right And Bottom: Nanaimo Bars, above
Centre Right: Chocolate Crisps, page 74

*Crisp and chocolaty. For a pretty contrast, drizzle melted white chocolate over top before cutting.*

# Mars Bars Squares

| | | |
|---|---|---|
| Mars candy bars (1 3/4 oz., 50 g, each, black and red label), chopped | 4 | 4 |
| Hard margarine (or butter) | 1/2 cup | 125 mL |
| Crisp rice cereal | 3 cups | 750 mL |
| Semi-sweet chocolate chips | 1 cup | 250 mL |
| Hard margarine (or butter) | 1/4 cup | 60 mL |

Heat and stir candy bar pieces and first amount of margarine in large heavy saucepan on low until smooth. Remove from heat.

Add cereal. Stir until coated. Press evenly in greased or foil-lined 9 x 9 inch (22 x 22 cm) pan.

Heat chips and second amount of margarine in small heavy saucepan on lowest heat, stirring often, until chips are melted. Spread evenly over cereal mixture in pan. Chill. Cuts into 36 squares.

*1 square: 92 Calories; 6.4 g Total Fat (3.5 g Mono, 0.5 g Poly, 2.1 g Sat); 1 mg Cholesterol; 9 g Carbohydrate; trace Fibre; 1 g Protein; 86 mg Sodium*

Pictured on page 73.

*Even the kids can make these. Fast and easy. Tastes like candy!*

# Chocolate Crisps

| | | |
|---|---|---|
| Smooth peanut butter | 1 cup | 250 mL |
| Liquid honey | 3/4 cup | 175 mL |
| Semi-sweet chocolate chips | 1 cup | 250 mL |
| Crisp rice cereal | 3 cups | 750 mL |
| Salted peanuts | 1 cup | 250 mL |

Heat peanut butter and honey in large heavy saucepan on lowest heat, stirring often, until melted. Bring to a gentle boil. Remove from heat.

Add chips. Stir until smooth.

Add cereal and peanuts. Stir until coated. Press firmly in greased or foil-lined 9 x 9 inch (22 x 22 cm) pan. Chill until firm. Cuts into 36 squares.

*1 square: 130 Calories; 7.5 g Total Fat (3.4 g Mono, 1.8 g Poly, 2 g Sat); 0 mg Cholesterol; 15 g Carbohydrate; 1 g Fibre; 3 g Protein; 96 mg Sodium*

Pictured on page 73.

# Shortbread

| | | |
|---|---|---|
| All-purpose flour | 2 cups | 500 mL |
| Icing (confectioner's) sugar (see Note) | 1/2 cup | 125 mL |
| Butter (not margarine), cut up | 1 cup | 250 mL |

Combine flour and icing sugar in large bowl. Cut in butter until mixture resembles fine crumbs. Press mixture together to form smooth ball. Press evenly in ungreased 9 x 9 inch (22 x 22 cm) pan. Prick entire surface of dough with fork through to bottom of pan. Bake in 300°F (150°C) oven for 50 to 60 minutes until just golden. Let stand in pan on wire rack for 5 minutes. Cuts into 36 squares.

*1 square: 81 Calories; 5.5 g Total Fat (1.6 g Mono, 0.2 g Poly, 3.4 g Sat); 15 mg Cholesterol; 7 g Carbohydrate; trace Fibre; 1 g Protein; 55 mg Sodium*

Pictured below.

*A favourite, no-fail recipe for shortbread.*

## scotch shortbread

Omit icing sugar. Use same amount of granulated sugar.

*The perfect ending to an evening meal.*

# Midnight Mints

### BOTTOM LAYER

| | | |
|---|---|---|
| Hard margarine (or butter) | 1/2 cup | 125 mL |
| Cocoa, sifted if lumpy | 1/3 cup | 75 mL |
| Granulated sugar | 1/4 cup | 60 mL |
| Large egg, fork-beaten | 1 | 1 |
| Graham cracker crumbs | 1 3/4 cups | 425 mL |
| Fine coconut | 3/4 cup | 175 mL |
| Finely chopped walnuts | 1/2 cup | 125 mL |

### MIDDLE LAYER

| | | |
|---|---|---|
| Icing (confectioner's) sugar | 2 cups | 500 mL |
| Hard margarine (or butter), softened | 1/3 cup | 75 mL |
| Milk | 3 tbsp. | 50 mL |
| Peppermint flavouring | 1 tsp. | 5 mL |
| Green liquid (or paste) food colouring | | |

### TOP LAYER

| | | |
|---|---|---|
| Semi-sweet chocolate chips | 2/3 cup | 150 mL |
| Hard margarine (or butter) | 2 tbsp. | 30 mL |

**Bottom Layer:** Heat margarine, cocoa and sugar in large heavy saucepan on low, stirring often, until sugar is dissolved. Add egg. Stir until thickened. Remove from heat.

Add graham crumbs, coconut and walnuts. Stir well. Press firmly in ungreased 9 x 9 inch (22 x 22 cm) pan.

**Middle Layer:** Beat first 4 ingredients in medium bowl until smooth, adding more milk or icing sugar as necessary until spreading consistency. Add enough food colouring until pale green. Spread evenly over bottom layer.

**Top Layer:** Heat chips and margarine in small heavy saucepan on lowest heat, stirring often, until chips are almost melted. Do not overheat. Remove from heat. Stir until smooth. Cool slightly. Spread evenly over middle layer. Chill until top layer is set. Cuts into 36 squares.

*1 square: 142 Calories; 9.1 g Total Fat (4.3 g Mono, 1.3 g Poly, 3.1 g Sat); 6 mg Cholesterol; 15 g Carbohydrate; 1 g Fibre; 1 g Protein; 90 mg Sodium*

Pictured on page 77.

*Millionaire means rich—exactly what these squares are!*

# Millionaire Squares

**BOTTOM LAYER**

| | | |
|---|---|---|
| Hard margarine (or butter) | 1/2 cup | 125 mL |
| Finely crushed crisp oatmeal cookies (such as Dad's) | 2 cups | 500 mL |

**FILLING**

| | | |
|---|---|---|
| Semi-sweet chocolate baking squares (1 oz., 28 g, each), chopped (or 1/2 cup, 125 mL, chocolate chips) | 3 | 3 |
| Hard margarine (or butter) | 1/2 cup | 125 mL |
| Large egg | 1 | 1 |
| Icing (confectioner's) sugar | 2 cups | 500 mL |
| Chopped walnuts (optional) | 1/2 cup | 125 mL |

**Bottom Layer:** Melt margarine in medium saucepan. Remove from heat. Add crushed cookies. Stir well. Reserve 1/4 cup (60 mL) crumb mixture for topping. Press remaining mixture firmly in greased 8 x 8 inch (20 x 20 cm) pan. Bake in 350°F (175°C) oven for 5 minutes. Let stand in pan on wire rack until cooled completely.

**Filling:** Heat chocolate and margarine in heavy medium saucepan on lowest heat, stirring often, until chocolate is almost melted. Do not overheat. Remove from heat. Stir until smooth. Add egg. Beat. Add icing sugar, 2 tbsp. (30 mL) at a time while beating, until smooth, adding more icing sugar as necessary until spreading consistency.

Add walnuts. Stir. Spread evenly over bottom layer. Sprinkle reserved crumb mixture over top. Chill until firm. Cuts into 25 squares.

*1 square:* 169 Calories; 10.6 g Total Fat (6.4 g Mono, 1.1 g Poly, 2.5 g Sat); 9 mg Cholesterol; 19 g Carbohydrate; trace Fibre; 1 g Protein; 129 mg Sodium

Pictured on page 79.

Top Left: Fudgy Macaroons, page 80
Top Right: Millionaire Squares, above
Bottom Right: Butterscotch Confetti, page 81
Bottom Left: Swirl Squares, page 80

*The swirl is made with chocolate chips. No need to ice these. The recipe is easily doubled.*

### variation

Omit the chocolate chips. Cool squares completely. Spread with your favourite icing.

# Swirl Squares

| | | |
|---|---|---|
| Hard margarine (or butter), softened | 1/2 cup | 125 mL |
| Brown sugar, packed | 1/2 cup | 125 mL |
| Granulated sugar | 1/4 cup | 60 mL |
| Vanilla | 1/2 tsp. | 2 mL |
| Large egg | 1 | 1 |
| All-purpose flour | 1 1/8 cups | 280 mL |
| Baking soda | 1/2 tsp. | 2 mL |
| Salt | 1/2 tsp. | 2 mL |
| Chopped walnuts | 1/2 cup | 125 mL |
| Semi-sweet chocolate chips | 1 cup | 250 mL |

Beat first 5 ingredients in large bowl until light and creamy.

Combine flour, baking soda and salt in small bowl. Add to margarine mixture. Stir until smooth.

Add walnuts. Stir. Spread evenly in greased 9 x 9 inch (22 x 22 cm) pan.

Scatter chips over top. Bake in 375°F (190°C) oven for 1 to 2 minutes until chips are very soft. Remove from oven. Swirl knife through batter to create marble effect. Return to oven. Bake for about 20 minutes until firm and wooden pick inserted in centre comes out clean. Let stand in pan on wire rack until cool. Cuts into 36 squares.

*1 square:* 94 Calories; 5.4 g Total Fat (2.5 g Mono, 1 g Poly, 1.5 g Sat); 6 mg Cholesterol; 11 g Carbohydrate; 1 g Fibre; 1 g Protein; 86 mg Sodium

Pictured on page 79.

*Crunchy butterscotch treats. Similar taste to brown sugar fudge.*

# Fudgy Macaroons

| | | |
|---|---|---|
| Granulated sugar | 1 1/2 cups | 375 mL |
| Evaporated milk | 1 cup | 250 mL |
| Hard margarine (or butter) | 1/4 cup | 60 mL |
| Butterscotch chips | 2 cups | 500 mL |
| Vanilla | 1 tsp. | 5 mL |

*(continued on next page)*

| Cornflakes cereal, lightly packed | 4 cups | 1 L |
| Medium unsweetened coconut | 2 1/2 cups | 625 mL |
| Chopped walnuts | 1 cup | 250 mL |

Heat and stir sugar, evaporated milk and margarine in large heavy saucepan on medium. Bring to a rolling boil. Immediately remove from heat.

Add chips and vanilla. Stir until smooth.

Add cereal, coconut and walnuts. Stir until coated. Press firmly in greased or foil-lined 9 x 9 inch (22 x 22 cm) pan. Chill until firm. Cuts into 36 squares.

*1 square: 198 Calories; 8.6 g Total Fat (1.8 g Mono, 1.6 g Poly, 4.6 g Sat); 3 mg Cholesterol; 29 g Carbohydrate; 1 g Fibre; 3 g Protein; 138 mg Sodium*

Pictured on page 79.

## Butterscotch Confetti

| Butterscotch chips | 1 cup | 250 mL |
| Smooth peanut butter | 1/2 cup | 125 mL |
| Hard margarine (or butter) | 1/4 cup | 60 mL |
| Package of miniature multi-coloured marshmallows | 8 oz. | 250 g |

Heat first 3 ingredients in large heavy saucepan on lowest heat, stirring often, until chips are almost melted. Do not overheat. Remove from heat. Stir until smooth. Let stand until bottom of saucepan is cool enough to touch.

Add marshmallows. Stir until coated. Press firmly in greased or foil-lined 9 x 9 inch (22 x 22 cm) pan. Chill until firm. Cuts into 36 squares.

*1 square: 73 Calories; 3.4 g Total Fat (1.8 g Mono, 0.7 g Poly, 0.7 g Sat); 0 mg Cholesterol; 10 g Carbohydrate; trace Fibre; 1 g Protein; 39 mg Sodium*

Pictured on page 79.

*There is no excuse not to have this treat on hand. Freezes well. Colourful!*

### variation

Line bottom of pan with whole graham crackers first. Proceed as directed in recipe.

### variation

Add 1/2 cup (125 mL) chopped walnuts and/or 1/2 cup (125 mL) medium unsweetened coconut to recipe ingredients.

*Make these when you're looking for something a little different.*

# Tweed Squares

| | | |
|---|---|---|
| Hard margarine (or butter), softened | 1/2 cup | 125 mL |
| Granulated sugar | 2/3 cup | 150 mL |
| All-purpose flour | 1 1/3 cups | 325 mL |
| Baking powder | 2 tsp. | 10 mL |
| Salt | 1/2 tsp. | 2 mL |
| Milk | 1/2 cup | 125 mL |
| Egg whites (large), room temperature | 2 | 2 |
| Semi-sweet chocolate baking squares (1 oz., 28 g, each), finely grated | 2 | 2 |
| **VANILLA ICING** | | |
| Icing (confectioner's) sugar | 1 1/2 cups | 375 mL |
| Hard margarine (or butter), softened | 3 tbsp. | 50 mL |
| Water | 1 1/2 tbsp. | 25 mL |
| Vanilla | 1/2 tsp. | 2 mL |
| Semi-sweet chocolate baking squares (1 oz., 28 g, each), chopped | 2 | 2 |
| Hard margarine (or butter) | 1 tbsp. | 15 mL |

Beat margarine and sugar in large bowl until light and creamy.

Combine flour, baking powder and salt in small bowl. Add flour mixture to margarine mixture in 2 additions, alternating with milk in 1 addition, beginning and ending with flour mixture.

Beat egg whites in separate small bowl until stiff peaks form. Fold into batter until no white streaks remain.

Fold in grated chocolate. Spread evenly in greased 9 x 9 inch (22 x 22 cm) pan. Bake in 350°F (175°C) oven for about 35 minutes until golden. Let stand in pan on wire rack until cooled completely.

**Vanilla Icing:** Beat first 4 ingredients in small bowl until smooth, adding more water or icing sugar as necessary until spreading consistency. Spread evenly over first layer. Let stand for at least 1 hour until set.

*(continued on next page)*

Heat chocolate and margarine in small heavy saucepan on lowest heat, stirring often, until chocolate is almost melted. Do not overheat. Remove from heat. Stir until smooth. Cool slightly. Spread evenly over icing. Chill until top layer is set. Cuts into 36 squares.

*1 square:* 107 Calories; 5 g Total Fat (2.9 g Mono, 0.4 g Poly, 1.4 g Sat); 0 mg Cholesterol; 15 g Carbohydrate; trace Fibre; 1 g Protein; 105 mg Sodium

Pictured below.

Top: Tweed Squares, page 82
Bottom: Chocolate Roll, page 84

*A colourful confection with a smooth texture. After a few slices are cut, you can pop it back in the refrigerator or freezer.*

### variation

Reduce coconut to 1/4 cup (60 mL). Add with rest of ingredients. Mix well. Press firmly in greased or foil-lined 8 x 8 inch (20 x 20 cm) pan. Cuts into 25 squares.

# Chocolate Roll

| | | |
|---|---|---|
| Semi-sweet chocolate chips | 1 cup | 250 mL |
| Hard margarine (or butter) | 2 tbsp. | 30 mL |
| Miniature multi-coloured marshmallows | 2 1/2 cups | 625 mL |
| Icing (confectioner's) sugar | 1 cup | 250 mL |
| Quartered maraschino cherries, well-drained | 1/2 cup | 125 mL |
| Chopped walnuts | 1/2 cup | 125 mL |
| Large egg, fork-beaten | 1 | 1 |
| Medium unsweetened coconut | 1/2 cup | 125 mL |

Heat chips and margarine in large heavy saucepan on lowest heat, stirring often, until chips are almost melted. Do not overheat. Remove from heat. Stir until smooth.

Add next 5 ingredients. Stir well. Let stand until cool enough to handle. Shape mixture into 2 1/2 inch (6.4 cm) diameter log.

Sprinkle coconut on waxed paper on work surface. Roll log in coconut until coated. Wrap in waxed paper or plastic wrap. Chill until firm. Cut into 1/2 inch (12 mm) slices, cleaning knife under hot water after each slice. Cuts into 24 slices.

*1 slice: 116 Calories; 6.3 g Total Fat (1.9 g Mono, 1.2 g Poly, 2.8 g Sat); 9 mg Cholesterol; 16 g Carbohydrate; 1 g Fibre; 1 g Protein; 18 mg Sodium*

Pictured on page 83.

*A light, summer treat. Freezes well so you can pull one out whenever you get a craving.*

# Lemon Bars

**BOTTOM LAYER**

| | | |
|---|---|---|
| All-purpose flour | 2 cups | 500 mL |
| Icing (confectioner's) sugar | 3/4 cup | 175 mL |
| Hard margarine (or butter), softened, cut up | 1 cup | 250 mL |

**TOP LAYER**

| | | |
|---|---|---|
| Large eggs | 4 | 4 |
| Lemon juice | 1/3 cup | 75 mL |
| Grated lemon peel | 1 tbsp. | 15 mL |

*(continued on next page)*

| Granulated sugar | 1 1/2 cups | 375 mL |
| All-purpose flour | 1/4 cup | 60 mL |
| Baking powder | 1 tsp. | 5 mL |

Icing (confectioner's) sugar, for dusting

**Bottom Layer:** Combine flour and icing sugar in medium bowl. Cut in margarine until mixture resembles fine crumbs. Press firmly in ungreased 9 x 13 inch (22 x 33 cm) pan. Bake in 350°F (175°C) oven for about 20 minutes until golden. Remove from oven.

**Top Layer:** Beat eggs in large bowl until frothy. Add lemon juice and peel. Stir.

Combine granulated sugar, flour and baking powder in small bowl. Add to egg mixture. Stir until just moistened. Spread evenly over bottom layer. Bake for about 25 minutes until set. Let stand in pan on wire rack for 5 minutes.

Dust evenly with icing sugar using sieve. Let stand until cool. Cuts into 48 bars.

*1 bar: 100 Calories; 4.5 g Total Fat (2.8 g Mono, 0.5 g Poly, 1 g Sat); 18 mg Cholesterol; 14 g Carbohydrate; trace Fibre; 1 g Protein; 60 mg Sodium*

Pictured below.

*Favourite date squares that are not as messy to eat as some others. These crumbs hold together well.*

# Matrimonial Squares

**CRUMB LAYERS**

| | | |
|---|---|---|
| Rolled oats (not instant) | 1 1/2 cups | 375 mL |
| All-purpose flour | 1 1/4 cups | 300 mL |
| Brown sugar, packed | 1 cup | 250 mL |
| Baking soda | 1 tsp. | 5 mL |
| Salt | 1/2 tsp. | 2 mL |
| Hard margarine (or butter), softened, cut up | 1 cup | 250 mL |

**DATE FILLING**

| | | |
|---|---|---|
| Chopped pitted dates | 1 1/2 cups | 375 mL |
| Water | 2/3 cup | 150 mL |
| Granulated sugar | 1/2 cup | 125 mL |

**Crumb Layers:** Combine first 5 ingredients in large bowl. Cut in margarine until mixture resembles very coarse crumbs. Press slightly more than 1/2 of mixture firmly in greased 9 x 9 inch (22 x 22 cm) pan. Set remaining mixture aside.

**Date Filling:** Combine dates, water and sugar in medium saucepan. Bring to a boil on medium. Reduce heat to medium-low. Simmer, uncovered, for about 10 minutes until dates are softened and water is almost evaporated, adding more water if necessary while simmering to soften dates. Spread evenly over bottom layer of crumbs. Sprinkle remaining crumb mixture evenly over top. Press down lightly. Bake in 350°F (175°C) oven for about 30 minutes until golden. Let stand in pan on wire rack until cool. Cuts into 36 squares.

*1 square: 139 Calories; 5.7 g Total Fat (3.6 g Mono, 0.7 g Poly, 1.2 g Sat); 0 mg Cholesterol; 21 g Carbohydrate; 1 g Fibre; 1 g Protein; 134 mg Sodium*

Pictured on page 87.

Top Right: Cherry Squares, page 88
Bottom Left: Matrimonial Squares, above

*This is one of our most popular bar cookies. After you've tried a piece, you'll understand why.*

# Cherry Squares

### BOTTOM LAYER

| | | |
|---|---|---|
| All-purpose flour | 1 1/4 cups | 300 mL |
| Brown sugar, packed | 1/3 cup | 75 mL |
| Hard margarine (or butter), softened, cut up | 1/2 cup | 125 mL |

### SECOND LAYER

| | | |
|---|---|---|
| Large eggs | 2 | 2 |
| Brown sugar, packed | 1 1/4 cups | 300 mL |
| All-purpose flour | 1 tbsp. | 15 mL |
| Baking powder | 1/2 tsp. | 2 mL |
| Salt | 1/8 tsp. | 0.5 mL |
| Medium unsweetened coconut | 1 cup | 250 mL |
| Chopped walnuts | 1/2 cup | 125 mL |
| Chopped red glazed cherries (or maraschino cherries, blotted dry) | 1/2 cup | 125 mL |

### VANILLA ICING

| | | |
|---|---|---|
| Icing (confectioner's) sugar | 2 cups | 500 mL |
| Hard margarine (or butter), softened | 1/4 cup | 60 mL |
| Milk (or water) | 2 tbsp. | 30 mL |
| Vanilla | 1 tsp. | 5 mL |

**Bottom Layer:** Combine flour and brown sugar in small bowl. Cut in margarine until mixture resembles fine crumbs. Press firmly in ungreased 9 x 9 inch (22 x 22 cm) pan. Bake in 350°F (175°C) oven for 15 minutes. Remove from oven.

**Second Layer:** Beat eggs in medium bowl until frothy. Add remaining ingredients, in order given, stirring after each addition. Spread evenly over bottom layer. Bake for about 25 minutes until golden. Let stand in pan on wire rack until cooled completely.

**Vanilla Icing:** Beat all 4 ingredients in small bowl until smooth, adding more milk or icing sugar as necessary until spreading consistency. Spread evenly over second layer. Cuts into 36 squares.

*1 square: 141 Calories; 6.4 g Total Fat (2.6 g Mono, 1.1 g Poly, 2.4 g Sat); 12 mg Cholesterol; 20 g Carbohydrate; trace Fibre; 2 g Protein; 62 mg Sodium*

Pictured on page 87.

# Apricot Zings

*A long-time favourite. Great to make ahead and freeze. Perfect choice for a bake sale.*

**BOTTOM LAYER**

| | | |
|---|---|---|
| Graham cracker crumbs | 1 cup | 250 mL |
| All-purpose flour | 1 cup | 250 mL |
| Brown sugar, packed | 1 cup | 250 mL |
| Hard margarine (or butter), melted | 3/4 cup | 175 mL |
| Medium unsweetened coconut | 1/2 cup | 125 mL |
| Salt | 1/2 tsp. | 2 mL |

**APRICOT FILLING**

| | | |
|---|---|---|
| Dried apricots | 1 cup | 250 mL |
| Water | | |
| Large eggs | 2 | 2 |
| Brown sugar, packed | 1 cup | 250 mL |
| Lemon juice | 1 tbsp. | 15 mL |
| All-purpose flour | 1/3 cup | 75 mL |
| Baking powder | 1/2 tsp. | 2 mL |
| Salt | 1/4 tsp. | 1 mL |

**Bottom Layer:** Combine first 6 ingredients in medium bowl. Reserve 1 cup (250 mL) crumb mixture. Press remaining mixture firmly in ungreased 9 x 9 inch (22 x 22 cm) pan. Bake in 350°F (175°C) oven for 10 minutes. Remove from oven.

**Apricot Filling:** Place apricots in small saucepan. Add enough water to cover. Bring to a boil on medium. Reduce heat to medium-low. Simmer, uncovered, for about 15 minutes until apricots are softened. Drain well. Chop.

Beat eggs in medium bowl until frothy. Add brown sugar and lemon juice. Stir well.

Combine flour, baking powder and salt in small bowl. Add to egg mixture. Stir. Add apricots. Stir well. Spread evenly over bottom layer. Sprinkle with reserved crumbs. Bake for 30 to 35 minutes until golden. Let stand in pan on wire rack until cool. Cuts into 36 squares.

*1 square: 135 Calories; 5.5 g Total Fat (2.9 g Mono, 0.5 g Poly, 1.7 g Sat); 12 mg Cholesterol; 21 g Carbohydrate; 1 g Fibre; 1 g Protein; 126 mg Sodium*

Pictured on page 91.

*Using soda crackers in this square gives it a bit of a different touch.*

# Lemon Crunch

**BOTTOM LAYER**

| | | |
|---|---|---|
| Crushed soda crackers | 1 1/3 cups | 325 mL |
| Hard margarine (or butter), softened | 3/4 cup | 175 mL |
| All-purpose flour | 3/4 cup | 175 mL |
| Granulated sugar | 1/2 cup | 125 mL |
| Medium unsweetened coconut | 1/2 cup | 125 mL |
| Baking powder | 1 tsp. | 5 mL |

**LEMON FILLING**

| | | |
|---|---|---|
| Large eggs | 3 | 3 |
| Granulated sugar | 1 cup | 250 mL |
| Lemon, grated peel and juice | 1 | 1 |
| Hard margarine (or butter) | 1/4 cup | 60 mL |

**Bottom Layer:** Combine all 6 ingredients in medium bowl until crumbly. Reserve 1 cup (250 mL) for topping. Press remaining crumb mixture firmly in ungreased 9 x 9 inch (22 x 22 cm) pan. Bake in 350°F (175°C) oven for 15 minutes. Remove from oven.

**Lemon Filling:** Beat eggs in heavy medium saucepan or top of double boiler. Add remaining 3 ingredients. Heat and stir on medium until thickened. Spread evenly over crumb layer in pan. Sprinkle reserved crumb mixture over top. Bake for about 20 minutes until golden brown. Let stand in pan on wire rack until cool. Cuts into 36 squares.

*1 square: 122 Calories; 7.1 g Total Fat (3.9 g Mono, 0.7 g Poly, 2.1 g Sat); 18 mg Cholesterol; 14 g Carbohydrate; trace Fibre; 1 g Protein; 120 mg Sodium*

Pictured on page 91.

Left: Apricot Zings, page 89
Right: Lemon Crunch, above

*Tastes like a famous candy bar.*

# Candy Bar Squares

| | | |
|---|---|---|
| Semi-sweet chocolate chips | 2 cups | 500 mL |
| Peanut butter chips | 1 cup | 250 mL |
| Granulated sugar | 1 1/4 cups | 300 mL |
| Hard margarine (or butter) | 1/3 cup | 75 mL |
| Milk | 1/3 cup | 75 mL |
| Coarsely chopped salted peanuts | 1/4 cup | 60 mL |
| Smooth peanut butter | 1/4 cup | 60 mL |
| Marshmallow creme | 1 cup | 250 mL |
| Vanilla | 1 tsp. | 5 mL |
| Coarsely chopped salted peanuts | 3/4 cup | 175 mL |
| Caramels | 40 | 40 |
| Water | 2 1/2 tbsp. | 37 mL |

Heat both chips in large heavy saucepan on lowest heat, stirring often, until chips are almost melted. Do not overheat. Remove from heat. Stir until smooth. Spread about 1/2 of mixture evenly in greased or foil-lined 9 x 13 inch (22 x 33 cm) pan. Let stand until firm.

Heat and stir sugar, margarine and milk in heavy medium saucepan on medium until boiling. Boil for 5 minutes, stirring often. Spread evenly over chip layer.

Sprinkle first amount of peanuts over top.

Heat and stir peanut butter in small heavy saucepan on lowest heat until melted. Remove from heat. Add marshmallow creme and vanilla. Stir until smooth. Spoon mixture in dabs, using 1 tsp. (5 mL) for each, over peanuts.

Sprinkle second amount of peanuts over top.

Heat and stir caramels and water in heavy medium saucepan on lowest heat until smooth. Spread evenly over peanuts. Reheat remaining 1/2 of chip mixture if necessary until spreading consistency. Spread evenly over caramel. Chill until firm. Cuts into 54 squares.

*1 square: 139 Calories; 6.7 g Total Fat (2.8 g Mono, 1 g Poly, 2.6 g Sat); 0 mg Cholesterol; 20 g Carbohydrate; 1 g Fibre; 2 g Protein; 70 mg Sodium*

Pictured on page 93 and on front cover.

*When unexpected company calls, whip these up. They're ready in a flash—and will be eaten just as quickly.*

# Chocolate Cherry Slice

**BOTTOM LAYER**

| | | |
|---|---|---|
| Sweet chocolate baking squares (1 oz., 28 g, each), or 1 1/3 cups (325 mL) chocolate chips | 8 | 8 |

**TOP LAYER**

| | | |
|---|---|---|
| Large eggs | 2 | 2 |
| Granulated sugar | 1/2 cup | 125 mL |
| Medium unsweetened coconut | 1 1/2 cups | 375 mL |
| Chopped glazed cherries | 1/4 cup | 60 mL |

Icing (confectioner's) sugar, for dusting (optional)

**Bottom Layer:** Heat chocolate in small heavy saucepan on lowest heat, stirring often, until almost melted. Do not overheat. Remove from heat. Stir until smooth. Spread evenly in bottom of greased 8 x 8 inch (20 x 20 cm) pan. Chill until firm.

**Top Layer:** Beat eggs and sugar in medium bowl until thick and pale. Add coconut and cherries. Stir. Spread evenly over bottom layer. Bake in 350°F (175°C) oven for 25 to 30 minutes until golden and firm to the touch. Let stand in pan on wire rack until cool. Cover and store in refrigerator.

Just before serving, dust with icing sugar using a sieve. Cuts into 25 squares.

*1 square: 112 Calories; 7.2 g Total Fat (1.3 g Mono, 0.2 g Poly, 5.2 g Sat); 17 mg Cholesterol; 13 g Carbohydrate; trace Fibre; 1 g Protein; 9 mg Sodium*

Pictured on page 95.

1. Saucepan Brownies, page 97
2. Chocolate Cherry Slice, above
3. Cream Cheese Brownies, page 96

*These are fussy to prepare, but are worth the extra time it takes. Very attractive.*

# Cream Cheese Brownies

### CHEESE LAYER

| | | |
|---|---|---|
| Block of cream cheese, softened | 4 oz. | 125 g |
| Large egg | 1 | 1 |
| Granulated sugar | 1/2 cup | 125 mL |
| All-purpose flour | 2 tbsp. | 30 mL |
| Chopped maraschino cherries, well-drained | 1/2 cup | 125 mL |

### BROWNIE LAYER

| | | |
|---|---|---|
| Large eggs | 2 | 2 |
| Granulated sugar | 1 cup | 250 mL |
| All-purpose flour | 3/4 cup | 175 mL |
| Chopped walnuts | 1/2 cup | 125 mL |
| Salt | 1/8 tsp. | 0.5 mL |
| Hard margarine (or butter), cut up | 1/2 cup | 125 mL |
| Cocoa, sifted if lumpy | 1/4 cup | 60 mL |

### CHOCOLATE COFFEE ICING

| | | |
|---|---|---|
| Icing (confectioner's) sugar | 1 1/3 cups | 325 mL |
| Cocoa, sifted if lumpy | 1/3 cup | 75 mL |
| Hard margarine (or butter), softened | 3 tbsp. | 50 mL |
| Hot prepared strong coffee (or hot water) | 1 1/2 tbsp. | 25 mL |

**Cheese Layer:** Beat cream cheese and egg in medium bowl until smooth. Combine sugar and flour in small bowl. Add to cream cheese mixture, 2 tbsp. (30 mL) at a time while beating, until smooth. Add cherries. Stir. Set aside.

**Brownie Layer:** Beat eggs in separate medium bowl until frothy. Add next 4 ingredients. Stir.

Heat and stir margarine and cocoa in small heavy saucepan on lowest heat until smooth. Add to egg mixture. Stir well. Spread about 2/3 of brownie mixture evenly in greased 9 x 9 inch (22 x 22 cm) pan. Spoon mounds of cream cheese mixture, using 1 tbsp. (15 mL) for each, over brownie layer. Spoon remaining brownie mixture in dabs, using 1/2 tsp. (2 mL) for each, over top. Mixtures will look patchy in pan. Bake in 350°F (175°C) oven for 30 to 35 minutes until edges pull away from sides of pan. Let stand in pan on wire rack until cooled completely.

*(continued on next page)*

**Chocolate Coffee Icing:** Beat all 4 ingredients in small bowl until smooth, adding more coffee or icing sugar as necessary until spreading consistency. Spread evenly over brownie layer. Cuts into 25 squares.

*1 square: 189 Calories; 9.4 g Total Fat (4.6 g Mono, 1.7 g Poly, 2.6 g Sat); 31 mg Cholesterol; 25 g Carbohydrate; 1 g Fibre; 3 g Protein; 97 mg Sodium*

Pictured on page 95.

## Saucepan Brownies

*A no-bake brownie with rich chocolate flavour.*

| | | |
|---|---|---|
| Semi-sweet chocolate chips | 2 2/3 cups | 650 mL |
| Evaporated milk | 1 cup | 250 mL |
| Vanilla wafer crumbs | 3 cups | 750 mL |
| Miniature marshmallows | 2 cups | 500 mL |
| Chopped walnuts | 1 cup | 250 mL |
| Icing (confectioner's) sugar | 1 cup | 250 mL |
| Salt | 1/2 tsp. | 2 mL |
| Evaporated milk | 2 tsp. | 10 mL |

Heat and stir chips and first amount of evaporated milk in large heavy saucepan on medium-low until smooth. Do not overheat. Remove from heat. Reserve 1/2 cup (125 mL) chocolate mixture. Set aside.

Add next 5 ingredients to remaining chocolate mixture. Stir well. Press firmly in greased or foil-lined 9 x 9 inch (22 x 22 cm) pan.

Add second amount of evaporated milk to reserved chocolate mixture. Stir well. Spread evenly over crumb mixture. Chill until firm. Cuts into 36 squares.

*1 square: 149 Calories; 7.7 g Total Fat (2.4 g Mono, 1.8 g Poly, 3.1 g Sat); 6 mg Cholesterol; 20 g Carbohydrate; 1 g Fibre; 2 g Protein; 66 mg Sodium*

Pictured on page 95.

*These do melt in your mouth.*

## Chocolate Coconut Melts

| | | |
|---|---|---|
| Can of sweetened condensed milk | 11 oz. | 300 mL |
| Unsweetened chocolate baking squares (1 oz., 28 g, each), chopped | 2 | 2 |
| Salt | 1/4 tsp. | 1 mL |
| Flake coconut | 2 2/3 cups | 650 mL |
| Vanilla | 1 tsp. | 5 mL |

Heat and stir condensed milk, chocolate and salt in heavy medium saucepan on medium-low until smooth. Remove from heat.

Add coconut and vanilla. Stir well. Spread evenly in greased 8 x 8 inch (20 x 20 cm) pan. Bake in 350°F (175°C) oven for about 20 minutes until set. Let stand in pan on wire rack until cool. Cuts into 25 squares.

*1 square: 129 Calories; 9.1 g Total Fat (1.1 g Mono, 0.2 g Poly, 7.4 g Sat); 5 mg Cholesterol; 12 g Carbohydrate; 1 g Fibre; 2 g Protein; 48 mg Sodium*

Pictured on page 99.

*You'll need two pans to make these. Wrap individual bars in plastic wrap for an easy take-along breakfast when you roll out of bed and have to run out the door!*

### note

To toast seeds, place in single layer in ungreased shallow pan. Bake in 350°F (175°C) oven for 5 to 8 minutes, stirring or shaking often, until desired doneness.

## Take-Along Breakfast Bars

| | | |
|---|---|---|
| Quick-cooking rolled oats (not instant) | 4 cups | 1 L |
| Medium unsweetened coconut | 2 cups | 500 mL |
| Lightly crushed cornflakes cereal | 1 cup | 250 mL |
| Chopped dried apricots | 1 cup | 250 mL |
| Raisins | 1 cup | 250 mL |
| Shelled sunflower seeds, toasted (see Note) | 2/3 cup | 150 mL |
| Hard margarine (or butter) | 1/2 cup | 125 mL |
| Can of sweetened condensed milk | 11 oz. | 300 mL |
| Golden corn syrup | 1/4 cup | 60 mL |
| Frozen concentrated orange juice | 2 tbsp. | 30 mL |

*(continued on next page)*

Combine first 6 ingredients in large bowl.

Melt margarine in medium saucepan. Add remaining 3 ingredients. Heat and stir on low until smooth. Slowly pour into rolled oat mixture while stirring until well combined. Mixture will be sticky. Divide and press firmly in 2 greased 9 x 13 inch (22 x 33 cm) pans. Bake in 325°F (160°C) oven for 20 to 30 minutes until edges are golden. Let stand in pans on wire racks for 5 minutes. Score top of each into 2 x 3 inch (5 x 7.5 cm) bars with knife. Let stand until cool. Each pan cuts into 18 bars, for a total of 36 bars.

*1 bar: 197 Calories; 9.4 g Total Fat (2.7 g Mono, 1.6 g Poly, 4.5 g Sat); 4 mg Cholesterol; 26 g Carbohydrate; 2 g Fibre; 4 g Protein; 79 mg Sodium*

Pictured below.

Top: Take-Along Breakfast Bars, page 98
Bottom: Chocolate Coconut Melts, page 98

## take-along breakfast cookies

Roll out mixture between 2 sheets of greased waxed paper to 1/2 inch (12 mm) thickness. Cut into shapes with cookie cutter. Carefully transfer to greased cookie sheets. Bake in 325°F (160°C) oven for 15 to 20 minutes until edges are golden. Let stand on sheets for 5 minutes before removing to wire racks to cool. Makes about 24 cookies.

*Brittle lovers take note: lots of peanuts covered in chocolate. A dream come true!*

# Chocolate Brittle

| | | |
|---|---|---|
| Granulated sugar | 1 cup | 250 mL |
| White corn syrup | 1/2 cup | 125 mL |
| Roasted salted peanuts | 1 cup | 250 mL |
| Hard margarine (or butter) | 2 tbsp. | 30 mL |
| Vanilla | 1 tsp. | 5 mL |
| Baking soda | 1 1/2 tsp. | 7 mL |
| **TOPPING** | | |
| Semi-sweet chocolate chips | 3/4 cup | 175 mL |
| Chopped unsalted peanuts | 1/3 cup | 75 mL |

Combine sugar and corn syrup in ungreased 2 quart (2 L) casserole. Microwave, uncovered, on high (100%) for about 4 minutes until sugar is dissolved and mixture is bubbling.

Add peanuts. Stir. Microwave, uncovered, on high (100%) for about 6 minutes, checking at 1 minute intervals, until golden.

Add margarine and vanilla. Stir. Microwave, uncovered, on high (100%) for 1 minute. Stir.

Add baking soda. Stir. Mixture will foam. Immediately turn out onto greased baking sheet with sides. Spread evenly into thin layer.

**Topping:** Sprinkle chips over hot peanut mixture. Let stand until chips are softened. Spread evenly. Sprinkle with chopped peanuts. Chill until set. Break into irregular-shaped pieces, about 1 1/2 x 2 inches (3.8 x 5 cm) each. Makes about 1 1/4 lbs. (560 g), or about 30 pieces.

*1 piece: 114 Calories; 5.5 g Total Fat (2.6 g Mono, 1.2 g Poly, 1.4 g Sat); 0 mg Cholesterol; 16 g Carbohydrate; 1 g Fibre; 2 g Protein; 120 mg Sodium*

Pictured on page 101.

Top Left: Chocolate Nuts, page 102
Top Right: Chocolate Marshmallows, page 102
Bottom: Chocolate Brittle, above

*These are a pleasant change from the usual mixed nut offering.*

# Chocolate Nuts

| | | |
|---|---|---|
| Pecan halves | 1 cup | 250 mL |
| Walnut halves | 1 cup | 250 mL |
| Chocolate syrup | 1/2 cup | 125 mL |
| Cooking oil | 4 tsp. | 20 mL |

Measure pecans and walnuts into medium bowl. Add chocolate syrup and cooking oil. Stir until nuts are well coated. Spread evenly in greased baking sheet with sides. Bake in 350°F (175°C) oven for 8 to 10 minutes, stirring halfway through baking time, until dry and crisp. Makes 2 cups (500 mL).

*2 tbsp. (30 mL): 117 Calories; 9.7 g Total Fat (4.5 g Mono, 4 g Poly, 0.9 g Sat); 0 mg Cholesterol; 8 g Carbohydrate; 1 g Fibre; 2 g Protein; 10 mg Sodium*

Pictured on page 101.

*Allow extra time for this impressive-looking candy dessert. Certainly worth the effort.*

## note

To toast nuts, place in single layer in ungreased shallow pan. Bake in 350°F (175°C) oven for 5 to 8 minutes, stirring or shaking often, until desired doneness.

# Chocolate Marshmallows

| | | |
|---|---|---|
| Can of sweetened condensed milk | 11 oz. | 300 mL |
| Jar of marshmallow creme | 7 oz. | 198 g |
| Semi-sweet chocolate chips | 2 1/3 cups | 575 mL |
| Large marshmallows | 60 | 60 |
| Finely chopped walnuts (or pecans), toasted (see Note) | 4 1/2 cups | 1.1 L |

Heat and stir condensed milk, marshmallow creme and chips in medium saucepan on low until smooth. Remove from heat.

Roll 1 marshmallow in chocolate mixture until coated using fork, allowing excess chocolate to drip back into saucepan. Roll in chopped walnuts in small bowl until coated. Place on waxed paper-lined baking sheet. Repeat with remaining marshmallows, chocolate mixture and walnuts. If chocolate mixture becomes too thick for dipping, reheat on low until desired consistency. Let marshmallows stand overnight until set. Makes 60 chocolate marshmallows.

*1 chocolate marshmallow: 147 Calories; 8.3 g Total Fat (2.1 g Mono, 3.8 g Poly, 1.9 g Sat); 2 mg Cholesterol; 18 g Carbohydrate; 1 g Fibre; 3 g Protein; 14 mg Sodium*

Pictured on page 101.

# Cranberry Almond Bark

| White chocolate bars (3 1/2 oz., 100 g, each), chopped | 5 | 5 |
| --- | --- | --- |
| Whole almonds (with skin) | 1 1/2 cups | 375 mL |
| Dried cranberries | 1 cup | 250 mL |

*Homemade chocolate bark may not be much less expensive than store-bought, but it tastes so much better!*

Heat chocolate in heavy medium saucepan on lowest heat, stirring often, until chocolate is almost melted. Do not overheat. Remove from heat. Stir until smooth.

Add almonds and cranberries. Stir until well coated. Spread on waxed paper-lined baking sheet with sides to 1/4 inch (6 mm) thickness. Chill until set. Break into irregular-shaped pieces, about 1 1/2 × 2 inches (3.8 × 5 cm) each. Makes about 56 pieces.

*1 piece: 75 Calories; 4.8 g Total Fat (2.2 g Mono, 0.5 g Poly, 1.8 g Sat); 2 mg Cholesterol; 7 g Carbohydrate; 1 g Fibre; 1 g Protein; 8 mg Sodium*

Pictured below.

*Whether they've been naughty or nice, your guests deserve these melt-in-your-mouth truffles.*

# Apricot Brandy Truffles

| | | |
|---|---|---|
| Whipping cream | 1/4 cup | 60 mL |
| Butter (not margarine) | 2 tbsp. | 30 mL |
| White chocolate bars (3 1/2 oz., 100 g, each), finely chopped | 3 | 3 |
| Finely chopped dried apricots | 3/4 cup | 175 mL |
| Brandy (or 1 tsp., 5 mL, brandy flavouring) | 1 tbsp. | 15 mL |
| White chocolate melting wafers | 1 cup | 250 mL |
| Medium unsweetened coconut | 1/4 cup | 60 mL |
| Dark chocolate melting wafers | 1 cup | 250 mL |

Heat and stir whipping cream and butter in small heavy saucepan on medium-high until boiling. Immediately remove from heat. Add chocolate bar pieces. Stir until chocolate is melted. Transfer to medium bowl.

Add apricot and brandy. Stir well. Chill, uncovered, for about 50 minutes, stirring twice, until just firm but not set. Roll into 25 balls, using 1 tbsp. (15 mL) for each. Chill for 30 minutes.

Heat white chocolate wafers in small heavy saucepan on lowest heat, stirring often, until almost melted. Do not overheat. Remove from heat. Stir until smooth. Dip 12 balls into white chocolate using fork, allowing excess to drip back into saucepan. Roll in coconut in small bowl. Place on waxed paper-lined baking sheet. If chocolate becomes too thick for dipping, reheat on low until desired consistency.

Heat dark chocolate wafers in separate small heavy saucepan on lowest heat, stirring often, until almost melted. Do not overheat. Remove from heat. Stir until smooth. Dip remaining balls into dark chocolate using fork, allowing excess to drip back into saucepan. Place on same baking sheet. If chocolate becomes too thick for dipping, reheat on low until desired consistency. Chill for about 30 minutes until set. Makes 25 truffles.

*1 truffle:* 168 Calories; 10.3 g Total Fat (3.1 g Mono, 0.3 g Poly, 6.3 g Sat); 10 mg Cholesterol; 19 g Carbohydrate; 1 g Fibre; 2 g Protein; 29 mg Sodium

Pictured on page 105.

Top: Rum Balls, page 106
Bottom: Apricot Brandy Truffles, above

*A classic sweet for Christmas gift-giving.*

## Rum Balls

| | | |
|---|---|---|
| Chocolate cake mix (1 layer size) | 1 | 1 |
| Brown sugar, packed | 1/4 cup | 60 mL |
| Cocoa, sifted if lumpy | 2 tbsp. | 30 mL |
| Apricot jam | 1/4 cup | 60 mL |
| Dark (navy) rum | 2 tbsp. | 30 mL |
| Boiling water | 1 tbsp. | 15 mL |
| Chocolate sprinkles | 1/2 – 3/4 cup | 125 – 175 mL |

Prepare and bake cake mix according to package directions. Let stand in pan on wire rack until cooled completely. Partially freeze. Crumble into large bowl.

Add brown sugar and cocoa. Stir.

Combine jam, rum and boiling water in small cup. Add to cake crumbs. Stir well. Shape into balls, using 1 1/2 tbsp. (25 mL) crumb mixture for each.

Roll each ball in chocolate sprinkles in small bowl. Chill. Makes 24 rum balls.

*1 rum ball: 74 Calories; 1.8 g Total Fat (0.8 g Mono, 0.1 g Poly, 0.9 g Sat); 1 mg Cholesterol; 14 g Carbohydrate; trace Fibre; 1 g Protein; 89 mg Sodium*

Pictured on page 105.

*So pretty and such a sweet treat!*

## Pinwheels

| | | |
|---|---|---|
| Icing (confectioner's) sugar | 2 1/2 cups | 625 mL |
| Mashed potatoes | 1/3 cup | 75 mL |
| Vanilla | 1/2 tsp. | 2 mL |
| Salt | 1/8 tsp. | 0.5 mL |
| Icing (confectioner's) sugar, for dusting | | |
| Smooth peanut butter | 1/3 cup | 75 mL |

Combine first 4 ingredients in large bowl.

*(continued on next page)*

Turn out onto work surface dusted with icing sugar. Knead until smooth, adding more icing sugar if necessary, until a pliable but not sticky dough forms. Divide into 3 equal portions. Roll out 1 portion on surface dusted with icing sugar to 5 × 8 inch (12.5 × 20 cm) rectangle, 1/8 inch (3 mm) thick.

Spread about 1 1/2 tbsp. (25 mL) peanut butter evenly over top. Roll up, jelly roll-style, from long side. Wrap with plastic wrap. Chill. Repeat with remaining portions. Cut each roll into 1/4 inch (6 mm) slices. Makes about 6 dozen (72) pinwheels.

*1 pinwheel:* 25 Calories; 0.7 g Total Fat (0.3 g Mono, 0.2 g Poly, 0.1 g Sat); 0 mg Cholesterol; 5 g Carbohydrate; trace Fibre; 0 g Protein; 13 mg Sodium

Pictured below.

*This is a soft, creamy fudge, so place in a sturdy container for gift-giving. A perfect blend of chocolate and peanuts.*

# Choco-Peanut Fudge

| | | |
|---|---|---|
| Granulated sugar | 2 cups | 500 mL |
| Cocoa, sifted if lumpy | 1/3 cup | 75 mL |
| Milk | 3/4 cup | 175 mL |
| Golden corn syrup | 2 tbsp. | 30 mL |
| Hard margarine (or butter) | 2 tbsp. | 30 mL |
| Salt | 1/8 tsp. | 0.5 mL |
| Smooth peanut butter | 1/3 cup | 75 mL |
| Chopped unsalted peanuts (or walnuts), toasted (see Note) | 1/2 cup | 125 mL |

Combine first 6 ingredients in large heavy saucepan. Bring to a boil on medium, stirring constantly. Reduce heat to medium-low. Brush side of saucepan with damp pastry brush to dissolve any sugar crystals. Simmer, uncovered, for about 30 minutes, without stirring, until mixture reaches soft ball stage: 234 to 240°F (112 to 116°C) on candy thermometer or until about 1/4 tsp. (1 mL) of mixture dropped into very cold water forms a soft ball that flattens on its own when removed. Let stand, without stirring, until bottom of saucepan is cool enough to touch.

Add peanut butter and peanuts. Beat with spoon until mixture loses its shine and pulls away from side of saucepan. Spread evenly in greased 8 × 8 inch (20 × 20 cm) pan. Chill until firm. Makes 1 1/2 lbs. (680 g) fudge. Cuts into 36 pieces.

*1 piece: 86 Calories; 3.2 g Total Fat (1.6 g Mono, 0.8 g Poly, 0.6 g Sat); 0 mg Cholesterol; 14 g Carbohydrate; 1 g Fibre; 1 g Protein; 32 mg Sodium*

Pictured on page 109.

*Marshmallow creme adds a definite creaminess to this rich, sweet fudge.*

# White Creme Fudge

| | | |
|---|---|---|
| Granulated sugar | 2 cups | 500 mL |
| Half-and-half cream | 2/3 cup | 150 mL |
| Hard margarine (or butter) | 1/4 cup | 60 mL |
| White corn syrup | 1 tbsp. | 15 mL |
| White chocolate baking squares (1 oz., 28 g, each), chopped | 8 | 8 |
| Jar of marshmallow creme | 7 oz. | 198 g |

*(continued on next page)*

| Quartered glazed cherries | 1/4 cup | 60 mL |
|---|---|---|

Heat and stir first 4 ingredients in large heavy saucepan on medium-low until boiling. Brush side of saucepan with damp pastry brush to dissolve any sugar crystals. Boil for about 30 minutes, without stirring, until mixture reaches soft ball stage: 234 to 240°F (112 to 116°C) on candy thermometer or until about 1/4 tsp. (1 mL) of mixture dropped into very cold water forms a soft ball that flattens on its own when removed. Remove from heat.

Add chocolate and marshmallow creme. Stir until chocolate is melted and mixture is smooth.

Add cherries. Stir. Spread evenly in greased 8 x 8 inch (20 x 20 cm) pan. Chill until firm. Makes about 2 lbs. (900 g) fudge. Cuts into 36 pieces.

*1 piece: 120 Calories; 3.7 g Total Fat (1.6 g Mono, 0.2 g Poly, 1.7 g Sat); 3 mg Cholesterol; 22 g Carbohydrate; trace Fibre; 1 g Protein; 26 mg Sodium*

Pictured below.

Inner Circle: White Creme Fudge, page 108
Outer Circle: Choco-Peanut Fudge, page 108

*The ultimate snack for those who love white chocolate and caramel corn. The perfect pick-me-up.*

### note

To toast nuts, place in single layer in ungreased shallow pan. Bake in 350°F (175°C) oven for 5 to 8 minutes, stirring or shaking often, until desired doneness.

*These take extra time, but are fun to make. Freeze in an airtight container.*

# White Chocolate Popcorn

| | | |
|---|---|---|
| White chocolate bars (3 1/2 oz., 100 g, each), chopped | 3 | 3 |
| Bag of caramel-coated popcorn and peanuts (about 5 cups, 1.25 L) | 7 oz. | 200 g |
| Slivered almonds, toasted (see Note) | 1/2 cup | 125 mL |

Heat chocolate in heavy medium saucepan on lowest heat, stirring often, until chocolate is almost melted. Do not overheat. Remove from heat. Stir until smooth.

Spread popcorn on foil-lined baking sheet with sides. Drizzle chocolate over popcorn. Stir. Sprinkle with almonds. Chill until set. Break into bite-size pieces. Makes about 5 1/2 cups (1.4 L).

*1/2 cup (125 mL): 255 Calories; 13 g Total Fat (5.2 g Mono, 1.5 g Poly, 5.3 g Sat); 6 mg Cholesterol; 33 g Carbohydrate; 1 g Fibre; 4 g Protein; 79 mg Sodium*

Pictured on page 111.

# Marshmallow Delights

| | | |
|---|---|---|
| Butterscotch toffee bars (such as Mackintosh's), 2 oz. (56 g) each, broken up | 3 | 3 |
| Sweetened condensed milk | 2/3 cup | 150 mL |
| Hard margarine (or butter) | 1/4 cup | 60 mL |
| Large marshmallows | 30 | 30 |
| Special K cereal | 4 cups | 1 L |

Heat and stir toffee, condensed milk and margarine in small heavy saucepan on medium until toffee is melted and mixture is smooth. Remove from heat.

Dip 1 marshmallow in toffee mixture until coated using fork. If toffee mixture becomes too thick for dipping, reheat on medium until desired consistency.

*(continued on next page)*

Roll coated marshmallow in cereal in medium bowl until coated using fork.
Place on waxed paper-lined baking sheet. Repeat with remaining marshmallows,
toffee mixture and cereal. Let marshmallows stand until set. Makes 30.

*1 marshmallow delight:* 95 Calories; 2.5 g Total Fat (1.3 g Mono, 0.2 g Poly, 0.8 g Sat); 3 mg Cholesterol;
18 g Carbohydrate; trace Fibre; 1 g Protein; 63 mg Sodium

Pictured below.

Top Left: Marshmallow Delights, page 110
Top Right: White Chocolate Popcorn,
page 110
Bottom: Crispy Roll, page 112

*Crisp cereal roll with a yummy chocolate filling.*

# Crispy Roll

| | | |
|---|---|---|
| White corn syrup | 1 cup | 250 mL |
| Smooth peanut butter | 1 cup | 250 mL |
| Granulated sugar | 1 cup | 250 mL |
| Hard margarine (or butter) | 3 tbsp. | 50 mL |
| Crisp rice cereal | 6 cups | 1.5 L |
| **FILLING** | | |
| Icing (confectioner's) sugar | 2 cups | 500 mL |
| Cocoa, sifted if lumpy | 1 cup | 250 mL |
| Hard margarine (or butter), softened | 1/2 cup | 125 mL |
| Water | 1/4 cup | 60 mL |
| Vanilla | 1 tsp. | 5 mL |

Heat and stir first 4 ingredients in large heavy saucepan on medium-high until boiling. Immediately remove from heat.

Add cereal. Stir until coated. Place sheet of waxed paper on damp work surface so paper will stay in place. Turn out cereal mixture onto waxed paper. Press into 10 x 15 inch (25 x 38 cm) rectangle. Let stand for 15 to 20 minutes until set, but still warm.

**Filling:** Beat all 5 ingredients on low in large bowl until combined. Beat on medium until smooth, adding more water if necessary until spreading consistency. Spread evenly over cereal mixture. Roll up, jelly roll-style, from long side, using waxed paper as guide. Wrap in plastic wrap. Chill. Cuts into 24 slices.

*1 slice: 273 Calories; 11.8 g Total Fat (6.5 g Mono, 2.1 g Poly, 2.6 g Sat); 0 mg Cholesterol; 41 g Carbohydrate; 2 g Fibre; 4 g Protein; 202 mg Sodium*

Pictured on page 111.

# Frozen Cheesecake Bites

*A creamy lemon cheesecake on a buttery shortbread base. Almonds add a crunch.*

### BOTTOM LAYER

| | | |
|---|---|---|
| All-purpose flour | 1 1/2 cups | 375 mL |
| Icing (confectioner's) sugar | 2 tbsp. | 30 mL |
| Sliced almonds | 3/4 cup | 175 mL |
| Hard margarine (or butter), softened, cut up | 1/2 cup | 125 mL |

### TOP LAYER

| | | |
|---|---|---|
| Blocks of cream cheese (8 oz., 250 g, each), softened | 2 | 2 |
| Container of lemon yogurt | 6 oz. | 175 mL |
| Large eggs | 2 | 2 |
| Granulated sugar | 1/2 cup | 125 mL |
| Cream of wheat (unprepared) | 2 tbsp. | 30 mL |
| Finely grated lemon zest | 1 tbsp. | 15 mL |
| Vanilla | 1/2 tsp. | 2 mL |
| Sliced almonds (optional) | 1/4 cup | 60 mL |

**Bottom Layer:** Combine first 3 ingredients in medium bowl. Cut in margarine until mixture resembles coarse crumbs. Press firmly in greased 9 x 13 inch (22 x 33 cm) pan. Bake in 350°F (175°C) oven for 10 minutes. Let stand in pan on wire rack for 5 minutes.

**Top Layer:** Beat first 7 ingredients in medium bowl until smooth. Spread evenly over bottom layer.

Sprinkle second amount of almonds over top. Bake for 25 to 30 minutes until set and edges are golden. Let stand in pan on wire rack until cooled completely. Cut into 15 rectangles with a wet knife. Cut each rectangle diagonally to make 2 triangles, for a total of 30 triangles. Arrange triangles 1/2 inch (12 mm) apart on ungreased baking sheet. Freeze for 2 to 3 hours until firm. Store in resealable freezer bags or tins, separating layers with waxed paper. Freeze until ready to serve. Makes 30.

*1 cheesecake bite: 157 Calories; 11 g Total Fat (4.9 g Mono, 0.9 g Poly, 4.6 g Sat); 33 mg Cholesterol; 12 g Carbohydrate; 1 g Fibre; 3 g Protein; 95 mg Sodium*

Pictured on page 115.

**Photo Legend next page**
1. Chipper Muffins, page 116
2. Butterscotch Muffins, page 116
3. Lemon Loaf, page 117
4. Frozen Cheesecake Bites, this page

*Imagine the cheers you'll receive when you bring these golden treats to the office for coffee break.*

# Butterscotch Muffins

| | | |
|---|---|---|
| Hard margarine (or butter), softened | 6 tbsp. | 100 mL |
| Brown sugar, packed | 1/4 cup | 60 mL |
| Large egg | 1 | 1 |
| Milk | 1 1/4 cups | 300 mL |
| All-purpose flour | 2 cups | 500 mL |
| Box of instant butterscotch pudding powder (4 serving size) | 4 oz. | 113 g |
| Butterscotch chips | 2/3 cup | 150 mL |
| Baking powder | 1 tbsp. | 15 mL |
| Salt | 1/2 tsp. | 2 mL |

Beat margarine and brown sugar in large bowl until light and creamy. Add egg. Beat. Add milk. Beat well.

Combine remaining 5 ingredients in medium bowl. Make a well in centre. Add margarine mixture to well. Stir until just moistened. Grease 12 muffin cups with cooking spray. Fill cups 3/4 full. Bake in 400°F (205°C) oven for about 18 minutes until golden, and wooden pick inserted in centre of muffin comes out clean. Let stand in pan for 5 minutes before removing to wire rack to cool. Makes 12 muffins.

*1 muffin: 231 Calories; 7.2 g Total Fat (4.1 g Mono, 0.8 g Poly, 1.7 g Sat); 20 mg Cholesterol; 39 g Carbohydrate; 1 g Fibre; 4 g Protein; 405 mg Sodium*

Pictured on page 114.

*A double chocolate treat. Great snacking.*

# Chipper Muffins

| | | |
|---|---|---|
| All-purpose flour | 1 3/4 cups | 425 mL |
| Semi-sweet chocolate chips | 1 cup | 250 mL |
| Granulated sugar | 3/4 cup | 175 mL |
| Cocoa, sifted if lumpy | 1/3 cup | 75 mL |
| Baking powder | 1 tbsp. | 15 mL |
| Salt | 1/2 tsp. | 2 mL |
| Large egg | 1 | 1 |
| Milk | 1 cup | 250 mL |
| Cooking oil | 1/3 cup | 75 mL |
| Vanilla | 1 tsp. | 5 mL |

*(continued on next page)*

Combine first 6 ingredients in medium bowl. Make a well in centre.

Beat egg in small bowl. Add milk, cooking oil and vanilla. Stir. Pour into well. Stir until just moistened. Grease 12 muffin cups with cooking spray. Fill cups 3/4 full. Bake in 400°F (205°C) oven for about 20 minutes until golden, and wooden pick inserted in centre of muffin comes out clean. Let stand in pan for 5 minutes before removing to wire rack to cool. Makes 12 muffins.

*1 muffin: 271 Calories; 12 g Total Fat (5.6 g Mono, 2.2 g Poly, 3.6 g Sat); 19 mg Cholesterol; 40 g Carbohydrate; 2 g Fibre; 4 g Protein; 210 mg Sodium*

Pictured on page 114.

## Lemon Loaf

*The glaze completes the delightful flavour of this loaf.*

| | | |
|---|---|---|
| Hard margarine (or butter), softened | 1/2 cup | 125 mL |
| Granulated sugar | 1 cup | 250 mL |
| Large eggs | 2 | 2 |
| Milk | 1/2 cup | 125 mL |
| All-purpose flour | 1 1/2 cups | 375 mL |
| Grated lemon peel | 1 tbsp. | 15 mL |
| Baking powder | 1 tsp. | 5 mL |
| Salt | 1/2 tsp. | 2 mL |
| LEMON GLAZE | | |
| Lemon juice | 1/3 cup | 75 mL |
| Granulated sugar | 1/4 cup | 60 mL |

Cream margarine and sugar in large bowl. Add eggs, 1 at a time, beating well after each addition. Add milk. Beat well.

Combine next 4 ingredients in small bowl. Add to margarine mixture. Stir until just moistened. Spread evenly in greased 9 x 5 x 3 inch (22 x 12.5 x 7.5 cm) loaf pan. Bake in 350°F (175°C) oven for about 60 minutes until wooden pick inserted in centre comes out clean.

**Lemon Glaze:** Heat and stir lemon juice and sugar in small saucepan on medium until sugar is dissolved. Spoon evenly over top of hot loaf. Let stand for 10 minutes before removing from pan to wire rack to cool. Cuts into 16 slices.

*1 slice: 177 Calories; 6.9 g Total Fat (4.2 g Mono, 0.7 g Poly, 1.5 g Sat); 27 mg Cholesterol; 27 g Carbohydrate; trace Fibre; 2 g Protein; 180 mg Sodium*

Pictured on page 115.

*A tender loaf with a delicate apple flavour.*

# Apple Loaf

| | | |
|---|---|---|
| Hard margarine (or butter), softened | 1/2 cup | 125 mL |
| Granulated sugar | 1 cup | 250 mL |
| Large eggs | 2 | 2 |
| Milk | 1/3 cup | 75 mL |
| Vanilla | 1 tsp. | 5 mL |
| Coarsely grated, tart cooking apple (such as Granny Smith), with peel, packed | 1 cup | 250 mL |
| All-purpose flour | 2 cups | 500 mL |
| Baking powder | 1 tsp. | 5 mL |
| Baking soda | 1/2 tsp. | 2 mL |
| Salt | 1/2 tsp. | 2 mL |
| Chopped walnuts, toasted (see Note) | 1/2 cup | 125 mL |

Cream margarine and sugar in large bowl. Add eggs, 1 at a time, beating well after each addition. Add milk and vanilla. Beat.

Add apple. Stir.

Combine remaining 5 ingredients in medium bowl. Add to apple mixture. Stir until just moistened. Spread evenly in greased 9 x 5 x 3 inch (22 x 12.5 x 7.5 cm) loaf pan. Bake in 350°F (175°C) oven for about 60 minutes until wooden pick inserted in centre comes out clean. Let stand in pan for 10 minutes before removing to wire rack to cool. Cuts into 16 slices.

*1 slice: 207 Calories; 9.2 g Total Fat (4.7 g Mono, 2.3 g Poly, 1.7 g Sat); 27 mg Cholesterol; 28 g Carbohydrate; 1 g Fibre; 4 g Protein; 219 mg Sodium*

Pictured on page 119.

*Comfort is sitting down and enjoying this muffin with a cup of your favourite hot beverage. Great served any time.*

# Apple Streusel Muffins

### TOPPING

| | | |
|---|---|---|
| Brown sugar, packed | 1/4 cup | 60 mL |
| All-purpose flour | 2 tbsp. | 30 mL |
| Ground cinnamon | 1/8 tsp. | 0.5 mL |
| Hard margarine (or butter), softened | 1 tbsp. | 15 mL |
| All-purpose flour | 1 1/2 cups | 375 mL |
| Granulated sugar | 1/2 cup | 125 mL |
| Baking powder | 1 tbsp. | 15 mL |
| Salt | 1/2 tsp. | 2 mL |
| Large egg | 1 | 1 |
| Milk | 2/3 cup | 150 mL |
| Cooking oil | 1/4 cup | 60 mL |
| Peeled, shredded cooking apple (such as McIntosh), packed | 3/4 cup | 175 mL |

**Topping:** Combine brown sugar, flour and cinnamon in small bowl. Cut in margarine until mixture resembles coarse crumbs. Set aside.

Combine next 4 ingredients in large bowl. Make a well in centre.

Beat egg, milk and cooking oil in small bowl. Add apple. Stir. Pour into well. Stir until just moistened. Grease 12 muffin cups with cooking spray. Fill cups 3/4 full. Divide and sprinkle topping over each. Bake in 400°F (205°C) oven for 15 to 20 minutes until golden, and wooden pick inserted in centre of muffin comes out clean. Let stand in pan for 5 minutes before removing to wire rack to cool. Makes 12 muffins.

*1 muffin: 196 Calories; 6.6 g Total Fat (3.7 g Mono, 1.7 g Poly, 0.4 g Sat); 19 mg Cholesterol; 29 g Carbohydrate; 1 g Fibre; 3 g Protein; 218 mg Sodium*

Pictured on page 121.

*Small melt-in-your-mouth mints. Cutting them with scissors gives them a pretty look.*

## After-Dinner Mints

| | | |
|---|---|---|
| Envelopes of unflavoured gelatin (1 tbsp., 15 mL, each) | 3 | 3 |
| Cold water | 1/2 cup | 125 mL |
| Icing (confectioner's) sugar | 2 cups | 500 mL |
| Peppermint flavouring | 1 1/2 tsp. | 7 mL |
| Baking powder | 1/4 tsp. | 1 mL |
| Icing (confectioner's) sugar | 4 cups | 1 L |

Sprinkle gelatin over water in medium saucepan. Let stand for 1 minute. Heat and stir on low until gelatin is dissolved. Remove from heat.

Add first amount of icing sugar, peppermint flavouring and baking powder. Stir well.

Add second amount of icing sugar. Stir. Mixture will be sticky. Turn out onto work surface dusted with icing sugar. Knead dough for about 1 minute until smooth. Divide into 4 equal portions. Cover 3 portions with plastic wrap to prevent drying. Roll out 1 portion into 1/2 inch (12 mm) diameter rope. Slice into 1/2 inch (12 mm) pieces with scissors or knife. Arrange in single layer on waxed paper-lined baking sheet. Repeat with remaining portions. Let stand for about 1 hour until firm. Store in resealable plastic bags. Makes about 168 mints.

*1 mint: 18 Calories; 0 g Total Fat (0 g Mono, 0 g Poly, 0 g Sat); 0 mg Cholesterol; 5 g Carbohydrate; 0 g Fibre; 0 g Protein; 1 mg Sodium*

Pictured on page 123.

*An all-chocolate, creamy, don't-have-to-wait-until-after-eight mint.*

### note

A few more drops of flavouring may be added to dough to increase mint flavour.

## Fudgy Chocolate Mints

| | | |
|---|---|---|
| Semi-sweet chocolate chips | 2 cups | 500 mL |
| Can of sweetened condensed milk | 11 oz. | 300 mL |
| Milk chocolate chips | 1 cup | 250 mL |
| Hard margarine (or butter) | 2 tbsp. | 30 mL |
| Vanilla | 1 tsp. | 5 mL |
| Peppermint flavouring (see Note) | 1/8 tsp. | 0.5 mL |

*(continued on next page)*

Heat and stir all 6 ingredients in large heavy saucepan on medium-low until chocolate is melted and mixture is smooth. Spread evenly in greased or foil-lined 9 × 9 inch (22 × 22 cm) pan. Let stand until set. Cut into 12 rows lengthwise and crosswise, for a total of 144 mints.

*1 mint: 28 Calories; 1.5 g Total Fat (0.5 g Mono, 0.1 g Poly, 0.9 g Sat); 1 mg Cholesterol; 4 g Carbohydrate; trace Fibre; 0 g Protein; 7 mg Sodium*

Pictured below.

## variation

For small candies, drop, using 2 tsp. (10 mL) for each, onto waxed paper. Let stand until set. If chocolate mixture becomes too hard to drop, reheat on low until desired consistency.

Left: Fudgy Chocolate Mints, page 122
Right: After-Dinner Mints, page 122

Throughout this book measurements are given in Conventional and Metric measure. To compensate for differences between the two measurements due to rounding, a full metric measure is not always used. The cup used is the standard 8 fluid ounce. Temperature is given in degrees Fahrenheit and Celsius. Baking pan measurements are in inches and centimetres as well as quarts and litres. An exact metric conversion is given on this page as well as the working equivalent (Metric Standard Measure).

## Pans

| Conventional – Inches | Metric – Centimetres |
|---|---|
| 8 x 8 inch | 20 x 20 cm |
| 9 x 9 inch | 22 x 22 cm |
| 9 x 13 inch | 22 x 33 cm |
| 10 x 15 inch | 25 x 38 cm |
| 11 x 17 inch | 28 x 43 cm |
| 8 x 2 inch round | 20 x 5 cm |
| 9 x 2 inch round | 22 x 5 cm |
| 10 x 4 1/2 inch tube | 25 x 11 cm |
| 8 x 4 x 3 inch loaf | 20 x 10 x 7.5 cm |
| 9 x 5 x 3 inch loaf | 22 x 12.5 x 7.5 cm |

## Oven Temperatures

| Fahrenheit (°F) | Celsius (°C) | Fahrenheit (°F) | Celsius (°C) |
|---|---|---|---|
| 175° | 80° | 350° | 175° |
| 200° | 95° | 375° | 190° |
| 225° | 110° | 400° | 205° |
| 250° | 120° | 425° | 220° |
| 275° | 140° | 450° | 230° |
| 300° | 150° | 475° | 240° |
| 325° | 160° | 500° | 260° |

## Spoons

| Conventional Measure | Metric Exact Conversion Millilitre (mL) | Metric Standard Measure Millilitre (mL) |
|---|---|---|
| 1/8 teaspoon (tsp.) | 0.6 mL | 0.5 mL |
| 1/4 teaspoon (tsp.) | 1.2 mL | 1 mL |
| 1/2 teaspoon (tsp.) | 2.4 mL | 2 mL |
| 1 teaspoon (tsp.) | 4.7 mL | 5 mL |
| 2 teaspoons (tsp.) | 9.4 mL | 10 mL |
| 1 tablespoon (tbsp.) | 14.2 mL | 15 mL |

## Cups

| | | |
|---|---|---|
| 1/4 cup (4 tbsp.) | 56.8 mL | 60 mL |
| 1/3 cup (5 1/3 tbsp.) | 75.6 mL | 75 mL |
| 1/2 cup (8 tbsp.) | 113.7 mL | 125 mL |
| 2/3 cup (10 2/3 tbsp.) | 151.2 mL | 150 mL |
| 3/4 cup (12 tbsp.) | 170.5 mL | 175 mL |
| 1 cup (16 tbsp.) | 227.3 mL | 250 mL |
| 4 1/2 cups | 1022.9 mL | 1000 mL(1 L) |

## Dry Measurements

| Conventional Measure Ounces (oz.) | Metric Exact Conversion Grams (g) | Metric Standard Measure Grams (g) |
|---|---|---|
| 1 oz. | 28.3 g | 28 g |
| 2 oz. | 56.7 g | 57 g |
| 3 oz. | 85.0 g | 85 g |
| 4 oz. | 113.4 g | 125 g |
| 5 oz. | 141.7 g | 140 g |
| 6 oz. | 170.1 g | 170 g |
| 7 oz. | 198.4 g | 200 g |
| 8 oz. | 226.8 g | 250 g |
| 16 oz. | 453.6 g | 500 g |
| 32 oz. | 907.2 g | 1000 g (1 kg) |

## Casseroles

| Canada & Britain | | United States | |
|---|---|---|---|
| Standard Size Casserole | Exact Metric Measure | Standard Size Casserole | Exact Metric Measure |
| 1 qt. (5 cups) | 1.13 L | 1 qt. (4 cups) | 900 mL |
| 1 1/2 qts. (7 1/2 cups) | 1.69 L | 1 1/2 qts. (6 cups) | 1.35 L |
| 2 qts. (10 cups) | 2.25 L | 2 qts. (8 cups) | 1.8 L |
| 2 1/2 qts. (12 1/2 cups) | 2.81 L | 2 1/2 qts. (10 cups) | 2.25 L |
| 3 qts. (15 cups) | 3.38 L | 3 qts. (12 cups) | 2.7 L |
| 4 qts. (20 cups) | 4.5 L | 4 qts. (16 cups) | 3.6 L |
| 5 qts. (25 cups) | 5.63 L | 5 qts. (20 cups) | 4.5 L |